Contents

Appendices

About the author

John Chard worked in local government for over 25 years and for the last ten has worked almost exclusively on school appeals. In the course of organising over 2,000 appeals, he has given advice and guidance to both sides of the appeal: to the admission authority and to parents/guardians. He has also given advice to appeal panels in his capacity as Clerk. As a result, he has gained extensive knowledge of the legislation and the evidence requirements that contribute to a successful appeal. He has also gained considerable insight into the way in which appeals can fail because parents/guardians are inadequately prepared for the appeal process, and because they do not have the know-how or confidence to give themselves the best chance of success.

In 2002, John launched School Appeals, a business established to help parents through the appeal process that has helped thousands of families. The School Appeals website, www.schoolappeals.org.uk, attracts well over 100,000 visitors each year. John represents parents successfully at appeals, as well as providing one-to-one services, and he is often approached to give lectures to existing and prospective panel members across the country. John has also been invited by admission authorities to check that their admission criteria meet current legislation.

John is regularly approached by the BBC's *Breakfast* to contribute to their *Chasing Places* programmes. He has been interviewed many times on national television and he often provides information about the admission and appeal process to both radio and television programmes, as well as national newspapers.

Acknowledgements

I am grateful to the following organisations who have very kindly given their consent to use extracts from their publications in the preparation of this book:

- The Department for Children, Schools and Families – Codes of Practice on School Admissions and School Admission Appeals.
- The Scottish Assembly – *Choosing a School – A Guide for Parents*.
- The Welsh Assembly – Codes of Practice on School Admissions and School Admission Appeals.
- The Commission for Local Administration in England – extracts from executive report summaries.

Jane Bell and Nadine de Souza at Lawpack have been enormously helpful in suggesting improvements to the text and in putting the book into shape for publication under very tight deadlines.

I would also like to thank my partner, Trisha, for her support and advice throughout and also my daughters, Sammy and Kelly, for putting up with my disappearing for hours on end while trying to meet editorial deadlines.

Introduction

I have been employed by a local authority for over 25 years and for the last ten years have been involved in the school admission appeal process, from arranging the hearing of appeal panels, on the one hand, to clerking those hearings, on the other. I have also been responsible for providing training for panel members. This has given me a unique insight into how appeal panel members make their decisions. In 2002, I established the website School Appeals (www.schoolappeals.org.uk), which provides help and guidance to parents who have to appeal because they have not been successful in securing a place at a school of their choice.

One of the most important issues facing parents is how they can make sure that their children benefit from the best education available. What constitutes the best education available will differ from one parent to another. However, the one thing that is constant is the lengths to which some parents will go to gain a place at their preferred maintained school. This will range from lawful methods, such as moving house or renting a property close to the school, to unlawful methods, such as using a false address.

First of all, let me dismiss one of the myths about choice. Both the major political parties are guilty of giving you, as a parent, the impression that you have a choice as to where your child is educated. Unless you pay for your child's education, you do not. But you do have the right to express a preference on which maintained school you would like your child to go to, and the admission authority has a legal obligation to meet that preference, unless to do so would cause prejudice (i.e. an additional admission would create problems for the school).

Every year approximately 1.5 million children start or transfer to a different school. For the vast majority of parents (approximately 90 per cent), the admission process results in their children obtaining a place at their preferred school. However, for the remaining ten per cent this can lead to several further months of uncertainty and anxiety. Unfortunately, there is nothing that you can do that will guarantee a place for your child at a particular school. But there are steps that you can take that will substantially improve your chances of success, both at the application stage and, if this is not successful, at the appeal stage.

This book takes you through the application stage and details what you can do to improve your chances of a successful application. Should you fail to get a place of your choice, it also outlines the steps that you can take to make a successful appeal. The application stage can be very confusing because of the different types of school and the variety of admission criteria used by admission authorities to determine places. I have broken these procedures into small sections to try to make them easier to understand. Once you understand them, you will find the process less daunting.

Education legislation is very topical and is always changing. Sometimes it is difficult to keep up with all the changes. At the time of writing, technically, there are four Codes on school admissions and appeals running concurrently in England. The advice in this book is based on the new Code on School Admissions which came into effect in February 2007 and which applies to admissions for children who are starting school from September 2008. However, the advice on appeals is based on the existing Code, which was published in 2003. A new Code, which replaces it, came into effect on 17 January 2008. There is always a period where the two Codes operate simultaneously. The new appeals Code applies to decisions communicated to parents on or after 1 March 2008. As a result, there are many parents who will have appeals conducted under the 2003 Code and others under the 2007 Code. There are many similarities in the two Codes, but where there are any significant differences the guidance in the new Code is shown in italics.

There are a number of appendices in this book that give a range of further useful information, including statements prepared for successful appeals; decisions of the Ombudsman and the courts that provide additional guidance; names, contact phone numbers and websites of all education authorities in England, Wales and Scotland; and a glossary explaining a number of terms used in admission circles.

This is the most comprehensive guide ever written, covering admissions to schools in England, Wales and Scotland. Do note, however, that this book does not cover independent schools.

You have purchased this book because you care about your child's education. Hopefully, this book's advice will help you to secure that goal.

CHAPTER 1

Applying for a place at a school of your choice

You, as a parent[1], have the right to express a preference about where you would like your child to be educated. But can you guarantee that your child will go to the school of your choice? Unfortunately – and this may surprise you – you cannot. Furthermore, you do not have the right to send your child to the school of your choice. The theme running through all legislation concerning primary and secondary school education is, simply, that there are no guarantees that any child will be able to attend the school preferred by his parents. However, every child between the ages of five and 16 is guaranteed a school place.

The good news is that there are things you can do to substantially improve your chances of obtaining your preferred school. You are already taking one very important step: you are reading this book. By doing so, you are gaining information on the three fundamental stages in preparing a successful admission application. These stages are:

1. Understanding how the school admission process works;

2. Obtaining the right information to assist you to make a successful admission application; and

3. Showing precisely how you meet your preferred school's admission criteria.

Other specific steps you should take appear in the **quick list** below. More information about these, as well as details of how the information can be obtained, is contained in this chapter. The **quick reference** below explains some of the terms frequently mentioned in this chapter.

You should prepare yourself mentally and emotionally for a long period of uncertainty. The 'admissions round', as the process of submitting application forms to the admission authority and waiting for its decision is known, can normally be expected to take over half a year; it starts in September one year and finishes in March – or even later – the following

---

[1] The word 'parent' is used throughout this book to denote any person who has legitimate care of a child, and who may be the child's guardian, carer or parent.

year. Normally, the Local Education Authority (LEA) will send you its admissions booklet at the beginning of the admissions round if your child is already in school. However, if your child is about to start school and the LEA is not aware of your child, you may need to contact the LEA to obtain a booklet. The admissions round is a long and often nerve-wracking time for parents and children to wait. Should you need, or decide, to appeal against the decision made at the admission application stage, the period of uncertainty will be lengthened even further.

However, obtaining the relevant information and doing the necessary research to provide the admission authority with the necessary information – in other words, doing your 'homework' on the admission criteria – is critical. By getting this part of the admission process right, you maximise the likelihood of timely success and minimise the possibility of needing to appeal against the admission authority's decision.

The issues covered in this chapter are as follows:

- The admission application deadline
- The LEA's admissions booklet
- The school prospectus
- Schools with specialist status
- How to work with the published admission criteria
- Special or exceptional reasons to attend a school
- Voluntary aided and foundation schools' and academies' admission criteria
- Grammar school applications
- Open evenings
- The equal preference system
- Co-ordinated admission arrangements
- The application form
- Sit back and relax!

So, what do you need to do next? Start by consulting the quick reference and the quick list below.

Quick reference

Understanding the meaning of these terms will help you to get the most from this chapter.

- ## The admission authority

  The admission authority is the body responsible for setting and applying the admission arrangement for a school (or schools).

- ## The Local Education Authority (LEA)

  The LEA is the local government body responsible for providing education for pupils of school age in a particular administrative area.

- ## The admission authority for community schools

  The LEA is the admission authority for community schools (also called 'state' schools) in England, Scotland and Wales. Each LEA in England & Wales publishes a booklet, which gives details of the admission arrangements for all the schools in the LEA's administrative area. This booklet can be obtained from your local LEA.

  England, Scotland and Wales each operate a separate system for school admissions. For details of how the admission process works in England, refer to this chapter; for Scotland, see Chapters 10 and 11; and for Wales, see Chapter 13. The details of all LEAs in England, Scotland and Wales appear in Appendix 8.

- ## The admission authority for voluntary aided and foundation schools and academies

  Voluntary aided schools, foundation schools and academies (definitions of these types of school can be found in the Glossary at the back of the book) differ from community schools in that in these schools the governing body, not the LEA, acts as the admission authority. The schools' governors are also responsible for setting the admission criteria and for the arrangements for any subsequent appeals. Information about voluntary aided schools, foundation schools and academies will appear in the LEA's admissions booklet. Guidance about the admission arrangements and the admission criteria for these schools may appear in the admissions booklet, or, if the admission arrangements and criteria are especially complex, the LEA may provide a summary only. The prospectus for each voluntary aided or foundation school or academy should give parents information about the school's admission arrangements. However, if you are in any doubt, it is safest to contact your preferred school and ask it to provide the information directly to you.

- ## Admission criteria

  When there are more applicants than there are school places available, the admission authority uses principles and rules known as admission criteria to determine which of its applicants can be offered a school place. In simple terms, admission criteria are practical, objective measures, such as the distance between an applicant's home and the school, whether or not the applicant already has siblings at the school, or if the applicant can demonstrate the necessary religious affiliation in the case of a faith school. All admission authorities are required to ensure that their admission criteria are explained clearly.

- ## Maintained schools

  Maintained schools include community, voluntary aided and foundation schools, because they are funded by the LEA. Academies are not maintained schools.

QUICK LIST

1. Have you obtained a copy of the LEA's admissions booklet, which deals with school admissions? If more than one LEA is involved, you should obtain all of the admissions booklets. This is important because you will find the admission criteria for your preferred school (or schools) in the admissions booklet. You will need this information to complete your admission application, which will be enclosed with the admissions booklet.

2. Have you studied the admission criteria for your preferred school (or schools)?

3. Have you checked to see how well you meet the admission criteria?

4. Have you researched the school (or schools) you are considering?

5. Have you looked at the school's (or schools') prospectus (or prospectuses)?

6. Have you visited your preferred school (or schools) and taken a look around to see what you think?

7. Have you spoken to parents whose children already attend the school (or schools) of your choice?

8. Have you spoken to pupils already attending the school (or schools) of your choice?

9. Have you talked to the teachers at the school (or schools)?

10. Have you listened to your child, to see what he thinks about the school (or schools)?

11. Have you used this book to assess your chances of making a successful admission application or admission appeal?

12. **Have you made sure that you have sent your application in on time?**

The admission application deadline

The admission authority will always publish the date and the time on that date by which it must receive applications. Case Study 4 (see page 15) shows how you could fall at the first hurdle, by failing to have your application considered because you did not meet the admission authority's published deadline. Remember, there is no appeal against the late submission of your application.

The LEA's admissions booklet

This is essential reading for anyone preparing a school admission application. Each LEA, as the admission authority for community schools, publishes a booklet which gives details of the admission arrangements for schools in the LEA's administrative area. This booklet can be obtained from the LEA, or it may be available from your public library. Voluntary aided schools, foundation schools and academies will produce prospectuses like other maintained schools, but the responsibility for providing an admissions booklet for the administrative area rests with the LEA.

The admissions booklet provides important information which can help you to prepare a successful application for your child's admission to your preferred school. The admissions booklet is where you can find out about the admission arrangements (the date and time by which applications must be received by the LEA, for example) and the admission criteria (the fair principles and rules used by the LEA when it is allocating school places) for all the maintained schools in your area.

It is very important that you study the admission criteria and provide the admission authority with as much information as you can, because this could help you to secure a place at your preferred school. It is, however, critical for you to be familiar with your preferred school's admission criteria if it is likely to be oversubscribed (i.e. there are fewer school places than there are applicants).

You can check to see if your preferred school is likely to be oversubscribed by consulting the LEA's admissions booklet. It gives each school's published admission number (also known as the published admission limit). The published admission number is the school's formal notification of the number of pupils it can admit. The admissions booklet also gives you the number of applications received by any school for the previous year. A comparison of these figures will allow you to assess whether or not your preferred school is likely to be oversubscribed.

You must refer to the current year's admission criteria when you are preparing your admission application. This is essential because what happened in last year's admissions round cannot be taken as a guarantee of what will happen this year. The admissions booklets always make this clear. For example, the majority of schools will use the distance factor (the distance between the child's home and the school) to determine who will be allocated a place. One school may choose to measure straight line distance (often referred to as 'as the crow flies'), while another school will measure the shortest safe walking route. The actual distance measured, whichever method of measurement is used, will not be the same every year. This is because physical changes may have been made to roads and pathways, or new construction may have altered routes, and so on. In addition, parents will be applying from different addresses. For more information on the distance factor, see the section 'How to work with the published admission criteria' on page 7.

The LEA's admissions booklet also gives the last admission criteria for those that were successful last year. The last admission criteria are the 'cut-off' points at which the final applicant was admitted to the school during the last admissions round. For example, if a secondary school is using the straight line measurement and the cut-off distance last year was 2.5 kilometres and you live five kilometres away from the school, it is unlikely that you will be able to secure a place through the admission process. But if you live two kilometres away, it is much more likely that your application will be successful.

The admissions booklet contains many other relevant details about the school, such as the maximum number of pupils on roll (i.e. at the school); the number of preferences for the school last year; and how the places were allocated last year. All of this information can help you with the preparation of an admission application. Admissions booklets are available from the LEAs in England and Wales. Do note that the arrangements in Scotland are completely different and that there is no obligation on an LEA to produce a booklet. All of the LEAs' contact details appear in Appendix 8.

The school prospectus

Every school produces a school prospectus. You may obtain a copy from the school's office. The school prospectus is the school's governors' opportunity to tell parents about the school.

The prospectus provides all of the key information about the educational activities of the school, such as the courses provided and the facilities available to the school's pupils. The school's governors may choose to give other information in the prospectus, including statements about the school's ethos and aspirations, perhaps, or a description of the various policies which the school is legally required to provide. It may also detail school policies, which range across all aspects of the school's operation, and it may encompass statements about how homework should be completed, as well as the accepted dress code, and discipline and bullying. It may give an indication of a school's attitude and approach to the education of its pupils. The prospectus is where parents can find information about how the school has been performing against national educational targets, such as the 'end of key stage' tests. The information contained in the school prospectus should help you to decide if the school is likely to suit your child, or not.

Schools with specialist status

Many secondary schools have obtained specialist status in a particular area of the National Curriculum. This means that they have been able to attract funding for specialised facilities, such as sports amenities. These special facilities can also be made available to the wider community in which the school is located. However, some schools may not explicitly draw attention to their specialist status in their prospectuses. A school's specialist status could be an important factor in your decision-making if you are looking for a school whose syllabus will suit your child's abilities; for example, should your child show a particular ability in sport, and you feel that he would benefit from attending the school with specialist status in this area of the curriculum, it would be wise to find out whether your preferred school has specialist status in sport. If it has, look closely at the school's admission criteria as the school may allocate some of its places to children with sporting ability.

Current legislation allows schools to allocate up to ten per cent of places to pupils with ability in the school's specialism. In practice, however, only about ten per cent of all schools do so. This means, of course, that only a very small proportion of children benefit from being allocated a school place on the basis of their particular ability in a specialised area of the school curriculum.

How to work with the published admission criteria

The published admission criteria are the factors which the admission authority (the LEA for a community school and the governing body for a voluntary aided school, a foundation school and an academy) states that it will use to decide which children will be offered a place at its school. Some examples of admission criteria are given in the section entitled 'The LEA's admissions booklet' earlier in this chapter.

It is the responsibility of each admission authority to determine the admission criteria it will use, and thus the criteria will vary from school to school and area to area. It is essential that you are fully aware of the current admission criteria when you are applying to your preferred school (or schools), and that you are able to show how well you satisfy these. Therefore, in order to make a successful admission application or appeal, it will be necessary for you to research the admission criteria in detail.

The 'distance factor' has been mentioned as one of the criteria relied upon by admission authorities when they allocate school places. Let us look at an example of why you need to fully understand how the published criterion, the straight line distance (or, 'how the crow flies') is applied. Unless you look very closely at the admission authority's distance calculations, you may find that the information provided could mislead you when you are preparing an admission application. Case Study 1 (see page 9) shows you why. Usually, the distance factor, whether straight line or some other method, will be used as the last main criterion to determine places or as a tie break (this is used if there are more applications that meet the terms of the criteria than there are places available). This will be used after the other main criteria, which is why the number of applicants allocated places using the distance factor can vary substantially from one year to the next.

This is best illustrated by using the simple example of a one-form entry school. Say the school in question admitted 30 pupils last year and there had been ten siblings applying for places. The siblings have a higher priority and were offered places. This left 20 places to be allocated using the distance factor. In this example the distance measured for the last successful applicant was 1.5 kilometres. In the preceding year there were 11 siblings, which meant that 19 places were decided on distance and the last successful applicant lived 1.4 kilometres from the school. The number of siblings will vary from year to year and also parents will be applying from different addresses. You live 1.3 kilometres from the school and you may, therefore, assess that you have a good chance of your application being successful. However, before you become too confident, you should contact the admission authority and determine the straight line distance accepted each year for the last five years. What you discover may confirm that your assumptions have a basis in fact or, on the other hand, that last year was an 'abnormal' year and that the usual accepted straight line distance is less than one kilometre. What this example illustrates is that nothing is guaranteed and that you can only make a best guess, or a reasonable assumption, based on historical information.

What should you do if the admission authority decides to apply the criterion of the shortest safe walking route? The definition of the shortest walking route will vary from one admission authority to another. The more common components include that the route must be paved and lit, and also that it is a route which is open to the general public. It may well include public footpaths, as well as roads. The important issue is to find out precisely what this means. The definition of the shortest walking route should be clear in the admission arrangements for the school. However, if you feel that it is unclear or you are not sure exactly how it applies, obtain a written explanation from the admission authority.

You may feel inclined to speak to someone in the school office to obtain a verbal definition of one or more of the admission criteria. However, I would urge caution here. You have every right to expect that the advice you are given by a representative of a school is accurate; regretfully, however, such responses have proved to be unreliable when they are later cited at an admission appeal. This may be because, for instance, the person to whom you spoke was trying to be helpful, but was not fully familiar with the full admission arrangements. When it comes to an admission appeal it will be 'your word against theirs' in the case of verbally issued advice, and who can reliably recall a conversation which took place some six to eight months earlier? A written explanation can, however, be produced at an admission appeal, and it will show whether or not you have been given reliable, accurate information in response to your enquiry.

The LEA is allowed to use whatever definition of the shortest walking route it wishes, but it must publish this definition and explain exactly how it will operate. Shortest walking routes may include any roads that are lit and paved, and are publicly accessible, but this must be checked with the relevant LEA. The case studies below show why this is necessary.

CASE STUDY 1

Mr and Mrs X lived reasonably close to the secondary school that they wished their child to attend. There was a large public park between their home and the preferred school. Mr and Mrs X checked the distance between their home and the school using software available on the internet and they found that the distance fell well within the distances for the safe walking route described in the school's published admission criteria. On this basis, Mr and Mrs X submitted an admission application and had every expectation that it would be successful.

To Mr and Mrs X's great surprise, their application was turned down. The reason given by the LEA was that Mr and Mrs X's child lived further away than the last successful applicant. Mr and Mrs X challenged the decision and found that while the route they had calculated themselves included the walk across the public park, the LEA had discounted the element of the walk that related to the route across the park. The park route was public and paved, but it was not lit and it did not, therefore, comply with the LEA's definition of a safe walking route. The parents subsequently appealed, but their appeal was not successful.

The LEA is there to help you and most LEAs are very willing to assist. Therefore, do not hesitate to ask the LEA to clarify any matters which you find unclear, or to provide additional information which will help you with an admission application or to make a choice about schools. You may wish to ask the LEA to plot your safe walking route in advance and also confirm the route plotted, because the admission authority can, on occasion, make mistakes. See Case Study 2.

CASE STUDY 2

Mr and Mrs Y applied to their preferred school, confident that their application on behalf of their child would be successful. Their application was rejected. The LEA stated that Mr and Mrs Y lived further from the school than the parents of the last successful applicant. The parents lodged an appeal and were able to illustrate that a new road that fulfilled the requirements for a safe walking route had not been included, which would have resulted in a place being offered. The appeal was not successful. For some reason, the appeal panel did not accept the integrity of the information supplied by the parents. In my view, if there was any doubt, the appeal should have been adjourned so that the information could be clarified. The investigation, which subsequently took place, should have been carried out before the panel reached their decision. This is why the original decision was flawed.

I discussed the LEA's decision, and the appeal decision, with Mr and Mrs Y and an investigation revealed that the LEA measuring software did not take into account a newly constructed road adopted by the local authority. Information demonstrating this omission was presented to the LEA, and it admitted that a mistake had been made in this regard. However, while it was not prepared to offer a school place to Mr and Mrs Y's child, the LEA did grant a further appeal. Mr and Mrs Y appealed again. After several months of uncertainty, they received notification that their second appeal had been successful.

CASE STUDY 3

Mr Z's admission application to the LEA of his granddaughter's preferred school was not successful. When he enquired why, Mr Z was told that he lived further away than the last successful applicant. Mr Z challenged this decision on the basis that a right of way discounted by the LEA did, in fact, meet its definition of a safe walking route. Had this factor been properly taken into account, the result would have been that the measured distance would have shown that Mr Z's granddaughter lived closer to the school than the last successful applicant.

The LEA inspected the right of way and agreed with Mr Z that it did comply with its definition of a safe walking route. In the circumstances, the LEA re-measured all the applications and found that several applicants, including Mr Z's granddaughter, had been mistakenly denied places at the school. The LEA subsequently offered places to several children, even though it exceeded its own published admission number, without the need for the parents to go through the appeal process.

Special or exceptional reasons to attend a school

Many community schools will feature an 'exceptional' or 'special reasons' criterion in their admission criteria. The exceptional reasons criterion has been designed to allow the admission authority to consider unusual or special circumstances which are not covered by other admission criteria. The admission authority must look at an application submitted under the exceptional reasons criterion from an objective point of view. The admission authority must also consider whether or not the exceptional circumstances cited by parents mean that their child can only attend the one school of their choice.

Should you wish to submit an admission application saying that exceptional circumstances dictate that your child must attend only the school of your choice, you will need to establish exactly what is required to satisfy this criterion. You may need to speak to the admission authority to see how it defines 'exceptional', or if it can give examples of what may be regarded as exceptional. However, such advice cannot be exhaustive, since by its very definition exceptional is, indeed, exceptional.

Many parents believe that their circumstances are exceptional, but this is rarely accepted by the admission authority. It should be noted that the LEA will look at exceptional reasons very carefully and apply its guidelines rigorously. Therefore, not many applicants meet this criterion.

Voluntary aided and foundation schools' and academies' admission criteria

The admission criteria are the same for all community schools within the same LEA area. However, the admission criteria for voluntary aided and foundation schools and academies differ from school to school because each school's admission policy is determined by that school's governors. You will need to look at each school's prospectus to see if you meet the admission criteria for the individual school.

Many voluntary aided schools have a religious ethos. This will be reflected in the school's published admission criteria. The school's governors may require you to complete a supplementary application form, in addition to the one required by the LEA, in order to obtain further information about how the applicant meets the element of the school's admission criteria concerned with religion. The governors of a church school will usually expect to see that the applicant demonstrates regular religious commitment. The governors will determine what they consider to be 'regular commitment'. For instance, the applicant, and also the child's family, may be required to show that he regularly attends church services. Applicants may be asked to provide documentary evidence of their religious membership (such as a baptismal certificate), and also provide a letter of support from their parish priest or minister of religion.

Below is an example of the admission criteria for a Roman Catholic (RC) secondary school, showing the basis on which places are allocated to applicants, with the greatest preference being given to those in category 1:

1 Baptised Roman Catholic children attending Catholic schools. The governors would expect each candidate to have the application form accompanied by a baptismal certificate and a statement of support written and signed by the applicant's parish priest.

2 Baptised Roman Catholic children who are not attending a Catholic school, but who otherwise meet the requirements of category 1.

3 Other baptised Catholic children; a baptismal certificate is essential in such cases.

4 Siblings in the same family (including those who are adopted or fostered) of children who are at the school at the time of entry.

5 Children of other denominations attending a voluntary aided church school. The governors would expect such Christians to have evidence of baptism and have support of worship written and signed by their parish priest or minister of religion.

6 Children of other Christian denominations not attending a voluntary aided church school, providing that they can satisfy the requirements in category 5.

7 Any other children whose parents wish them to be educated at the school.

Notes

1 'Baptised Roman Catholics' is defined.

2 'Other Christian denominations' is defined.

3 A tie-break using distance is applied where appropriate. (This is used in any criteria when there are more applications than places available.)

4 'Looked after' children are given priority in each category (looked after children are cared for by the local authority and are given priority above all children in every school).

The example shows that you may, relatively simply, assess the category into which you fall with respect to this criterion. This will give you an indication of how successful your admission application is likely to be. You must, of course, take other factors into account, such as the number of available places (the published admission number) in your preferred school.

If you speak with the admission authority to obtain advice or information, remember that it is always worthwhile to ask for its response to be given in writing. A written document can always be produced at a later admission appeal, if necessary. It will also show the information you used when you made your decision to apply to a particular school (or schools).

Grammar school applications

The admission arrangements for applying to a grammar school are exactly the same as those for applications to a non-grammar school. You will, however, need to contact the relevant school (or schools) in order to make arrangements for your child to sit the grammar school tests. The admission authority will make arrangements for the tests, which usually take place in October/November. Because of the timing of the tests, it is unlikely that you will know the outcome of your child's tests before the LEA's deadline for the submission of application forms or preference forms. The decisions will be sent to parents at different times depending on the timetable set by the school, but usually these will be in December or January.

Other relevant information

Open evenings

All schools will arrange open evenings for parents. Open evenings are your opportunity to look around the school and see the facilities for yourself. You will be able to speak with the head teacher and the staff, and to ask them any questions you may have about the school. The school naturally wishes to attract pupils, so bear in mind that the head teacher and staff may give a positive slant to the school's achievements. Many students will also be on hand and you should speak to them, as well as to the staff. This will enable you to get an idea of the students' views of the school and the opinions of the school given by the staff.

It is important that you attend the open evening. You can assess first hand whether or not the school is suitable for your child, and if it has an atmosphere which will promote your child's educational development. Your child should also see the school because his views will be important when you decide which school (or schools) you would prefer him to attend.

The equal preference system

From the September 2008 intake, LEAs must operate what is referred to as an equal preference system. What will happen is this: You will rank the schools to which you are applying in order of preference, with your first choice at number 1. The LEA will simply receive a list of all applicants who have included the school as one of their preferences. The LEA will then allocate places to applicants in accordance with the LEA's published admission criteria, regardless of the order of preference indicated on the application form. At the same time the LEA will send lists of pupils to the governors of voluntary aided and foundation schools, and academies, where those schools have been listed as a preference. The governors will then advise the LEA which pupils the school is proposing to offer places to, based on the application of the school's own admission criteria.

Under the equal preference system, some applicants may be eligible to receive more than one offer of a school place. Should this happen, the LEA will offer your child a place in the school that has an available place and that has also been ranked highest (although not necessarily first) on your list of preferred schools. The school places which you do not need to accept will be allocated to other pupils.

Co-ordinated admission arrangements

All LEAs operate what is known as co-ordinated admission arrangements. What this means is that you must complete and return the application form for any school (or schools) to your own LEA. Under current legislation, you are entitled to express up to three preferences for schools. In some areas you can express more preferences. In London, for example, you can express up to six preferences.

What happens, therefore, if you live in the London Borough of Lewisham and you want to apply for two Lewisham community schools, two voluntary aided schools in Lewisham, and two community schools in Greenwich? The simple answer is that you apply on the Lewisham co-ordinated preference form – that is, the application form (which is included in the admissions booklet) – giving details of all six schools ranked in order of preference. You must ensure that you provide any supporting documentation required by any of the schools. Finally, you must make sure that the application form is received by the LEA by the closing time on the closing date. Case Study 4 shows why it is important to meet the LEA's deadline.

If it is at all possible, take the application form in to the LEA personally, and ask for a receipt. If you are unable to do this, make sure that your application form is posted well before the closing date. Telephone the LEA to check that it has been received. This is very important, because LEAs may claim that proof of posting is not proof of receipt. Thus, even if you can demonstrate that you posted your application form, there is no guarantee that it was received by the LEA.

The application form

An application form, also called the preference form, will normally be included in the LEA's admissions booklet. Many LEAs now enable you to apply online. Applications made online are usually acknowledged by an automatic message. The acknowledgement message should be printed and kept, so that it may be produced if necessary. If you do not receive acknowledgement of an online application, you should check with the LEA that the application has been received.

If you are applying for a place at a secondary school, some LEAs make provision for application forms to be handed in to the primary school currently attended by your child. If this is the case, ask the primary school for a receipt. If you are applying for a primary school place, some LEAs allow you to return the application form to the first preference primary school, as well as directly to the LEA.

But, whatever you do, do not leave returning your application form to the LEA until the last minute! If you do, something unexpected may happen. This could mean that your application form is not received until after the LEA's deadline. Case Study 4 shows that, in a 'worst case scenario', your child may be denied a place at your preferred school, simply because you missed the deadline.

CASE STUDY 4

Mrs N, who happened to be a teacher at a secondary school, gave the preference form to her son and asked him to hand it in at his primary school. The school noticed that it had not received a form from Mrs N and it left an urgent message on her mobile phone to let her know that the closing time for receipt of the forms was 3pm that day. Mrs N retrieved the message at approximately 1pm. In haste, Mrs N went to the primary school attended by her son and found the form in his locker. However, the primary school had already returned the forms to the LEA, as it was required to do. Mrs N then rushed the form straight to the LEA's offices. Unfortunately, by the time the LEA received the form it was 3.15pm and the form was, correctly, deemed to be late.

The preferred school was oversubscribed and was not in a position to offer Mrs N's son a place. Mrs N lodged an appeal, but it was not successful. If the application form had been received on time, her son would have secured a place at his preferred school.

The LEA will start to process the application forms as soon as it receives them. If any preferences have been received for schools other than the community schools in its administrative area, such as voluntary aided schools, it will advise the relevant admission authorities to see if they are able to offer places to the applicants; these lists will not be sent to those authorities until after the closing date.

Please bear in mind that if you are seeking a place at a voluntary aided school, foundation school or academy, you may also need to complete a governors' form (which can be obtained from the school concerned), in addition to the usual LEA application form. It is important that you provide whatever information is required, in order to avoid any delay to the LEA's decision-making process and thus to your being informed where your child will be offered a school place.

Sit back and relax!

Having done all your homework and submitted your application (or preference) form, there is nothing more that you can do. Except to wait! Decisions relating to secondary school applications are published on 1 March every year. Decisions regarding primary school applications will usually be published later in the year, although some primary schools do issue their decisions before 1 March.

Remember that approximately 90 per cent of all parents secure a place at one of their preferred schools. The children of the remaining ten per cent of parents will be offered places at alternative schools. If your child is offered a place at a school which you feel is unacceptable, you will be offered the opportunity to appeal against the LEA's decision. If you did not get offered a place at any of your preferred schools, or if you were offered a place at a school but not at your highest preference, you have a right to a statutory appeal in front of an independent appeal panel.

CHECKLIST 1

1   Have you obtained a copy of the LEA's admissions booklet?

2   Have you obtained the prospectus (or prospectuses) for the school (or schools) which interest(s) you?

3   Do you understand how places will be allocated if there are more applications than available school places?

4   After studying the published admission criteria for last year's admission, is it your opinion that your child will be allocated a place in your preferred school?

5   Have you attended your preferred school's (or schools') open evening(s), and spoken to the staff and the students?

6   After consulting the current year's admission criteria, is your choice of school realistic and reasonable?

7   Do you understand how the equal preference system will operate?

8   Have you obtained details of successful admissions for the last five years?

9   Have the admission criteria been amended recently? You can find this out by asking the admission authority.

10 Have you obtained any advice from the LEA or from the school in writing, and if so, have you kept this information to hand?

11 If you are applying to a grammar school, have you arranged for your child to sit the entrance tests?

12 If you are applying to a faith school, are you certain that you can demonstrate your religious affiliation?

13 If you are applying to a faith school, have you asked your parish priest or minister of religion for a letter of support?

14 Have you obtained all the documentation to support your admission application?

15 Have you checked to make sure that you have enclosed **all** of the necessary information with the application form?

16 Have you ensured that your application was submitted on time?

17 Have you checked to ensure that your application was received by the admission authority?

Chapter 2

Schools' admission criteria

Every year admission authorities are required to consult and publish criteria that they will use to decide which applications will be successful if more applications are received than there are places available. This is commonly referred to as admission criteria. Admission authorities are required to consult the Local Education Authority (LEA) and other adjoining admission authorities by 1 March and determine such admission criteria by 15 April for the admissions round starting in the following September. This means that if an admission authority wishes to change its admission criteria, it will take at least 18 months, and often longer, to do so.

The following sections will look at what is regarded as being permissible and how such admission criteria will operate in practice.

The issues covered in this chapter are as follows:

- Setting admission criteria
- Children with special educational needs
- Siblings
- Social and medical needs
- Random allocation
- Home to school distance
- Catchment areas
- Faith-based admissions
- Additional guidance for boarding schools
- Additional guidance for primary schools
- Additional guidance for secondary schools
- Banding

Quick reference

- Special educational needs
  The term 'special educational needs' has been defined as children who

have learning difficulties or disabilities that make it harder for them to learn or access education than most children of the same age.

- ## Siblings

  These are usually brothers and sisters of the same family living at the same address. However, it may include any children living at the same address. The published admission criteria will define siblings.

- ## Comprehensive schools

  These are schools that do not use selection by ability or aptitude as part of their published admission arrangements. Most secondary schools will be deemed comprehensive and can include community, voluntary aided and foundation schools, as well as academies.

- ## Oversubscription criteria

  These are also referred to as admission criteria and they are the priorities that the admission authority will use if the school receives more applications than there are places available.

- ## Oversubscribed school

  This is a school which is very popular and every year receives more applications than available places.

- ## First preference first

  This is where all first preferences applications are considered before second and third preferences are considered. Such arrangements have been replaced by equal preference arrangements (see Chapter 1 for more information).

QUICK LIST

1   Does your child have a statement of special educational needs (see page 25) that gives him priority in the admission criteria?

2   Have you checked the admission criteria of the school (or schools) that you prefer to see how best you meet them?

3   Is the school using any admission criteria that are not permissible?

4   Is the school that you are interested in within the statutory walking distance?

5   Does your child have special medical, or other exceptional, reasons to attend the school, and have you any third party support for the application?

6   According to your child's age, which key stage does he fall into?

7   Do you understand how the admission criteria will be applied?

8   Do you understand the admission criteria that will be used at the school of your choice?

Setting admission criteria

In February 2007, the Department for Education and Skills (now the Department for Children, Schools and Families, and in future referred to as the DCSF) published a new School Admissions Code that applies to admissions for children who are starting school from September 2008. The new Code sets out the ground rules for establishing and changing admission criteria and what issues the admission authority must take into consideration.

2.4 When determining oversubscription (admission) criteria all admission authorities must ensure that they take account of their statutory responsibilities in respect of children with statements of special educational needs and children in care. Admission authorities must ensure that their determined admission arrangements for admissions in September 2008 and subsequent years comply with the mandatory provisions of this Code.

The School Admissions Code 2007

The Code explains good and bad practice in admission criteria and it gives examples. It also refers to common criteria that are in use at the moment. Admission authorities have considerable discretion about the admission criteria that they use, and the examples in this book cannot cover every possibility. The different types of admission criteria that are commonly used will be discussed later in this chapter.

It is important that you understand what is regarded as being good practice, so that you can judge for yourself whether your application is likely to be successful or not. This will help you to decide which schools to choose when you submit your application form to the LEA, and also how to lodge a successful appeal if your application is not successful.

Admission authorities are encouraged to use admission arrangements that are easy to understand so that you are able to assess whether you have a reasonable prospect of gaining a place at a particular school. The problem is that the more they try to make it apply equally to everyone, the more complicated it becomes and, consequently, the more difficult it is to understand.

Many admission authorities, usually voluntary aided and foundation schools, have used interviews to assess the pupils' suitability for a place at the school. The new Code has banned the use of interviews, except for assessing suitability for boarding at boarding schools. Interviews now have no place in the admission arrangements and if they are used, they are against the Code and are unlawful.

Some admission authorities (usually foundation and voluntary aided schools and academies) use complicated points systems as part of their admission criteria and they award points according to their relative importance. For example, some authorities award points for regular attendance at church – the more frequently you attend church the more points you will be awarded – and then places will be offered to the parents with the most points.

Although you cannot be guaranteed a place at a particular school, you must be given the opportunity to express a preference for the school (or schools) you want for your child (or children). It is important that other policies used by schools (e.g. school uniforms) do not inadvertently discourage applications from poorer families. This can occur when schools allow only a few outlets, or in some cases, only one, to stock uniforms and the cost is beyond some parents. Other schools are less specific about where school uniforms and other school garments can be purchased.

So what does the DCSF describe as admission criteria which should not be used to allocate school places?

> 2.13 In setting oversubscription (admission) criteria the admission authorities for all maintained schools **must not**:
>
> a) Stipulate any conditions that affect the priority given to an application, such as taking account of other preferences for schools. For example, by saying that priority will be given if all or some other preferences are for a school with particular characteristics (e.g. other schools are of a particular religious denomination). This includes criteria often referred to as 'conditionally';
>
> b) Give priority to children according to the order of other schools named as preferences by their parents, including 'first preference first' arrangements;
>
> c) Giving priority to children according to their parents' willingness to give practical support to the ethos of the school or to support the school financially or in some other way;
>
> d) Give priority to children according to the occupational, financial or marital status of their parents;

e) Give priority to children according to the educational achievement or background of their parents;

f) Take account of reports from primary or nursery schools about the children's past behaviour, attendance or achievement;

g) Discriminate against or disadvantage children with special educational needs or disabilities;

h) Allocate places at a school on the basis that the siblings of the children, or other relatives, **are former pupils**, including siblings who were on roll at the time of application but will have left by the time the children start school;

i) Take account of the behaviour of other members of the children's families, whether good or bad, including good or bad attendance records of other children in the same family;

j) Give priority to children whose parents are current or former staff or governors, or who have another connection to the school, subject to paragraph 2.14 below;

k) Give priority to children according to the children's, or their parents', particular interests, specialist knowledge or hobbies. This does not include taking account of membership of, or participation in, religious activities for faith schools, providing that this is consistent with the Code and guidance issued by the faith provider body/religious authority;

l) Give priority to children based on the order in which applications were received;

m) In the case of designated grammar schools, that rank all children according to a pre-determined pass mark and allocate places to those who score highest, or give priority to siblings of current or former pupils;

n) In the case of schools with boarding places, take account of the children's suitability for boarding.

2.14 The prohibition in 2.13 does not prevent an admission authority from offering a place (or places) to the children of a new appointee to a post at the school after the published offer dates for primary schools, or the national offer day for secondary schools, where there is a demonstrable skills shortage for the vacant post in question, even where this will be in excess of the published admission number, provided that all other relevant law is complied with. Alternatively, admission authorities may, in these circumstances, place the children of new appointees at the top of any waiting list for places at the school.

The School Admissions Code 2007

All of the admission criteria above (detailed in paragraphs 2.13 and 2.14) are not permitted for admissions for children who are starting school from September 2008. It is certainly possible that some admission authorities, either through ignorance or otherwise, will still continue to use admission criteria that are not permissible. However, if you are unsuccessful with your original application, and an admission authority is still using admission criteria that are not permitted, this will not necessarily result in a place being offered through the appeal process. What you will need to show is that the use of such criteria has resulted in a place being denied. These issues will be dealt with in more detail in the section on admission appeals (see page 59).

Often, parents are not aware that a school is using admission criteria that are not permissible, and it is important that you are aware because the use of such criteria could be a ground for lodging an appeal. The only way that you can find out about this is to check the criteria against what is permissible in the School Admissions Code 2007.

CASE STUDY 1

I acted for a parent who was a teacher at a school where her son was seeking a place. According to the admission criteria, children of teachers were given priority and, quite naturally, she expected that her son would gain a place at the school. In the year before her son was due to be admitted, the school was challenged about the legitimacy of the admission criteria. As a result, the school was no longer able to give priority to the children of teachers.

The teacher did not secure a place for her son because she lived approximately 15 miles from the school. I was asked to help with the appeal, which was successful. One of the reasons that were put forward at the appeal was that the teacher had every expectation that a place would be secured and this did not happen as a result of the admission criteria being changed at such a late stage. If the admission criterion was amended earlier, the teacher could have moved in an effort to improve her son's chance of a successful application.

So what oversubscription criteria are permissible? There is a range of commonly used criteria that most admission authorities will apply. These are now discussed in more detail.

Children with special educational needs

Children with special educational needs are defined as children who have learning difficulties or disabilities that make it harder for them to learn or access education than most children of the same age. Children with special educational needs fall into three categories. These are School Action, School Action Plus and children with a statement of educational needs. If a child has special educational needs, he may need extra help in a range of areas. These might include:

- schoolwork;
- reading, writing, number work or understanding information;
- expressing himself or understanding what others are saying;
- making friends or relating to adults;
- behaving properly in school;
- organising himself;
- sensory or physical needs which may affect them in school.

School Action

When children start school they will be assessed to see if they have any special educational needs. If it is decided that they fall into one of the above areas, they will be provided with extra help and this will be met from within the school's existing budget. School Action is where a need has been identified but it is not regarded as being serious. No priority is given to pupils with School Action in the admission arrangements.

School Action Plus

This is the next level up where the needs identified are more significant and cannot be met from the school's existing budget. The needs are such that outside agencies, such as social services, specialist teachers, or speech and language specialists, have to be called upon. No priority is given to pupils with School Action Plus in the admission arrangements.

Children with a statement of special educational needs

This is where a child has been identified with substantial learning difficulties and has been the subject of a formal process. The statement will identify the school where the child should be educated. Children with a statement will be awarded a place at the named school, even if it means that the published admission number will be exceeded. The special educational needs process is outside the scope of this book. Further details can be obtained from the Special Educational Needs Tribunal website at www.sendist.gov.uk.

Siblings

The use of siblings as an admission criterion is one that is commonly used by many community schools and, to a lesser extent, faith schools. Many admission authorities rightly believe that children in the same family should be given priority. This view is endorsed by the main political parties, who feel that families are an important institution who need to be supported.

For those admissions for pupils who were being admitted before September 2008, admission authorities could take into consideration siblings, at the school in question, if they were attending the school either at the time of the application or at the time that the younger child was due to start school. However, from the September 2008 intake, a sibling can only be taken into consideration if he will still be attending the school when the younger sibling starts. A sibling who is attending the school at the time of application but will not be at the school when the younger sibling starts, will no longer be recognised as a sibling in the admission arrangements.

The definition of a sibling is now not as straightforward as it used to be. In modern society a sibling could be a blood relative, an adopted child, or indeed any child living at the same address as the qualifying sibling. The admission authority will need to define a sibling in its admission arrangements and, therefore, you will need to look carefully at this definition to see if your child qualifies.

Siblings at primary schools

The government sees the family to be at the heart of the admissions system and it encourages admission authorities to take into account the needs of parents and young children when they are establishing their admission criteria. With this in mind, admission authorities are encouraged to allow siblings to attend the same school, particularly multiple birth children (e.g. twins or triplets), providing that this does not conflict with the infant class size legislation. This will be discussed in more detail in Chapter 6.

You may wish to note that some authorities place a distance factor on recognising siblings. The statutory walking distance for children under the age of eight is two miles; and for eight and over is three miles. The statutory walking distance will determine if your child qualifies for assistance with travel to and from school. You will qualify for assistance if you live further than the statutory walking distance to the school, which you have been allocated by the LEA, providing that the school is not one of your expressed choices. Some authorities will not recognise siblings if they live further than a certain distance from the school and they will often use the statutory walking distance as the qualifying factor. You will need to consider this when applying for a school and also if you consider moving house after you have established a sibling connection at the school.

CASE STUDY 2

Mr and Mrs X had two children and applied for their older child to attend their first preference primary school. The application was successful. Afterwards, they moved to a house that was located approximately eight miles from the school. They applied for their younger child to attend the same school as his sibling. The application was not successful because the admission authority had placed a two-mile limit on recognising siblings and, as the parents lived further than two miles from the school, they were not given priority under the siblings rule. The parents were then considered under the distance criteria which gave priority to children living nearest to the school. The parents lived further away than the last successful applicant based on distance criteria. The parents appealed but it was unsuccessful.

Moral: Before you think about moving house, check the admission criteria for the school to make sure that a change of address will not adversely affect any subsequent application for the school.

Siblings at secondary schools

In 1996 there were 3,594 maintained secondary schools in England of which 164 were selective (i.e. schools where places are allocated by ability). Schools which are not selective are commonly known as 'comprehensive' schools. Some comprehensive schools have successfully applied for specialist status (that attracts additional funding from the government), which allows the governors' discretion to select up to ten per cent of their admissions by ability or aptitude. However, 90 per cent of these schools have chosen not to exercise this discretion. The School Admissions Code has accepted that it is good practice to give priority to siblings at secondary schools.

The government is committed to not introducing any more grammar schools. There are currently 164 grammar schools in England and the government has allowed such schools to continue to select by ability. There are some grammar schools that select all of their pupils by ability. If this is the case, the school will only give priority to siblings who achieve the required pass mark.

However, having an older sibling at the school of your choice does not necessarily mean that a younger sibling will secure a place at the school.

Unlike primary schools, secondary schools will not normally use a distance factor for siblings, but they may place conditions on such applications. For example, if you are applying to a grammar school, a younger sibling will only be given priority if he passes the grammar school test. Also, if you live outside of the catchment area for a school, a younger sibling may not be given priority over anyone living in the catchment area.

Social and medical needs

Many authorities give priority to pupils that have a social or medical need to attend a particular school. Social or medical reasons would normally mean that there is a compelling need for the child to attend a particular school and those needs cannot be met by any other school. This is usually a very stringent test that only a very small percentage of applicants, if any, will be able to meet. It is difficult to define such needs because the definition will differ between different admission authorities. Examples of this may include a child who has been sexually or physically abused and needs a close network of friends who all attend the same school, or a child with a rare medical condition who needs to be in close proximity to his parents' home or work in the case of an emergency.

Admission authorities that use such a criteria must explain what information would be required in order to support such an application and, indeed, exactly what they mean by social or medical reasons. This is important because the definition may well vary between different admission authorities. Such information would normally include a supporting letter from a health professional or social worker. The supporting evidence must explain why the school in question is the most suitable school and the difficulties that would be caused if the child was to attend another school. The admission authority must also explain in its admission arrangements how this information will be objectively assessed. The admission arrangements will be set out in the school's prospectus.

If a pupil has an ability or interest in the activity covered by the specialist status of the school (e.g. sport or music), admission authorities must not use the social or medical admission criteria to admit pupils because of a need related to the specialist status. Such an interest or ability would not be regarded as an exceptional reason to attend the school. Each school will use objective tests to determine which applicants will be successful. For example, if the school is a specialist sport school, such tests may include running or jumping tests, which can be objectively assessed. For more information on specialist status schools, see the section on 'Partially selective schools' at page 38.

CASE STUDY 3

Mr and Mrs X were applying to a secondary school for their daughter. Although their daughter had strong medical grounds to attend the school, the parents did not disclose this information on the application form and they did not provide supporting medical evidence. This was because, having looked at the successful applications in the previous years, they saw that they lived considerably closer to the school than the last successful application. They were reluctant to disclose this medical information because they did not want their daughter to be tagged with a medical condition.

Unbeknown to the parents, there were a considerable number of siblings applying for admission at the same time as them and, as a result, the number of places available using the distance factor was considerably less than the previous year. As a consequence, the distance measured for the last successful applicant this year was much closer to the school.

As a result, Mr and Mrs X's application was not successful and they then had to appeal. The admission authority confirmed that if the medical information had been supplied with the application, it would have been successful. Fortunately, a subsequent appeal was successful, but if the medical information had been supplied with the original application, Mr and Mrs X would have avoided months of stress and anxiety, not to mention the uncertainty that their daughter had to endure at a crucial time when she was sitting her SATS (i.e. Standard Assessment Tests, which are the statutory tests that are taken at the end of each key stage to determine a pupil's progress against national targets).

Moral: Always disclose all the information available with your application and make sure that you send in any supporting documentation to ensure that you give yourself the best chance of a successful application. This may avoid months of uncertainty and anxiety. The information disclosed will be kept entirely confidential.

Random allocation

Random allocation has been accepted as a fair way of determining places. It is not clear, at the moment, exactly how this will operate, since it is believed that only a few admission authorities have formally decided to allocate places on this basis, although it is understood that another admission authority has been using it on a limited basis; these authorities are located in Brighton, London, Hertfordshire, Derbyshire and

Northampton. Random allocation can be used either as a tie break (this is used if there are more applications that meet the terms of the criteria than there are places available) or as an admission criterion in its own right. Other admission authorities are waiting to see how successful this method of allocating places will be before they decide whether to introduce similar arrangements. Random allocation simply means that all applicants will have an equal chance of securing a place irrespective of where they live. It is understood that computer software will be used to allocate places which will be subject to independent scrutiny. All such eligible places will be allocated by inputting the applicants' data into a computer and using software to produce a priority list, and the places will then be allocated according to that list.

Brighton & Hove City Council decided to offer places using this method after incorporating random allocations as a tie break. The council received a lot of local and national publicity as it is the first admission authority to incorporate random allocation as a fundamental part of its admission criteria. Many admission authorities are watching the situation to see how it develops because the criteria may need to be reviewed in the light of experience. It is possible that some unforeseen problems may emerge after the first year of operation and they will need to be addressed in the future. The criterion was introduced following a review that aroused a lot of public reaction, both for and against its introduction. It will be interesting to see if any other admission authorities introduce similar criteria in the future.

If random allocation is used by admission authorities, they must set out clearly how this will operate and ensure that arrangements are transparent.

Home to school distance

Without doubt, the vast majority of school places throughout the whole country are allocated by using a distance factor of some kind. It meets the provisions of the Code inasmuch as it is clear, fair and objective, which is why so many admission authorities use it. In addition, it also gives priority to children living closest to the school. The distance factor differs from catchment areas, which are described below, in that catchment areas are defined before applications are sought from parents. The way that the area is drawn may mean that successful applicants may not necessarily live closest to the school. The distance factor will be determined after applications have been received from parents and the school will allocate places according to those applicants that live nearest to it.

Most admission authorities will use computer software to measure the distance between the child's home and school. Such software can measure either the shortest straight line distance (i.e. 'as the crow flies') or the shortest walking route. If an admission authority uses the latter method, it will need to identify which roads and footpaths meet its definition of a safe walking route. For example, is the route lit, paved and a public right of way? Whatever definition the admission authority uses as a safe walking route, it must be set out clearly in its admission arrangements, which will be included in the school's prospectus for voluntary aided and foundation schools, and academies, and in the LEA's admissions booklet for community schools. If you are in any doubt whatsoever about what constitutes a safe walking route, you should contact the admission authority.

A distance factor can be used either as an admission criterion in its own right or as a tie-break. The School Admissions Code states that when determining admission criteria, admission authorities must use a tried and tested system which parents can understand.

Regretfully, there are many circumstances, where following a family breakdown, a child lives with both parents on a shared basis. The Code says that where a child lives with parents with shared responsibility and he spends part of the week with both of them, the admission authority must make it clear which address will be used as the home address for the purpose of allocating places.

Catchment areas

A catchment area is a predefined area which is established before applications are sought from parents and it does not necessarily give priority to children living closest to the school. However, living in a catchment area does not guarantee a place at a school. No admission criteria can give such a guarantee. The catchment area criterion differs from the distance factor in that the home to school distance is defined after applications have been received. Catchment areas and home to school distance are two separate admission criteria and authorities can use either one or the other.

Some admission authorities use, what is referred to as, inner and outer catchment areas. In this situation priority is, first of all, given to pupils living in the inner catchment area; such an area will usually be drawn very close to the school. If there are still places available after offering places to all those living in the inner catchment area, then pupils living in the outer catchment area are considered. If there are places available after the school offers places to all pupils living in both the inner and outer catchment areas, then places will be offered to pupils that live outside both areas. Alternatively, the admission authority may limit the number of places available to pupils living in the inner catchment area. This will allow admission authorities to give priority to a specified number of places in the inner catchment area and the remaining places in the outer area. Another practice is to establish a number of small catchment areas which may be some distance from the school. This will mean that priority is not given to pupils that live nearest to the school.

If admission authorities use catchment areas or distance in their admission criteria, they should provide a map of the area, which is usually included in the admissions booklet published by the admission authority. Alternatively, the admissions booklet will explain where the map can be inspected or a copy obtained. Catchment areas must be established in advance of the normal admissions round.

Admission authorities are required to review their admission criteria annually and therefore you could make representations about possible changes that the authority were proposing to introduce. You can contact the admission authority to see how you can do this. Admission authorities are encouraged to involve parents when they are reviewing their admission arrangements. You can also lodge an objection with the Schools Adjudicator, who will then be required to make a decision on the proposed admission criteria.

Faith-based admissions

2.41 It is unlawful under section 49 of the Equality Act 2006 for maintained, non-maintained or independent schools to discriminate against a child on the grounds of the child's religion or belief in the terms on which they offer to admit him as a pupil, or by refusing to accept an application for a place at the school. However, those schools, designated by the Secretary of State as having a religious character (faith schools), are exempt and are permitted to use faith-based oversubscription criteria in order to give priority in admissions to children who are members of, or who practise, their faith or denomination. This only applies if the school is oversubscribed.

The School Admissions Code 2007

It is important that, while faith schools are given this exemption, their admission criteria must be clear, fair and objective. It is for the admission authority to decide exactly how membership of a faith or religious practice is to be demonstrated. It is good practice for the governing bodies of all faith schools that are their own admission authority to consult with their own religious authority before consulting other admission authorities. The admission criteria will vary from one school to another. Authorities are required to consult other admission authorities because it is possible that the introduction of any new or amended admission criteria may have an adverse effect on adjoining authorities. Admission authorities are required to consult before 1 March in every year and determine such arrangements by 15 April. Any changes that have been agreed will apply to the admissions round that commences in the following September and relates to admissions 12 months later.

CASE STUDY 4

Mrs X applied to a religious-based school and part of the admission criteria required the applicant to show regular attendance at church. However, the governors' support form simply asked for the minister of religion's comments and the comment was, 'I fully support this application'. This is a subjective judgement made by the priest and is difficult to assess objectively. In this case it was difficult for the appeal panel to make an assessment of the religious commitment when checked against the admission criteria for the school, which determined that regular attendance meant once a week.

Having listened to all the details of the appeal, including the personal issues raised by the parent, the panel was not persuaded that there were compelling reasons to attend the school and therefore the appeal was not successful.

Moral: If you are thinking of applying to a religious-based school, always check the admission criteria of the school carefully. Some admission authorities require you to attend church regularly for a period of time before the admissions round starts – sometimes for up to two years.

As part of their admission arrangements, many admission authorities require applicants to demonstrate attendance at church on a regular basis. This may be once a week, once a fortnight or once a month. For this to be an objective criterion, your minister of religion must complete a form provided by the admission authority with a tick box against each possibility. This is objective because the responses are simply 'yes' or 'no' and they cannot be coloured by the minister's feelings or opinions. The minister of religion knows what is expected of him and the admission authority can objectively assess his answers.

However, some admission authorities will ask the minister of religion to sign a form where he comments on the applicant's suitability. This requires the minister of religion to interpret what the admission authority needs; and it also requires the admission authority to interpret what the religious minister has said. This is subjective and against the Code of Practice.

You will not normally see the minister of religion's response until after the completion of the admission arrangements. You may well be able to challenge the response if your application is not successful and you believe that a mistake has been made when you lodge an appeal.

New voluntary aided or foundation faith schools

2.50 The governing body of a voluntary aided or foundation school, which is established after Part 2 of the Education and Inspections Act 2006 comes into force, **must** obtain the consent of the appropriate diocesan authority or other body or person representing the religion or religious denomination, as may be prescribed under section 89(2)(e) for consultative purposes, before proposing or determining admission arrangements which give priority for a proportion of places to children otherwise than on the basis of whether that child is a member of or practises the relevant religion or religious denomination.

The School Admissions Code 2007

If a new voluntary aided or faith school is established, it must obtain the consent of its appropriate diocesan authority before introducing admission criteria that will give priority to children not of the same faith. Usually faith schools will give priority to children of the same faith before other faiths.

Additional guidelines for boarding schools

There are around 35 state-maintained or grant-maintained schools. The School Admissions Code explains that such schools provide a stable educational environment for those children that need it, including those whose parents have jobs or careers which require them to work abroad. If such places are made available, priority must be given in the admission criteria for children with a 'boarding need'. What is regarded as a boarding need must be made clear in the school's published admission arrangements. If you consider that boarding is appropriate for your child, you will need to contact the school concerned in order to determine eligibility for admission.

Additional guidelines for primary schools

Although most admission authorities allow for children to start school at the beginning of the academic year in which they reach the age of five, which is commonly referred to as 'rising fives', and is also referred to as the reception or foundation year, the law states that children do not need to start school until the term following their fifth birthday. Years 1 and 2 are referred to as Key Stage 1. There are four key stages which are directly linked to the National Curriculum as follows:

Age of the child at the end of the school year	Year group at school	Key stage
5	Reception	-
6	1	1
7	2	1
8	3	2
9	4	2
10	5	2
11	6	2
12	7	3
13	8	3
14	9	3
15	10	4
16	11	4

The compulsory school age is five years old. For many children this could mean starting school in Year 1, rather than the reception or foundation year. Admission authorities will usually try to contact parents who have children who are three or four to advise them about the admission arrangements for their area. Authorities do this by advertising in public areas, such as nurseries or libraries, and using lists provided by the health authorities. Most admission authorities expect children to start full-time education in the term during which they reach the age of five. Therefore, children whose birthdays are between 1 September and 31 December would start full time in the autumn term; those whose birthdays are between 1 January and 31 March would start full time in the spring term; and those whose birthdays are between 1 April and 31 August would start full time in the summer term.

Date of birth	Start school part time	Start school full time
1 September to 31 December	-	September
1 January to 31 March	September	January
1 April to 31 August	September	March/April

You will need to check the local arrangements because sometimes the admission authority may use different arrangements.

Deferred entry to primary schools

The School Admissions Code allows admission authorities for primary schools to offer places in reception classes to children before they reach the compulsory school age. If an LEA offers you a place early, it should also offer you the option of deferring entry until later in the academic year. However, you would not be able to defer entry beyond the term following your child's fifth birthday and you would not be able to defer it until a later academic year. The effect of this is that the place would be offered to you as normal and the place would be held open until you take up the place.

Infant classes

The government introduced legislation in 1999 that limited class sizes in Key Stage 1 to no more than 30 with a single school teacher. This means that in infant classes, which includes reception and Years 1 and 2, children must not be taught in classes of more than 30, unless there is more than one school teacher present. Therefore, it is possible to have a class of 45, providing that there are two school teachers present. These issues will be covered in more detail in Chapter 6.

2.58 The class size legislation makes allowance for the entry of an additional child in very limited circumstances where not to admit the child would be prejudicial to his interests ('excepted pupils'). However, every effort must be made to keep over large classes to a minimum. These circumstances are where:

a)   a child moved into an area outside the normal admissions round and no other school would provide suitable education (i.e. provide access to the National Curriculum) within a reasonable distance of the child's home. Before admitting children under this exception, admission authorities must consult their local authority who are in a position to advise whether these conditions apply;

b)   the school is named on a child's statement of special educational needs when that child has either been assessed or moved into the area outside the normal admissions round;

c)   a child in care is admitted outside the normal admissions round;

d)   a child wins an appeal, having initially been refused entry as a result of an error in implementing the school's admission arrangements, or because the decision to refuse admission was not one which a reasonable admission authority would have made in the circumstances of the case;

e)   a child normally educated in a special school or special educational needs unit attached to a mainstream school attends an infant class in the mainstream school, where this has been deemed as beneficial to the child. This also applies to those children registered both at special and mainstream schools.

2.59 In the first four cases, the class may only be above 30 for that school year or the remainder of that school year. Qualifying measures must be taken for the following year, or the class will be unlawfully large.

The School Admissions Code 2007

Additional guidelines for secondary schools

Feeder primary schools

Some LEAs use feeder schools as a means of allocating places. What this means is that if your child attends a particular primary school or group of schools, he will be given priority when allocations are made to secondary schools, but this does not provide a guarantee of a place. If the secondary school receives more applications than there are places available, first consideration will be given to children attending the designated feeder school. If there are more children attending the designated feeder school than there are places available, the published admission criteria will be used to determine which applicants will be successful.

Grammar schools

Admission authorities for grammar schools are permitted to select children on the basis of high academic ability and are able to leave places unfilled if they do not have sufficient applicants of the appropriate standard. It is quite normal for such schools to use tests to establish eligibility for places. Most authorities use tests designed by the National Foundation for Educational Research and they usually comprise verbal and non-verbal reasoning tests, and sometimes Maths and English. However, demonstrating that your child meets the required standard does not guarantee a place at a school and this must be made clear in the published admission arrangements.

Admission authorities can use a variety of methods for selecting applicants. Some authorities will have a designated number of places and will offer them to the top ranked applicants. In these circumstances, there will not be a predetermined pass mark. While other authorities will use a pass mark and, if there are more successful applicants than places, they will then apply admission criteria, which are much the same as for non-grammar schools.

Some admission authorities operate an internal review system for those pupils that only just missed the pass mark and marginally failed to reach the required standard. Such reviews do not form part of the published admission arrangements and do not replace your right of appeal against the school's refusal to offer your child a place. If such reviews are used, the school will need to explain how and when such reviews will take place.

Partially selective schools

Grammar schools are fully selective and all places are filled on the basis of academic ability. However, there are some schools that are referred to as 'partially selective' and they select a proportion of places by ability or aptitude. They will usually determine a pupil's ability by using some form of test. If there are insufficient applicants that satisfy the selective places, then they must be offered to other applicants. Partially selective places cannot remain unfilled if there are applicants for them. These schools should make it clear in their admission arrangements that they are partially selective.

Schools which operate a grammar stream alongside a comprehensive system are considered to be partially selective schools. The admission arrangements for the school should make it clear whether your child will be considered for a comprehensive place, if you are unsuccessful with a grammar stream application.

2.71 The School Standards and Framework Act 1998 and supporting regulations allow the following forms of partial selection:

a)   Priority for up to ten per cent of pupils on the basis of aptitude in certain subjects in limited circumstances and where the school has a specialism; however, new selection in design and technology and Information and Communications Technology (ICT) is prohibited from entry in 2008/09;

b)   Partial selection by ability or aptitude that existed at the beginning of the 1997/98 school year and which could not now be lawfully introduced (pre-existing partial selection). Admission authorities may continue to use this form of selection but only if the proportion of children selected does not exceed the lowest proportion at any time since the beginning of the 1997/98 school year and the basis for selection has remained unchanged.

The School Admissions Code 2007

Prior to The School Standards and Framework Act 1998 the law permitted schools to operate admission arrangements that allowed for some places to be allocated on the basis of ability or aptitude which would not now be permitted. However, those forms of selection have been allowed to continue, providing that the number of children to be admitted does not exceed the numbers that were admitted prior to 1997/98. The number of schools that continue to operate under these arrangements is small, although there are no published figures of numbers. The more common basis for partial selection is described in the next section. If, for any reason, you believe that a school is operating in breach of these provisions, then it is best to consult the LEA for advice. You may also need to speak to DCSF or the Schools Adjudicator.

Section 102 of the School Standards and Framework Act 1998 allows all admission authorities to give priority of up to ten per cent of available places to children who can demonstrate an aptitude in the relevant subject.

2.74 The relevant subjects are:

a)   physical education or sport, or one or more sports;

b)   the performing arts, or any one or more of those arts;

c)   the visual arts, or any one or more of those arts;

d)   modern foreign languages, or any such language;

e)   design and technology, and ICT. Schools already selecting in those subjects before the 2008 school year may continue to do so, but no further selection in these subjects can be introduced in respect of subsequent years.

The School Admissions Code 2007

What this means is that after the 2008 school year, schools will no longer be able to apply for specialist status in design and technology and ICT, but existing arrangements will be allowed to continue.

When considering whether your child has an aptitude for a relevant subject, the admission authority must decide whether your child can demonstrate a particular capacity to learn or to develop skills in that subject, and that he can benefit from the particular expertise and facilities that the school is able to offer. If you wish to apply to a school on the basis of a specialism that is offered, the school will provide details of how your child's ability and aptitude will be tested. Such tests will normally be carried out and the results known before the closing date for applications.

Some schools have been designated with more than one specialism. However, the overall limit of places reserved for the specialisms must not exceed ten per cent. If a school has more than one specialism, the total number of places available must not exceed ten per cent of the overall admission number.

Banding

Grammar schools select high ability pupils and comprehensive schools are non-selective and are described as all ability schools. However, all schools can use their admission arrangements to enable them to allocate places that ensure a proportionate spread of children with different abilities. Banding systems are seen as good practice, providing that they are fair and objective and are not used as a means of unlawfully admitting a disproportionate number of pupils with higher ability.

What will normally happen is that prospective applicants will be tested and then placed in one of usually three, four or five bands. The admission authority will determine the basis of the tests, which will usually be verbal reasoning or non-verbal reasoning or both, and these tests will usually be carried out in October or November prior to admission in the following September. If a school operates three bands, it may allocate the bands as follows:

Band 1   Pupils achieving 75 per cent and above

Band 2   Pupils achieving between 25 and 75 per cent

Band 3   Pupils achieving below 25 per cent

The school will then allocate places according to each ability band. Say the school has 160 places available. It will allocate 40 places (25 per cent) of the places to Band 1; 80 places (50 per cent) to Band 2; and 40 places (25 per cent) to Band 3.

Schools that operate a banding system must not apply any other tests once the applicants are allocated to bands. In addition, banding will only operate if the school receives more applications than places available. If there are fewer applicants than available places, all of the applications will be successful. Schools must not give priority within bands according to the tests' scores. If there are more applicants in a band than there are places available, the school must use published admission criteria in order to determine which applicants will be successful. Such criteria may include catchment or distance factors. If one band has more applicants than places and another band has places available, first of all, the places in the band with more applications will be allocated using the published admission criteria. When this exercise has been completed, those applicants who were unsuccessful will be considered for the available places in the next adjacent band, either above or below. Those places will be allocated using the same admission criteria and ranked accordingly.

So how does the banding system operate?

Banding can be adopted in relation to a particular school, two or more schools, or across a local authority area. Banding arrangements that were already in place before 1998 may continue, even though they may disproportionately favour high ability pupils. Banding arrangements introduced after 1998 are subject to much more stringent monitoring to ensure that places provide a proportionate spread of children with different abilities. Admission authorities for a school, or a group of schools working together, may now adopt arrangements that band applicants to produce an intake that is representative of:

- the full range of ability of applicants for the school (or schools); or
- the range of ability of children in the local area; or
- the national ability range (see example below).

The nationally representative sample of the results of the 2006 Qualifications and Curriculum Authority optional Year 5 tests showed the following results:

- 19 per cent of children achieved level 5 (Band 1)
- 40 per cent of children achieved level 4 (Band 2)
- 24 per cent of children achieved level 3 (Band 3)
- 17 per cent of children achieved below level 3 (Band 4)

In this example, 19 per cent of the children admitted to a school would be from Band 1, 40 per cent from Band 2, and so on. Therefore, in a school which admitted 120 pupils, 23 places (19 per cent) would be allocated to pupils from Band 1; 48 places (40 per cent) would be allocated to pupils from Band 2; 29 places (24 per cent) allocated from Band 3; and 20 places (17 per cent) from Band 4.

If places become available, and there are no other applicants in that band on the waiting list, places should be filled by applicants in the next nearest band, either above or below. If there is more than one applicant in a band on the waiting list, the order will be determined by using the published admission criteria for the school. However, if more than one place becomes available, then if the first place is filled from the band above, then the subsequent one should be filled from the band below, and so on.

Partial selection by aptitude and banding

2.83 Section 101(5) of the School Standards and Framework Act 1998 allows admission authorities, which use banding also, to admit up to ten per cent of children in total on the basis of aptitude for one or more of the prescribed subjects. So, for example, admission authorities are able to admit the first ten per cent of children on the basis of aptitude and band the remaining 90 per cent, or they can band children first and then admit ten per cent of each band on the basis of their relevant aptitude.

The School Admissions Code 2007

This section of the Code means that in schools which operate banding, it is open to the school to allocate up to ten per cent of places by ability or aptitude. The school can either admit this ten per cent by ability or aptitude and then allocate the remaining 90 per cent by using the banding method, or the school can band all the applicants and then select ten per cent from each band. Either way the school will achieve the objective of admitting ten per cent of its admission by ability or aptitude.

Test arrangements for banding and partial selection by aptitude

The School Admissions Code gives guidance about such tests, but it is a matter for each individual admission authority to decide what tests will be used to decide which band a particular child will be allocated to. However, whatever testing arrangements are used, the admission authority must explain clearly to parents what the arrangements are and it must ensure that adequate notice is given on the location and length of the tests. The Code also states that if there are a number of schools in an area, they must use a common test to ensure that children are not required to take more than one test.

The tests that will be used will vary from school to school. For those schools which operate a banding system, the tests will usually be verbal reasoning tests, which are the same as those used for grammar school tests.

For those schools which use partial selection by aptitude, the tests will be designed to test that ability. For example, those schools that have a specialism in sport will usually use tests which assess the children's sporting prowess, such as running, jumping, throwing, etc. For those whose specialism is performing arts, the tests may comprise a dance routine, a musical piece, a song or an audition.

In addition, whatever test is devised, it must be designed to give an accurate reflection of the abilities of all children, irrespective of sex, race or disability.

> 2.87 Tests, assessment or auditions used to identify whether a child has an aptitude for a particular subject **must** be objective, have a distinct subject focus and **must not** discriminate against applicants on the grounds of sex, race, disability or family background. The assessment **must** test only for the subject aptitude concerned and not for ability or any other aptitude or for prior learning or experience in the subject. If there are two or more schools using tests in an area, the same aptitude test **should** be used.
>
> *The School Admissions Code 2007*

The Code states that tests for children should be held at times that are likely to be convenient to parents with varying work patterns. In addition, the Code also states that admission authorities must not adjust the scores achieved by any child in a test in order to take into consideration any admission criteria, such as siblings at the school.

The Code also reminds admission authorities that it is unlawful to levy a fee in connection with admission to any maintained school. Such fees would include those designed to cover the costs of selection and testing arrangements, even if they are refunded to successful candidates. Even though such fees are unlawful, some schools may still try to levy such fees. Any request for voluntary contributions to support the school, however conditional, before decisions on admissions have been taken could be seen as a disguised fee and therefore unlawful.

Finally, admission authorities must ensure that any such tests carried out as part of the admission arrangements are accessible to children with special educational needs and disabilities. This would include making arrangements for the test material to be available in different formats or allowing additional time, depending on the needs of the individual.

CHECKLIST 2

1. Do you understand the difference between permissible and non-permissible criteria?

2. Do you understand how the admission criteria will be applied?

3. Has the admission authority published a definition of a sibling?

4. Do you want your child to attend a grammar school?

5. Do you know what tests will be conducted?

6. Have you obtained copies of the test papers so that your child can practise? Practice papers can be obtained from good bookshops or the internet.

7. Do you want your child to attend a faith school?

8. Does your child meet the faith criteria?

9. Do you understand how any distance factor will be measured?

10. Does the school give priority to pupils with a specialism?

11. Does your child have ability, or potential, in the specialism offered by the school?

12. Have you checked out the facilities at the school?

13. Having considered the admission criteria, is your choice of school reasonable?

A summary of school admissions in England

1. Get admissions booklet from the Local Education Authority

2. **DECIDE WHAT YOUR PRIORITIES ARE FOR YOUR CHILD**

3. Decide which schools best meet those priorities and go to the open evenings

4. Talk to the teachers and pupils to get their views about the school

5. Assess the facilities at the school to see if they meet your expectations

6. Look through the most recent Ofsted report and the performance figures for the school

7. **LOOK AT THE ADMISSION CRITERIA FOR THE SCHOOL AND ASSESS YOUR CHANCES OF SUCCESS**

8. Check to see if you would have secured a place at the school in the last five years, based on the admission criteria

9. List your preferences in order with the one that offers the best chance of success at the top

10. **MAKE SURE THAT THE PREFERENCE FORM IS SUBMITTED BY THE DEADLINE SET BY THE ADMISSION AUTHORITY**

Chapter 3

Admissions during the school year

The previous chapter explained what should happen for admissions that take place at the time when children either start school, or when they transfer to the next stage of education during the normal admissions round. For some parents, transfers do not always occur at these prescribed times and arrangements are in place to deal with admissions that arise at other times of the year. Such transfers can occur as a result of a house move to a different area or families may have moved to, or returned from, abroad. It is also possible that parents may wish to move their children because of unresolved problems at their existing school. The Code on School Admissions 2007 has made some important changes on how these transfers should be dealt with by the admission authority.

The issues covered in this chapter are as follows:

- General issues
- Information sharing when a child moves school
- Children looked after by the local authority
- Children who have been permanently excluded
- Children with challenging behaviour
- In-year fair access protocols (formerly 'hard to place pupil protocols')
- Local authority decisions to admit a child to a community or voluntary controlled school
- Admission of children of UK Service personnel and other Crown Servants
- The timing of admissions
- Waiting lists

Quick reference

- ## Schools Adjudicator

  The Schools Adjudicator is a statutory officer appointed by the Secretary of State for Education, but is independent of him. He makes decisions on objections to published admission arrangements and the variations of determined admission arrangements.

- ## 'Looked after children'

  'Looked after children' are defined in section 22 of the Children Act 1989, and are also referred to as children in care and children in public care. In relation to school admissions legislation, a 'looked after child' is only considered as such if the local authority confirms that he will be in public care when he is admitted to the school.

- ## Pupil Referral Unit

  The purpose of Pupil Referral Units is to provide a suitable and appropriate education to children of compulsory school age who, because of illness, exclusion or otherwise, are unable to attend a maintained (i.e. mainstream or special) school.

- ## Children with challenging behaviour

  Challenging behaviour is any behaviour that interferes with children's learning, development and success at play; which is harmful to the child, to other children or adults; or puts a child at high risk for later social problems or school failure.

- ## Admission forum

  Forums include representatives of the local authority, local schools and other interested parties. They have a key role in ensuring a fair admissions system that promotes social equity, does not disadvantage one child compared to another, and which is straightforward and easy to understand for parents. Forums are also responsible for monitoring compliance with the Code.

- ## Normal admissions round

  This is the period of time between 1 September and the date when decisions are issued in the academic year prior to admission in reception, or transfer in the case of junior, middle and secondary schools. These dates will be included in the LEA's admissions booklet.

- ## Undersubscribed school

  An undersubscribed school is where a school has fewer pupils at the school than the published admission number. A school will be described as undersubscribed if the school historically receives fewer applications for places than the published admission number,

- **Special measures**

  This occurs if a school has been underperforming against national standards assessed by the inspectors from Ofsted (the official body for inspecting schools) and is receiving extra support to increase standards to an acceptable level.

- **'Fresh start' school**

  A 'fresh start' school is where a school has been identified as underperforming and is closed and subsequently reopened on the same school site with additional support to increase standards to an acceptable level.

QUICK LIST

1 Do you know the reasons for the school turning down your application?

2 Do you know the rights of a permanently excluded child?

3 Do you know what a looked after child is in the context of school admissions?

4 Are your circumstances covered by the fair access protocol?

5 Are you a UK Service personnel or Crown Servant applying outside of the normal admissions round?

6 Do you know how waiting lists should operate?

7 Is your child on the admission authority's waiting list?

General issues

The vast majority of places will be allocated during the normal admissions round. However, for a small, but not insignificant, number of parents, they will be looking to obtain places at times other than the normal admissions round. For most parents, the reason for this will be due to their moving house and, therefore, to a different area, where it is not possible for their children to commute to the existing school. Alternatively, parents may be moving to, or back to, this country from abroad and they will be looking for a school so that their children can continue their education.

The Code sets out the arrangements that must be put in place to deal with applications that are received outside of the normal admissions round, whether this occurs at the start of the school year or at any other time of the year. Admission authorities must give you the right to complete an application form and they must give you a response in writing, advising you of your right to an appeal if the application is unsuccessful. You must not be refused the opportunity to make an application, or be advised that you can only be put on a waiting list rather than making a formal application.

There are three reasons why an admission authority can refuse an application:

1. The admission will be prejudicial to efficient use of resources, i.e. an oversubscribed school taking away resources from an undersubscribed school.

2. The admission will be prejudicial to efficient education, i.e. overcrowding causing inefficiency of teaching methods and facilities.

3. The application will be incompatible with the admission arrangements of the school, i.e. the child has failed the entrance exam (in the case of selective schools).

The following reasons cannot be given by an admission authority as grounds for its refusing to offer a place at the school:

- You have applied after other applications (this relates to late applications and applications received after the normal admissions round).

- You are not of the faith of the school, in the case of faith schools (even though faith schools give priority to their own faith, they also admit pupils from other faiths).

- The school follows a different curriculum to your previous school.

- No information has been received from the previous school (see below).

- Your child has missed the entrance test (in the case of secondary schools).

It is not possible to set out every ground that may be used, but it does include examples of reasons for refusal that admission authorities have used in the past.

Information sharing when a child moves school

When your child moves from one school to another it is important that the receiving school obtains your child's education records from the former school. Such records must be sent by the governors of the school that your child has moved from within 15 school days after your child ceases to be registered there. If the governors do not know which school your child is to be registered at, they should send a common transfer file for your child to the Secure Data Transfer website (www.teachernet.gov.uk/S2S) giving the destination of the school as unknown. This information is then stored on the lost pupil database, which local authorities can research if common transfer files are not received.

Under equal opportunities legislation, admission authorities must not adopt procedures which disadvantage children who arrive outside the normal admissions round. Admission authorities must ensure that arrangements for Gypsy, Roma and Traveller children are in place so that they can be quickly registered at a school, whether they are residing permanently or temporarily in the area.

Children looked after by the local authority

The law requires admission authorities to give children in care and looked after by the local authority the highest priority in their admission arrangements, thus ensuring that they are guaranteed admission to preferred schools at the normal time of entry; such children are normally referred to as 'looked after children'.

The law also allows local authorities to direct admission authorities of maintained schools to admit a child to a school that is best suited to his needs, which occurs outside the normal admissions round. Such action must be taken in the best interests of the child. Before giving such a direction, the local authority must consult the admission authority concerned and give that authority seven days to indicate that it is willing to admit the child without being directed to do so.

3.8 If, following consultation, the local authority decides to issue the direction, it must inform the admission authority, the governing body (if the governing body is not the admission authority), the head teacher and, if the school is in another local authority area, the maintaining local authority. If the admission authority (or the governing body if it is not the admission authority and only in relation to a child in care who has previously been excluded from at least two schools) considers that admission of the child would seriously prejudice the provision of efficient education or efficient use of resources, the admission authority has seven days in which to refer the case to the Adjudicator. The Adjudicator may either uphold the direction, or, if the local authority that looks after the child agrees, determine that another school in England must admit the child. The Adjudicator's decision is binding. The Adjudicator may not direct an alternative school to admit the child when the child has already been excluded from that school or when admission would seriously prejudice the provision of efficient education or efficient use of resources.

The School Admissions Code 2007

Children who have been permanently excluded

If a child has broken the school rules or is in breach of the school's disciplinary policy, the head teacher of the school may decide to permanently exclude the child. The process for permanent exclusions is outside the scope of this book. If your child has been permanently excluded, you do have the right to an appeal and the governing body of the school should provide details of the appeal process. There is also guidance on the Department for Children, Schools and Families (DCSF) website at www.dcsf.gov.uk.

If your child is permanently excluded once, it does not affect your rights in relation to expressing a preference about where he will be educated. You can still express a preference for your child, even if he has been excluded from two or more schools. However, although the LEA must find a school for your child, the admission authority does not have to comply with your preference for a period of two years from the date on which the last permanent exclusion took place. But this provision does not apply in the following circumstances:

- Children with a statement of special educational needs.

- Children who were below the compulsory school age when excluded.

- Children who were reinstated following a permanent exclusion (arising from a successful appeal).

- Children who would have been reinstated following a permanent exclusion had it been practical to do so (arising from a successful appeal).

A permanent exclusion is regarded as taking effect from the first day the head teacher has told your child not to attend school. The admission authority, for the school which you have expressed a preference for, may refuse to admit a child who has been excluded twice, or, in the case of a community or voluntary controlled schools which are run by the LEA, the governing body may appeal against the decision of the local authority as the admission authority to admit the child (this is covered in the Code of Practice on School Admission Appeals). Whatever the circumstances, the local authority is still responsible for providing suitable full-time education for these children and it may need to use its powers of direction or provide a place at a Pupil Referral Unit, which is run for pupils that have been permanently excluded, if a place cannot be found for them in a maintained school. Pupils that have been permanently excluded will normally attend a Pupil Referral Unit for a period of time before they are reintegrated into a mainstream school. The length of time will be determined by the needs of the pupil.

Children with challenging behaviour

Challenging behaviour is any behaviour that interferes with children's learning, development and success at play; that is harmful to the child, other children or adults; or that puts a child at high risk for later social problems or school failure. Admission authorities must not refuse to admit a child to a school because of his behaviour at a previous school, unless such behaviour has resulted in two permanent exclusions covered in the section above. This applies whether you are applying either in or outside of the normal admissions round.

An admission authority cannot refuse to admit your child because he is thought to be potentially disruptive, or thought to exhibit challenging behaviour. It may be that the admission authority may have some evidence that your child has special educational needs, but it will not know for sure until an assessment has been carried out. If your child is refused admission on these grounds, you will be able to appeal and put your case to an independent appeal panel.

If, following admission, your child begins to demonstrate challenging behaviour, the school may consider disciplinary action that may involve either temporary or permanent exclusion. If this is the case, the admission authority must follow the guidance provided by the DCFS.

A child who exhibits challenging behaviour may also be disabled, as defined under the Disability Discrimination Act 1995. If this is the case, the school may need to make reasonable adjustments for him and possible particular support for any special educational needs that he might have.

In the past, undersubscribed schools may have been required to admit an undue proportion of children with challenging behaviour. The introduction of an 'in-year fair access protocol' will result in a more even distribution of such children, including children excluded from other schools. The issues here are covered in the next section.

If your child exhibits challenging behaviour, admission authorities may refuse to admit him on the basis that admission will cause prejudice either to the efficient use of resources or efficient education, even where there are places available. This will normally occur where a school has a high concentration of children with challenging behaviour or previously excluded children, and one or more of the following exceptions applies:

- The school requires special measures or has come out of them within the last two years (this is where Ofsted inspectors have identified that the school is not providing suitable education and measures have been put in place to remedy the situation).

- The school has been identified by Ofsted as having serious weaknesses or requires significant improvement, and has therefore been given 'notice to improve'.

- The school is subject to a formal warning notice (issued by the Ofsted inspectors stating that if the school does not improve, it will be placed in special measures).

- The school is a fresh start school (designated by Ofsted as special measures or significant improvement and the school is closed and then re-opened on the same site under normal school reorganisation procedures) or an academy open for less than two years.

- The school is a secondary school where fewer than 30 per cent of pupils are achieving five or more GCSEs at grades A* to C, or a primary school where fewer than 65 per cent of pupils achieve level 4 or above at Key Stage 2 in both English and Maths for four or more consecutive years.

In-year fair access protocols (formerly 'hard to place pupil protocols')

In-year fair access protocols exist to ensure that there are procedures in place so that access to education is secured quickly for children who do not have places at school, and they also enable all schools in an area to admit their fair share of children with challenging behaviour. By September 2007, all admission authorities and admission forums must have had fair access protocols in place. All schools and academies must have participated in their local authority's protocol to ensure that unplaced children are offered a place at a suitable school as quickly as possible. In some cases this may involve admitting children above the published admission number for the schools that are already full. The Code suggests that admission appeal panels should not accept that because a child has been admitted to an oversubscribed school this in some way indicates that additional pupils can be admitted without causing problems for the school.

Admission authorities must ensure that all children applying for places outside the normal admissions round who may have difficulty finding places are covered by the protocol. Children with special educational needs but without statements (see Chapter 2) should be treated in the same way as other applicants. Children with statements that name a school must be admitted, even if the school is full. Where a local authority, as corporate parent for a looked after child, directs an admission authority to admit a child in care, the governing body must admit the child to the school at any specified time during the year, even if the school is full, unless the Adjudicator upholds an appeal from the admission authority.

The governing body of an admission authority may refer a local authority's decision to direct the admission of a child in accordance with the locally agreed protocol to the Schools Adjudicator. The Adjudicator will then determine which school will be required to take the child. The governing body of the determined school must admit the child. If the governing body refuses to comply with such a direction, the local authority may refer the matter to the Secretary of State for consideration. A local authority cannot make a direction if such an admission will result in the school breaching the class size legislation of 30 pupils per school teacher.

Looked after children come first on admission criteria for all schools except academies, and the admission to academies depends on their funding agreements. Local authorities can ask academies to admit looked after children. Where such a request is refused, the local authority can refer the matter to the Secretary of State to consider whether or not it should direct the academy to admit the child.

In-year fair access protocols cover any child who does not have a place at school, but most will be from the categories identified above. However, the protocols do cover children who have moved into an area and there are no places available at a school within a reasonable distance from their new home.

Local authority decisions to admit a child to a community or voluntary controlled school

The governing body of community and voluntary controlled schools must implement any decision made by the local authority relating to the admission of children, except where this relates to the admission of a child that has been excluded twice. Note that LEAs are the admission authority for community and voluntary controlled schools, so this does not apply to voluntary aided and foundation schools.

Admission of children of UK Service personnel and other Crown Servants

Families of UK Armed Service personnel and other Crown Servants (including diplomats) are subject to frequent movement often at very short notice and therefore admission authorities should make provision for dealing with such applications as quickly as possible. Usually admission authorities will not act until a confirmed address or date for moving has been agreed, but in such cases it should be possible for admission authorities to allocate places to children and their families in advance of the approaching school year, providing that such requests are accompanied by an official Ministry of Defence, Foreign and Commonwealth Office or Government Communications Headquarters letter declaring a relocation date. Admission authorities should also consider notifying results by email, if this is acceptable to the applicant, especially where families are still abroad.

3.23 Local authorities and admission authorities **must**:

a) ensure that the needs of the children of these families are taken into account;

b) allocate a school place in advance, if the applicant would meet the criteria when he is relocated;

c) invite a Service representative or representative of other Crown Servants (e.g. Government Communications Headquarters personnel) to join the admission forum where there are significant concentrations of such personnel in an area; and

d) accept a postal address for the Unit (i.e. the Unit where the person is employed) for applications from service personnel in the absence of a new postal address.

3.24 Admission authorities **must not**:

a) reserve places for blocks of these children; or

b) refuse a place to such a child because the family does not currently live in the local authority area.

The School Admissions Code 2007

The timing of admissions

The law permits the deferment of admission to the start of the school term. In cases involving school transfers which are not the result of a house move, or where there is no need for an immediate move, admission authorities may wish to arrange for a child to join the school at the beginning of term in order to minimise the disruption to his own and other children's education. However, if the parent wants his child to move because he is, for example, being bullied, the admission authority may allow this.

Waiting lists

There is no obligation on an admission authority to maintain a waiting list for vacancies that arise either during or outside of the normal admissions round. If it does not, then it will deal with applications on a first-come first-served basis. If this is the case, then it is important to contact the admission authority to see how casual admissions are dealt with.

However, most admission authorities do use waiting lists and they must operate in exactly the same way as the published admission criteria. Waiting lists must be clear, fair and objective and they must not give priority to children based on either the dates that their applications were received or when their applications were added to the waiting list. For example, if your child has moved into an area and has a higher priority against the published admission criteria, he must be ranked above those children with lower priority already on the list.

The admission authority is required to notify you if your child has been placed on the waiting list but it does not have to give any indication as to the prospect of a place being offered, as the position may well change. You may find it surprising if your child has been on the waiting list for a school for some time, and when a place does become available it is offered to a child who may have only just joined the waiting list. However, you are entitled to apply and appeal each and every academic year, and these issues may well add weight to your case when they are viewed by the appeal panel.

As soon as a place becomes available, the admission authority must fill it straight away and it must not wait until any forthcoming admission appeals have been heard. When the appeals take place there will not be any vacancies at the school. If there are, because they remain unfilled, the appeal panel will fill the vacancies from the appeals being heard using the published admission criteria and it will then consider any outstanding appeals. The panel will be aware of any vacancies because of the difference in numbers between the number of pupils at the school and the published admission number, which is set out in the admission authority's statement.

Putting your child on a waiting list does not affect your statutory right to an appeal. Children who are the subject of a direction by the local authority to be admitted or who are allocated to a school in accordance with an in-year fair access protocol will take precedence over those children on the waiting list. This must be made clear in the admission arrangements published by the admission authority. However, if it is not, there is legislation in place to ensure that this is done immediately, without the need to apply to the Schools Adjudicator for a variation in the published admission arrangements, which would otherwise be the case.

CHECKLIST 3

1. Is your child's circumstances covered by this chapter?

2. Do you understand how the in-year fair access protocol will work?

3. Do you understand the position if you are a member of the UK Service personnel or a Crown Servant, including diplomats?

4. Does your child suffer from challenging behaviour covered by this chapter?

5. Has your child's admission been dealt with in accordance with the issues covered by this chapter?

6. Has your child been placed on the school's waiting list?

7. If you have not been offered a place, have you lodged an appeal?

Chapter 4

The statutory appeal process

This chapter will help you if you have not been successful in securing any of your preferred schools or you have not obtained a place at your first preference school. If you are in this situation, you can use the statutory appeal process. This chapter explains what will happen so that you know what to expect and the subsequent chapters explain in more detail how to prepare for the appeal you are likely to face.

The appeal process is described in the Code of Practice on School Admission Appeals issued by the Department for Education and Skills (now called the Department for Children, Schools and Families (DCSF)) in 2003, which provides statutory guidance as to how appeals should be conducted. The DCSF has now published a new Code that applies to decisions issued on or after 1 March 2008. Where appropriate, any differences between the existing and the new Codes will be explained. Also any references to either Code will be disclosed. *The new Code and any issues that arise are shown in italics.*

The issues covered in this chapter are as follows:

- The decision letter
- Lodging an appeal
- The notice to be given to appellants by the Clerk to the Appeal Panel
- The Clerk to the Appeal Panel
- The appeal panel
- The presenting officer
- The venue for the appeal
- Arrangements for the appeal
- The preparation and production of evidence
- Representation
- The principles of natural justice

- Other Acts of Parliament
- Individual or multiple appeals

Quick reference

- ## Principles of natural justice

  Essentially, this means that both sides, the admission authority and you, will be treated exactly the same. You will be given the same opportunity to submit your case and challenge the admission authority's case. It also means that the appeal panel is completely independent and not biased towards either you or the admission authority.

- ## Multiple appeals

  This is where more than one appeal has been received for the same school and arrangements have been made for the admission authority's case to be heard in the presence of all of the parents that are appealing.

- ## Working days

  Working days include Mondays to Fridays, but they do not include Saturdays and Sundays. They also exclude public and bank holidays.

- ## School days

  The term 'school days' means, literally, what it says. School holidays are excluded, so this means that the 30-day period within which an appeal should be heard will be extended considerably if your appeal arrives just before the end of term or just before half term.

QUICK LIST	
1	Have you looked through the decision letter to find out the grounds why the admission authority refused your application?
2	Have you gathered all your supporting documents and made sure that the appeal has been submitted within the prescribed time limit?
3	Do you understand the role of the appeal panel?
4	Do you understand the role of the Clerk to the Appeal Panel?
5	Do you understand the role of the presenting officer?
6	Has the admission authority sent you its statement within the prescribed time limit?

7   Do you know what should be included in the admission authority's statement?

8   Do you feel that you need to be represented at the appeal?

9   Has the appeal been dealt with in accordance with the principles of natural justice?

10 Do you know if your appeal will be dealt with as an individual or as a multiple appeal?

The decision letter

If your application for a school was unsuccessful, the admission authority (the Local Education Authority (LEA) for community schools and the governors of the school for voluntary aided and foundation schools and academies) should have either sent you an appeal form or advised you how you can obtain one. The letter from the admission authority should also advise you when the appeal form should be returned. The date must not be less than ten working days (*the new Code says ten school days*) from the date that you were notified that your application was not successful.

The letter that you receive from the admission authority should also explain, in detail, why your application was not successful. For LEAs which may be sending out several thousand letters, this can cause some problems and they may try to overcome this by sending letters that include only very general information. For example, the letter may say that the schools you applied for received more applications than places available and all the places were filled by applicants with a higher priority than yours. The letter may not explain in detail why your application was not successful and it may not give reasons which you could challenge at an appeal and, as a result, such a letter would not comply with the Code. How can you possibly mount a serious appeal if you do not know why your application was unsuccessful? If this is the case, you can write to the admission authority and ask for clarification as to why your application was unsuccessful.

There are some authorities that demonstrate good practice. For example, Hertfordshire County Council can provide a pupil audit report on request. Such a report gives details of the number of applications submitted for your preferred schools and it also explains how many applications were successful in each admission category, and it will also show why an application was not successful.

For the vast majority of parents, the reason why their applications are unsuccessful is because they live too far away from the school. But even if this occurs in your case, you will still need to know the distances involved.

How much further away do you live than the last successful applicant? The answer may well determine how you approach your appeal.

Lodging an appeal

The most important thing you must do is make sure that you send in your appeal within the prescribed period. If you do not, you run the risk that there may be a delay in your appeal being heard. This will prolong the period of uncertainty for you and the admission authority may be reluctant to hold your appeal unless you can provide a very good reason for missing the deadline. You may feel that ten working days (*ten school days for decisions notified on or after 1 March 2008*) are not long enough to prepare for an appeal after you have received the decision. **However, do not panic!** This is an administrative deadline. It does not mean that you have to submit all of the information at this stage, which may be impractical. If you are seeking written support from a third party (e.g. a doctor), it may not be possible to organise this within two weeks.

In order to trigger the appeal process, all you need to do is return the appeal form filling in the basic details of your name and address and contact details. Where the form refers to the grounds for your appeal, all you need to say is 'details of grounds for appeal will follow shortly'. This will give you the opportunity to consider and articulate the grounds of appeal very carefully and it will also ensure that any supporting documentation is also available.

The Code of Practice also encourages admission authorities to produce guidance notes for parents which explain about the appeal process. It is important that you receive this guidance as soon as possible so that you can familiarise yourself with the various issues involved and make preparations for the appeal.

Once you have submitted your appeal form, make sure that it has been received. You can do this either by asking for a receipt, if you deliver it personally, or by asking the admission authority to acknowledge it. If you have heard nothing within five working days or if the closing date for appeals is imminent, contact the appeals office to check if the appeal has been received and if not, submit another form. Forms can go missing and you need to protect your position.

The notice to be given to appellants by the Clerk to the Appeal Panel

Having lodged your appeal, the admission authority is required to give ten

working days' notice (*the new Code states that you must receive at least ten school days' notice in advance of the hearing*) of the date of your appeal. The Code allows you to waive this period and accept shorter notice if this is acceptable to you. You must only agree to waive this notice if you are confident that your appeal will not be compromised due to lack of time to prepare for it.

Appeals should be heard within a reasonable period and this is defined as 30 school days, either from the receipt of the appeal or from the closing date for appeals, whichever is the later. *The new Code states that, in relation to secondary school appeals for on-time applications where decisions were sent on the national offer day of 1 March, appeals must be heard by 6 July or the next working day if 6 July falls on a weekend.*

The Clerk to the Appeal Panel

Every appeal will have a Clerk available. The Clerk plays a very important role at the appeal. The Clerk is independent and is appointed, but should not be employed, by the admission authority. *According to the new Code, if the admission authority is the LEA, the Clerk is regarded as being independent provided that he is not connected in any way with education or children's services, but he may be employed in a different department.*

Being independent, the Clerk is able to give advice to you, the admission authority and also the appeal panel. The Clerk should be familiar with the law and guidance and he must ensure that the appeal is conducted in accordance with the Code of Practice on School Admission Appeals. The Clerk should not answer questions asked by either the admission authority or the parent, but he may clarify a response from either side.

Most LEAs use Clerks who have a professional background in committee administration, since they will have already developed the skills necessary to fulfil the role of the Clerk and will be used to giving advice and guidance on the law. It is not necessary for the Clerk to be legally qualified, but he must have received regular training so that he is familiar with any changes in the law or guidance.

Most appeals held by LEAs will be conducted in accordance with the provisions of the Code of Practice because they will be involved in arranging hundreds of appeals every year. However, this does not necessarily mean that you will have received a fair hearing. It is far more likely that voluntary aided and foundation schools and academies that are responsible for arranging their own appeals may not be as familiar with the Code as they should be and this often leads to maladministration.

4.22 The Clerk's key tasks are to:

- explain the basic procedures to appellants and deal with any questions they may have;

- ensure that the relevant facts, as provided by both the appellants and the admission authority, are presented and recorded (e.g. where there is an inexperienced chairperson, the Clerk may tactfully intervene to assist the panel or the parents with the procedure);

- order the business (i.e. he will decide the order in which the cases will be heard);

- be an independent source of advice on procedure, the Code of Practice and the law on admissions (usually giving any advice in the presence of the parties to the appeal);

- record the proceedings, decisions and reasons; and

- notify all parties of the decision.

The Code of Practice on School Admission Appeals 2003

1.28 The Clerk's role is wider than that of note-taker. His key tasks are to:

a) *make the necessary administrative arrangements for hearings, including appointing panel members (unless this has been done by a separate independent appeals administrator);*

b) *explain the basic procedure to appellants and deal with any questions they may have before the hearing (the Chair or Clerk, as appropriate, may deal with questions raised during the hearing);*

c) *be an independent source of advice (or to seek appropriate advice) on procedure, on both the School Admissions and School Admission Appeals Codes, and on the law on admissions, giving any advice in the presence of all parties where practicable;*

d) *ensure that both the appellants and the admission authority have the opportunity to present relevant facts at the hearing. The Clerk's role is to assist the panel, admission authority or parents with procedure and obtain advice where directed by the Chair to do so, but otherwise he should not participate in the hearing;*

e) *record the proceedings, attendance, voting outcomes, panel decisions and reasons in such a form that the panel and Clerk agree is appropriate. This record does not need to be verbatim, but it **must** record the points raised at the hearing and make clear what view the panel took in coming to its decision about important points raised by the appellants; and*

The appeal panel

The Code states that the appeal panel will comprise either three or five people. The panel is appointed by the admission authority from a list of persons that have been authorised to act as panel members. All panel members will be completely independent.

The situation is that, for the vast majority of appeals, the panel will comprise three members. This being the case the make-up of the panel will comprise at least one person experienced in education and one layperson. The person experienced in education will usually be either an existing or retired head or deputy head, but who has had no involvement with the school concerned. The layperson cannot have been employed in any paid capacity at a school; he can be a governor or even a classroom assistant, providing that he has not been paid and has no connection with the school which is the subject of the appeal. Admission authorities are required to advertise for laypersons once every three years in a local paper. If they have sufficient time, parents can apply to become panel members, although, curiously, they would sit on panels as a person experienced in education! However, once your child leaves school you will revert to being a lay member, unless you have developed knowledge in education. The third member of the panel can either be a second layperson or a person experienced in education.

The Chair of the appeal panel is either appointed by the admission authority or from within the panel members for the appeal. The Chair must have received training in chairing meetings. The Code provides that panel members must be trained before they sit on panels and they must also receive regular training so that they can keep abreast of any changes or developments in guidance.

CASE STUDY 1

Some years ago I was asked to clerk a number of appeals for a voluntary aided school. The school had appointed the panel. There were approximately 16 appeals and towards the end of the second day it became clear that something was not right. It subsequently became clear that the panel member who had been appointed as the lay member was, in fact, a retired teacher and therefore he could not sit in that capacity. Unfortunately, the other two panel members were also experienced education professionals and therefore the panel did not comply with the Code of Practice.

I spoke to the governors about the situation and I explained that the only possible solution would be for the appeals to be reheard with a different panel. The governors were not prepared to contemplate this and therefore offered places to all the appellants.

This illustrates how important it is to ensure that the panel is properly constituted and it is wise to check.

The presenting officer

The admission authority must provide a presenting officer at the appeal who is able to explain the authority's decision and also answer any detailed questions that may be put by either the panel or you about the admission arrangements. The presenting officer must be present throughout the hearing to be able to do this.

CASE STUDY 2

A parent approached me after being unsuccessful with an appeal. I asked her to explain what happened at the appeal and it became clear that there was no presenting officer present at the appeal. I advised her that this amounted to maladministration and urged her to make a complaint to the Local Government Ombudsman. The Ombudsman agreed and she was offered a fresh hearing, but this was some weeks later. She subsequently won her fresh appeal.

The venue for the appeal

It is up to the admission authority to make arrangements for the appeal, including the venue. As the appeal is independent it is unlikely, if the appeal is held at the school which is the subject of the appeal, that you would presume that the appeal is truly independent. While the Code of Practice does not expressly forbid appeals being held at the school, the Local Government Ombudsman, which is the body that investigates complaints about appeals, does not look favourably on such a situation. It is my experience that appeals are held at the school, which is the subject of the appeal, where the admission authority is a voluntary aided or foundation school and this is usually for convenience or financial reasons, neither of which I feel are legitimate reasons for holding the appeal there. It is much better if the appeal is held on neutral premises. You can object to the appeal being heard at the school, but the effect will be to delay the appeal, which may not be in your best interests, since it will only extend the period of uncertainty for you.

Arrangements at the appeal

The Code of Practice gives very practical advice about the facilities that should be available at the appeal.

> 4.13 Points to consider when setting up the accommodation for the appeal are as follows:
>
> - There should be a room to allow parties and their representative or advisor to have private discussions.
> - There should be arrangements (such as a notice on the door) to ensure that the hearing is not interrupted.
> - The location of the room should not be such that there is likely to be disturbance from noise going on outside.
> - It is particularly important that those waiting outside should not be able to hear what is going on inside.
> - The room layout for the appeal hearing should ensure structure, comfort and informality.
> - Drinking water, or other refreshments, should be available.
> - Toilets should be conveniently located.
> - There should be name plates for the panel and the Clerk.
> - Adequate time should be allowed for the hearing, especially if an interpreter is present to act on behalf of the parents.
>
> *The Code of Practice on School Admission Appeals 2003*

> *2.23 The venue must:*
> a) *be reasonably accessible to parents and well sign-posted;*
> b) *be accessible to public transport;*
> c) *be accessible for people with disabilities, with consideration given to the provision of spaces for car parking; and*
> d) *have a suitable waiting area for parents and presenting officers to wait separately from the appeal panel before and between the appeals.*
>
> *The Code on School Admission Appeals 2007*

If the arrangements are not in accordance with the above provisions, it could potentially be grounds for an unfair hearing. These issues will be dealt with in Chapter 9.

CASE STUDY 3

I was acting for a client at an appeal for a voluntary aided school and, as part of the guidance notes, the admission authority indicated that ten minutes would be allocated for the appeal. I attended the appeal and it actually lasted 90 minutes, including two adjournments. The appeal was unsuccessful and the appellant made a complaint to the Local Government Ombudsman following my advice. In this particular hearing, there were about 15 breaches of the Code of Practice, which resulted in an unfair hearing. The Ombudsman agreed that the appellant did not receive a fair hearing and she was offered a fresh hearing.

As to whether ten minutes is or is not unreasonable depends on the hearing itself. In one complaint to the Ombudsman the finding was that there was no maladministration as, during the ten-minute hearing, the appellant had said all that he had wanted to say. I would suggest that on average an appeal would normally last between 30 to 45 minutes. This will enable sufficient time for both sides to put their case and for questions to be asked to clarify any issues which are unclear.

The point here is not the length of time that the hearing lasted for, but whether you, as an appellant, were able to raise and say all that you wanted to say at the hearing. If you did, it is unlikely that maladministration will be found, but if you did not, then it is likely that the Ombudsman will find maladministration that caused injustice. Given these circumstances you may be offered a fresh hearing, or a place at the school if the Ombudsman believes that the hearing was so flawed that the appeal panel would have offered a place if the maladministration had not taken place. The advice here is for you not to say anything at the appeal, but make notes about what happened which you can use later in the event that your appeal is unsuccessful.

Appeal panel Chairs are trained to ask at the end of the hearing whether all parties have been able to say all that they wanted to say. Before you say 'yes', make sure that you have said all that you wished to and that you have covered all the necessary issues.

At the hearing, and before the appeal panel consider the issues that have been raised, some panel Chairs may ask if you have had a fair hearing. I would urge you not to answer this question! If you say yes and then lose the appeal and subsequently make a complaint, the admission authority will state that you had confirmed at the appeal that you had received a fair hearing and this will undermine any subsequent action that you may want to take. If you are asked this question, I would suggest that you respond by saying that you have said all that you want to say, if indeed this is the case.

The preparation and production of evidence

At least seven days (five working days) before the hearing, the admission authority should send you a copy of its statement detailing the reasons why it turned you down for a place. The admission authority will operate their own timetable and in the vast majority of cases the statement will be sent out as late as possible. Your authority is very unlikely to provide it before it has to, even if you request it to do so. If there is more than one appeal, the statements will all be sent out at the same time to be fair to everyone.

The statement is also sent to the appeal panel. If the statement turns up late, you will have to consider either whether you have sufficient time to respond to the statement or whether you should seek an adjournment in order to allow more time for you to prepare for the appeal.

You may be asked if you want to waive the ten-day period for notice of the appeal and the five-working day period when the statement should be sent to you. If you waive this period, you will still receive the statement but not within the prescribed period. Before waiving this period, think very carefully and make sure that you have sufficient time to prepare a response to the details of the statement, which you would make at the appeal.

What should be included in the statement always seems to cause discussion. This is what the Code says about documents to be supplied to you and also the appeal panel:

Paragraph 4.28

- A written statement summarising how the admission arrangements for the school apply to your application, with any relevant background information. Where your appeal relates to the LEA's administration of co-ordinated arrangements (e.g. because an error has allegedly been made, or because the application of those arrangements has led to your child not being offered a place at one of two or more preferred schools you could have been offered), the details of the co-ordinated arrangements or a statement from the LEA should be provided;

- A written statement summarising the reasons for the decision; for instance, full supporting information that would cause prejudice to the provision of efficient education or use of resources which would arise from the admission of your child. (In laymen's terms, what problems would be caused if an additional pupil was admitted to the school.) A statement referring to accommodation, class sizes, capacity, etc. should be supported by factual information, as panel members cannot be led on 'tours' of schools to make their own assessments – this would call into question their independence, and could lead to allegations of lobbying (if considered necessary, evidence can be produced in the form of photographs or a video, as well as layout plans of a building);

- Where another place has been offered, as identified under co-ordinated arrangements, either the relevant extract of the published scheme or a statement from the LEA should be provided;

- Copies of any information or documents which are to be put to the panel at the hearing, including anything which has been submitted by you.

The Code of Practice on School Admission Appeals 2003

Under the new Code the Clerk must send out the appeal papers to you, the presenting officer and the panel at least seven working days before the hearing. The seven days does not include the date of the hearing or the day that the papers are sent out. This means that the Clerk should send you the appeal papers nine working days before the hearing. The papers sent out include:

Paragraph 2.19

a) *a written statement summarising how places at the school were allocated (without disclosing personal details of applicants which would enable identification of individuals) and how the admission arrangements for the school apply to the parents' application, accompanied by any relevant background information and documents on which the admission authority places substantial reliance (such as the parents' application form or references from religious ministers). Where distance criteria have been used to allocate places, the admission authority **should** demonstrate how this was applied to the parents' application compared to those offered a place:*

b) *a written statement summarising the reasons for the decision (and attaching a copy of the decision letter), explaining how the admission of an additional child would cause prejudice to the provision of efficient education or use of resources, making it clear*

> *whether or not the admission authority is defending its decision on the basis of infant class size legislation. The statement* **should** *include a summary of the school's net capacity and could also include a map/plan of the school, if this would be helpful. Any statement referring to accommodation, class sizes, capacity, etc.* **should** *be supported by factual information, as panel members cannot undergo 'tours' of schools to make their own assessments, as it could call into question their independence and lead to allegations of lobbying;*
>
> c) *the relevant extract of the area's co-ordinated admission scheme, where this is relevant to the appeal (e.g. a parent appealing for a place at a school that he ranked lower on his common application form than the one offered under the scheme (e.g. most parents will appeal for a higher ranked school for which they were unsuccessful. However, sometimes a parent appeals for a lower ranked school, maybe a grammar school, because he does not think that his child will pass the 11 plus, but the child does and then the parent wants him to have a grammar school education) and, in the case of a voluntary aided or foundation school or an academy, a statement from the local authority explaining how the scheme was applied;*
>
> d) *details of how the locally agreed in-year fair access protocol operates, where relevant; and*
>
> e) *copies of any information or documents that will be supplied to the panel at the hearing, including any documents that have been submitted by parents.*
>
> *The Code on School Admission Appeals 2007*

Despite what appears to be fairly firm guidance about statements, admission authorities appear to have some doubts about what should be included in their statements. In the circumstances, the Local Government Ombudsman issued a Special Report in March 2004 which covers a range of issues that it has come across when investigating complaints. It has issued further guidance about statements and this is as follows:

> The content of the authority's statement must be adequate. The Appeals Code gives good guidance on this point. We would like to highlight some points and add some supplementary points as follows:
>
> • the document must explain, with full supporting information, why the admission authority considers that the admission of an additional child or children would cause prejudice to efficient education or the efficient use of resources;

- the document must demonstrate the nature of the prejudice (that is, specifically what harm would be caused by additional admissions);

- information should include how the year group will be organised and the size of the classes (because, for example, there would be a significant difference in how a parent would need to approach the appeal, depending whether the intake of, say, 240 children would be organised in eight classes of 30 or nine classes of 26/27);

- if classes are small, some reference should be made to the reason for that (e.g. that the classrooms are small);

- in respect of the school appealed for, there should be a statement of the breakdown of successful admissions (that is, how many were admitted under each criterion);

- the document for each individual parent should explain why the child was refused a place, with relevant supporting information (e.g. if the distance from home to school was the explanation, there should be information about what that is and what was the furthest distance from home to school for children accepted under the distance criterion);

- there should be sufficient information to enable the parent to reach a proper view on whether the admission criteria were correctly applied, and for parents to be able to prepare any questions and points that they want to put.

The Local Government Ombudsman Special Report 2004

There is no statutory deadline for the submission of information about your appeal; however, any written information should be submitted as soon as possible. The admission authority must be given an opportunity to consider and respond to any information that you have submitted. The risk you run by submitting information, either just before or at the hearing, is that the admission authority may seek an adjournment so that it can properly consider and respond to the information. Both sides must have the opportunity to see the other side's case and comment on it. *The new Code has clarified this by stating that it may be necessary to adjourn the hearing if significant information is received less than three working days before the hearing.*

You can ask the admission authority for the answers to any questions or any information that you feel is necessary to enable you to prepare your case at any time. The admission authority must provide all the information that you reasonably ask for, so that you are in a position to question the admission authority. There should be no grounds for the admission authority to produce substantial new information at the appeal because it should all be included in its statement. However, this does not apply to you because you may have only received the admission authority's statement seven days before the hearing.

Representation

You should be encouraged to attend the appeal and make oral representations to clarify or supplement your written submission. However, you do have the right to be accompanied by a friend or to be represented by a friend or relative, a professional in school admission appeals or a solicitor. The panel will try to ensure that the appeal is as informal as possible and therefore it is normally not necessary for you to have legal representation. However, you may feel that you would like some professional help and to be represented because you may not feel sufficiently confident. The appeal can be a traumatic experience because it is an environment that may make you feel uncomfortable, but with proper preparation you will feel more assured and able to present a sufficiently robust case.

The principles of natural justice

Appeals must operate under the principles of natural justice. Below is what the Code of Practice says about natural justice.

4.42 Appeal panels perform a judicial function. They must be, and be seen to be, both independent and impartial. They must operate in accordance with the principles of natural justice, which means that they must be fair to all parties at all times. The principles of natural justice most directly relevant to appeals are as follows:

- No member of the panel should have a vested interest in the outcome of the proceedings or any involvement in an earlier stage of the proceedings.

- Each side should be given the opportunity to state their case without unreasonable interruption.

- Written material must be seen by all parties. If a new issue arises during the proceedings, parties should be offered an opportunity to comment on it.

The Code of Practice on School Admission Appeals 2003

There are a number of other principles that the appeal panel should follow. The overriding principle is that the appeal panel must act independently. Panel members must do everything possible to demonstrate to all parties that they are independent. In addition, panels must follow interpretations of law laid down by the courts and, although they are part of the legal system, panels must ensure that hearings are as informal as possible. Panels should enable both parties to be able to say what they want to say and also to be able to question and challenge the other side. However, informality should not lead to lack of structure which is there to ensure that natural justice prevails.

Appeals are evidence-based forums and it is important that any evidence presented that may be unreliable must be treated with caution by the appeal panel. Panels should check the evidence wherever possible; this is usually done at the hearing by questioning either party or cross-checking with evidence already submitted. However, if it is not possible to check any information at the hearing, the panel may require an adjournment. If there is a conflict of evidence, then panels should use their knowledge and experience to assess which information to rely on.

Other Acts of Parliament

When they are considering appeals, panel members must also be aware of the implications of other legislation which may impact on the admission authority's original decision, and also on their own decision. The panel must be aware of the implications of the Sex Discrimination Act 1975 and the Race Relations Act 1976, as well as the Disability Discrimination Act 1995. Admission criteria should not discriminate against anyone on the grounds of sex, race or disability.

In addition, the panel should also be aware of the implications of the Human Rights Act 1998 and the duties in accordance with the European Convention on Human Rights. Under the European Convention, your child has a right to an education and for your wishes to be considered. For example, you have a right for your religious convictions to be considered, but this does not confer a right for your child to be educated at a religious school of your choice.

Individual or multiple appeals

When organising appeals the admission authority can decide whether to hold individual or multiple appeals. If it is an individual appeal, the panel will hear the admission authority's case followed by your case. This approach is relatively straightforward. However, if there is more than one appeal for the same school, the admission authority may decide to hold multiple appeals. The Code of Practice provides for different approaches. The usual approach will be to invite all the parents together to hear the school's case and then to move into individual hearings where the panel will consider your individual case without other parents being present. The approach taken may well determine how you approach your appeal. These issues will be discussed in the following chapters.

CHECKLIST 4

1   Did you receive at least ten working days' notice of the appeal?

2   Was the admission authority's statement sent to you at least seven working days before the appeal?

3   Are you prepared to waive this if not?

4   Did you receive a guidance note from the admission authority?

5   Have you made a list of the persons you want to contact because you would like them to support your case? (Sometimes witnesses do have to attend the appeal, but usually a written statement is enough.)

6   Have you started to make a list of the issues that you want to raise at the appeal?

7   Do you know what type of appeal to expect?

8   Do you understand the role of the Clerk to the Appeal Panel?

9   Do you understand the role of the presenting officer?

10   Do you understand what should be included in the authority's statement?

11   Do you know whether your appeal will be dealt with as an individual or as a multiple appeal?

12   Do you understand the principles of natural justice?

13   Do you feel that you need to be represented?

14   Do you feel confident about representing yourself?

15   Have you obtained all the supporting documentation for your appeal?

Chapter 5

Normal prejudice appeals

What is a normal prejudice appeal? Well, put simply, it is the appeal that you will face if it is not a class-size appeal (a class size appeal relates to Key Stage 1 appeals only, covering reception and Years 1 and 2 – see Chapter 6) or a grammar school appeal (see Chapter 7). The vast majority of appeals fall into this category.

When you apply for a place at a school and there are more applications than places, the admission authority will apply the admission criteria and will offer places up to and including the published admission number. It will use the published admission criteria to determine which applications will be successful. Those applications which are unsuccessful will be refused and the admission authority will have to explain in detail why your application was refused and also explain why, in its view, an additional admission will cause prejudice, whether it is normal prejudice or class size prejudice (see Chapter 6).

When the admission authority cites normal prejudice, the reason it gives is that your admission will cause prejudice to either efficient use of resources or efficient education. In laypersons' terms, this means that the admission authority has determined the number of admissions that the school can admit without causing problems for the school. This is the only legal reason why any application is unsuccessful and it will always be used by the admission authority as the formal reason as to why an application was refused. It will not cite the use of the admission criteria because, ultimately, that is not the legal reason why the application was not successful. The admission authority will only admit pupils up to, but not exceeding, the published admission number.

The issues covered by this chapter are as follows:

- What decisions do the panel have to make?
- Have the admission arrangements been applied correctly?
- Can the school take any more pupils?
- How is the net capacity worked out?
- Is the school overcrowded?
- Pupil/teacher ratios

- Health and safety issues
- Pupil/teacher contact time
- What does Ofsted have to say?

Quick reference

- Prejudice

  This is the term used by admission authorities to describe the effect of admitting additional pupils above the expected number.

- Published admission number

  This is the number of pupils that the admission authority has agreed to admit to each year group.

- Net capacity

  This is the total number of pupils that are expected to be at the school for all of the year groups based on the size of the school. The net capacity is agreed by the governors of the school.

- Work spaces

  This is a term used in calculating the net capacity of the school. A work space is the area that has been designated for one pupil. If the net capacity is 1,500 work spaces, this means that the school can accommodate 1,500 pupils.

- Building Bulletin 98

  This is the document issued by the Department for Children, Schools and Families (DCSF) that sets out the guidance for new-build schools and extensions to existing schools.

- Registration class

  In schools where there is more than one class being admitted, pupils will be allocated to a class which is referred to as a registration class. In primary schools, pupils will remain in these classes while they are taught most subjects excluding, for example, physical education. In secondary schools, pupils will be allocated to a registration class, but will then be streamed by ability into subject classes.

QUICK LIST
1 Was your application dealt with in accordance with the published admission arrangements?

2   Can the school take any more pupils?

3   What is the net capacity for the school?

4   Have you checked the performance of the school?

5   Has the school's performance deteriorated?

6   What does Ofsted say about the school?

7   Have you checked the classroom sizes?

8   Have you checked the pupil/teacher ratio?

9   How many issues can you challenge in the admission authority's statement?

10   Do all the figures in the statement add up?

11   Are there any issues that you can challenge?

What decisions do the panel have to make?

In normal prejudice appeals, the appeal panel has to make three decisions. Firstly, the panel has to decide if the admission arrangements were correctly applied in your case. Secondly, the panel will have to decide if the school can accommodate any more pupils without causing any problems for the school. Thirdly, the panel will have to decide if, notwithstanding the prejudice issues, the personal reasons that you have for your child wanting to attend the school are compelling enough to outweigh any prejudice that may be caused to the school.

Have the admission arrangements been applied correctly?

The panel will have to decide if the admission authority has correctly applied the admission arrangements. In other words, did the admission authority make a mistake when it applied the admission criteria, which has resulted in a place being denied? To enable the panel members to do this, they have to understand the admission criteria and how they have been applied. For example, if a distance factor has been applied, the admission authority will need to explain how the distances have been measured; and from which point on your property to which point at the school? How has the distance factor been defined in the published admission criteria? Is the distance measured manually or by computer? How accurate is the measurement?

Some of these may seem fairly simplistic questions, but it could mean the difference between a successful and an unsuccessful application. I have attended appeals where an applicant has been refused a place at a school because the distance measurement was judged to be two metres more than the last successful applicant! This is why it is very important that the admission authority explains in detail how the admission criteria have been applied in general and also how they have been applied in your particular case. This is also why it is important that the decision letter that you originally received explains in detail why your application was not successful so that you can decide the basis of your appeal.

If the panel decides that your application was not dealt with correctly and you were unfairly denied a place, the appeal panel will allow your appeal. If the panel decides that your application was dealt with correctly, the panel will take into consideration any strong personal reasons you may have why your child should attend the school and it will decide whether any more additional admissions will cause prejudice or problems for the school.

Can the school take any more pupils?

The admission authority will decide how many pupils the school can admit without adversely affecting efficient and effective education of the pupils at the school. The number that the school will admit is the published admission number (otherwise referred to as the 'published admission limit'). The admission authority will argue that to go beyond this number will cause problems and it will explain in its statement to the appeal panel what those problems are. So how does the admission authority decide what is the optimum number that the school can admit without causing such problems? The government decided some time ago that there should be a uniform basis for deciding the optimum number of pupils that can be admitted, bearing in mind the physical size of the school. This is known as the 'net capacity' for the school.

How is the net capacity worked out?

Net capacity is the formula that determines the maximum number of pupils that the school can accommodate based on the physical size of the school. In very simple terms, all the areas of the school are measured and logged and the maximum number of work spaces is determined. These are then added together to arrive at the maximum number of work spaces for the school. This figure is then multiplied by 90 per cent, which then determines the minimum number of work spaces. The governing body of the school then determines where the capacity will be within these two figures by considering a number of matters, such as the size and shape of classrooms, the size of the communal areas and the size of corridors. In addition, it will also consider the school resources, the number of classes and the general infrastructure of the school. The net capacity is then divided by the number of year groups, which determines the indicated admission number, which is also known as the 'published admission number'. See the example below.

Maximum number of work spaces	1,300
Minimum number of work spaces **(1,300 multiplied by 90 per cent)**	1,170
Net capacity range	1,170 – 1,300
Net capacity	1,200
Indicated admission number (1,200 divided by five)	240

In the example given, the figures are based on a secondary school with five year groups from Year 7 to Year 11. In this example, the published admission number for the school will be 240.

If the secondary school has a sixth form, the formula becomes more complicated. In the following example, the assumption is that the school is for 11 to 18 year olds.

Maximum number of work spaces	837
Minimum number of work spaces **(837 divided by 90 per cent)**	753
Net capacity range	753 – 837
Net capacity	834
Number of year groups	6.95
Indicated admission number (834 divided by 6.95)	120

In the example given, the number of year groups is established by using a complicated formula, which is included in the net capacity assessment method for secondary schools. There is also a similar formula for primary schools; however, the published admission number may be influenced by the infant class size regulations, which will be covered in Chapter 6. You can download the booklet on net capacity from the DCSF website at www.dcsf.gov.uk.

The admission authority may use the net capacity for the school as grounds for not increasing the admission number. However, it may well use other grounds.

Is the school overcrowded?

If the school has historically been oversubscribed, it is very likely that there have been successful appeals in the past which means that some, if not all, of the year groups have more pupils than the published admission number. The admission authority may well cite the fact that the size of the classrooms cannot cope with more pupils. As with most public services, the government strives to increase standards and facilities in schools. For many years, the yardstick for the size of classrooms for classes of 30 was 54 square metres, which was based on 1.8 square metres per child. This made it more difficult for the admission authority to argue that a classroom was full if it exceeded 54 square metres and 30 pupils were present, or if there were fewer than 30 pupils in the room. Note that a class can exceed 30 pupils in number for Year 3 and above.

However, the government has published guidance for new-build accommodation, whether this is for brand new schools or for extending existing schools or indeed replacing temporary classrooms. In Building Bulletin 98, which sets out the guidance for new-build accommodation built after 1998, the figures quoted are different. The recommended area for a group of 30 pupils is 51 square metres for a small classroom, 60 square metres for a standard sized classroom and 66 square metres for a large classroom. The difference in these approaches does provide a possible route for you to challenge the admission authority's case. Further guidance will be given in Chapter 8.

Admission authorities have to make subjective judgements about their admission number and capacity, often in consultation with the governors, for community schools, and with the LEA, for aided and foundation schools and academies. Of course, the admission authority will believe that it has established the published admission number after taking into consideration a range of issues and that this is a reasonable number. However, at the appeal, the admission authority will have to justify its reasons to the appeal panel.

4.61 It is not enough for the admission authority to show that the admission number has been reached; it should also demonstrate what prejudice would be caused by the additional admission. In order to establish whether or not there is prejudice, the panel will wish to consider a number of factors, such as the school's published admission number, and for applications made for admission to a later year group, and whether any changes have been made to the school's physical accommodation or staffing level since the admission number was set for that year group when it was the normal year for admission to the school. The appeal panel should be satisfied that the school's published admission number is a justified limit. The parent may question the case presented by the admission authority and raise points of his own in support of a contention that admission of an additional child would not cause prejudice.

The Code of Practice on School Admission Appeals 2003

3.2 b) The panel **must** consider whether or not there would be prejudice caused by the additional admission of the child. Where this is the case, the admission authority **must** be able to demonstrate this over and above the fact that the published admission number has already been reached. The panel **must** consider a number of factors in reaching a decision as to whether or not there would be prejudice. This may include considering, in the light of current school organisation (i.e. 'future prejudice') or, if the application was for a year group other than the normal year of entry, whether any changes have been made to the school's physical accommodation or organisation since the admission number was originally set for that year group. The panel can decide what weight to give to the arguments presented.

The Code on School Admission Appeals 2007

Note: Future prejudice occurs not only in relation to the year to which the pupil is to be admitted but also any subsequent years.

Pupil/teacher ratios

What is the pupil/teacher ratio for the school? The situation is often more straightforward at primary schools because most subjects are taught in registration classes and there is no setting or streaming. The situation is very different in secondary schools where the head teacher has much more flexibility and pupils will often be streamed by ability at different stages. Some schools operate streaming in all years, whereas others do not until Years 8, 9 or 10.

In practice, most schools will set in the core subjects of Maths, English and Science in Years 7 or 8 and set in the other subjects in later years. For example, if the published admission number for a school is 300 and there are ten forms of entry, then the class size or registration group is 30. However, if there are 11 forms of entry, this brings the figure down to 27. This may suggest that there is room in the school to admit more pupils and it is an issue that you may be able to challenge at an appeal. Again, this issue will be covered in more detail in Chapter 8.

It is also helpful if you can establish the pupil/teacher ratio for the school and make comparisons with other similar-sized schools. The pupil/teacher ratio is simply the pupil numbers divided by the number of teachers. If the pupil/teacher ratio is lower than average, this suggests that there is more flexibility than the school is prepared to admit and this may convince an appeal panel that the school can admit more pupils without causing any problems. Details of pupil/teacher ratios can be found on the DCSF website at www.dcsf.gov.uk.

Health and safety issues

These issues are often used by admission authorities to justify why they cannot admit any more pupils. They will usually cite issues such as crowded corridors, small classrooms, a high level of accidents, specialist classrooms being unable to accommodate more pupils, problems with means of escape in case of fire, issues identified by health and safety inspectors, adopting one-way systems (used by schools so that pupil movement is all one way round certain corridors to avoid too many pupils moving in opposite directions down the same corridor) and the very fact that the school was not designed for the number of pupils currently at the school.

Any one of these issues may be considered by the admission authority to justify not admitting any more pupils. However, in my experience, many statements make claims about health and safety issues but do not provide any evidence to support such claims. For example, it is very easy to say that there has been a substantial increase in the number of accidents at the school, but where is the evidence of this? If the statement contained details of serious accidents that have been directly attributable to the high numbers at the school, this may be persuasive, but, in the vast majority of cases, such information is not provided. As has been mentioned previously, the appeal panel exercises a quasi-judicial function and it is not enough to make such claims without supporting them with firm evidence to verify them.

The situation is that the vast majority of schools were built many years ago when the demands on them were very different. Many statements refer to the historical development of schools and state that they were built for substantially fewer pupils. However, most of these schools have been extended, and in any event, the net capacity has been determined, having taken into consideration the size of the accommodation. So while the admission authority may try to convince an appeal panel that additional admissions should not be permitted because of health and safety issues, parents can challenge this and argue that such issues should not prevent the admission of additional pupils. You can do this by finding out from the school concerned about the level of reported health and safety incidents and questioning any reason given by the authority about health and safety concerns. You can also look at the most recent Ofsted inspection report to see if the inspectors raised any concerns about health and safety issues.

Pupil/teacher contact time

Some schools may argue that if they are required to take an additional pupil, this will reduce the contact time with pupils; this is the time that the teacher has available to spend with each pupil. However, the question here is what effect, if any, has the increased numbers had on the school's performance? This is a major issue. You will no doubt have read over the years about performance figures and the extent to which schools argue that they do not necessarily show the whole picture. But if a school is doing particularly well, what is the first thing that schools quote? The answer is the performance figures!

Therefore, if the school genuinely believes one additional admission will adversely affect how the education is delivered, then one would expect the school's performance to be compromised. But in the vast majority of cases, this does not occur. The better performing schools continue to perform better. Of course, there comes a point where the numbers of pupils will cause problems and there will be tell-tale signs. The school will suffer from teacher retention and recruitment problems and the school's performance figures will also begin to suffer.

If the admission authority should use this reason as a defence, then it is up to the authority to demonstrate that pupil/teacher contact time has suffered, rather than your having to demonstrate that it has not.

What does Ofsted have to say?

Her Majesty's inspectors will inspect schools on a regular basis and it is recognised that the inspectors' work represents an independent assessment of a range of educational issues. Inspectors will grade the school against a range of predetermined targets. The method of inspection has recently changed in the hope that inspections will be carried out more frequently. Inspections are now based on self-assessments carried out by the governors and the inspectors determine whether these assessments are accurate. The inspections take less time than previously, but this does not mean that they are any less valid.

If the school receives a positive inspection, the governors are the first to include this in their prospectus. It is also likely that the school will include

Ofsted comments in its statement. If the inspectors are concerned about any aspect of school life, they will comment on it in their report.

It is important that you look at the most recent Ofsted report to see the conclusions of the inspectors before you attend the appeal so that you can anticipate what issues might be raised by the school. You can look at and download Ofsted reports from its website at www.ofsted.gov.uk.

CASE STUDY 1

At an appeal for Year 7, the head teacher submitted a statement that referred to concerns raised by Ofsted at an inspection carried out in 2002. These concerns involved limited communal areas, a shortage of classrooms and a range of health and safety issues. Since the report in 2002, the school had a range of improvements carried out following a private finance initiative that sought to address the shortfall in the school's accommodation.

In a statement to the appeal panel, the head teacher referred to the concerns in the Ofsted report and while he acknowledged that improvements had been carried out, he sought to convince the appeal panel that most of the concerns still existed. What the head teacher failed to reveal was that a further Ofsted inspection had been carried out in 2006 and none of the concerns were referred to in the latest report.

When he was challenged about this by the appeal panel, the head teacher stated that the most recent report was less valid because the basis on which the report had been produced had changed significantly and it was based on a self-assessment. Not surprisingly, this claim was not accepted by the appeal panel, and the panel members were concerned that the head teacher had sought to mislead the panel. The outcome was that the panel did not accept that the school could not accommodate more pupils and it allowed 26 appeals.

Moral: It is important that you do not simply accept what the governors have said, but that you question and challenge it. Also, carry out your own research and see what you can find out.

Generally, the admission authority will seek to justify its decisions but, in practice, its arguments can be carefully dismantled. Details of how this can be done are shown in Chapter 8.

Many parents seek professional help with their appeals and an example of a professionally prepared response to an admission authority's statement, which was successful, is shown in Appendix 2. You will see that the response draws on relevant paragraphs in the Code of Practice on School Admission Appeals, which was published in 2003, and which explains what is expected in an admission authority statement. This advice has been further endorsed by the Ombudsman in his Special Report published in 2004. You will see that the response also uses the performance figures for the school, along with extracts from the most recent Ofsted inspection, to help to undermine the admission authority's statement.

CHECKLIST 5

1 Do you understand what normal prejudice is?

2 Have you checked to see if the admission arrangements have been correctly applied?

3 Do you understand how the net capacity is worked out for the school?

4 What is the net capacity for the school?

5 How many pupils are on roll at the school?

6 What is the pupil/teacher ratio for the school? You can work this out by dividing the number of pupils by the number of teachers at the school.

7 What is the pupil/teacher ratio for other similar schools?

8 What is the school's performance compared to other schools?

9 How many successful appeals have there been for the school in the last five years? You can obtain this information from the admission authority.

10 What effect has this had on the school's performance?

11 Have you checked to see what Ofsted has said about the school following the last inspection?

12 Is there anything in the report that you can use to challenge the school?

Chapter 6

Infant class size appeals

This chapter explains the issues over class size appeals, which relate to Key Stage 1 appeals only. A class size appeal is where the admission authority refuses a school place because it would result in a class size of more than 30 for children aged five, six and seven or it would result in a ratio of more than 30 children to one teacher. The vast majority of Key Stage 1 appeals will be class size appeals; although there are some exceptions of smaller schools which have admission numbers below 30 and which operate their appeals as normal prejudice.

Because of the limited grounds for a successful appeal, class size appeals are not easy to win. However, the guidance described below will help to give you the best chance of success.

The issues covered in this chapter are as follows:

- What is a class size appeal?
- Has the admission authority made a mistake?
- Was the decision unreasonable?
- Is it, or is it not, a class size appeal?
- Schools with one-form entry
- Schools with two or more forms of entry
- What about multiple birth children?
- Guidance issued by the Department for Children, Schools and Families (DCSF)

Quick reference

- ### Qualifying measures
  There are two qualifying measures. One is the employment of an additional teacher by the admission authority to ensure that the class size limit of 30 is not exceeded. The second is the provision of additional accommodation. This is where the existing classroom is not big enough to accommodate an additional pupil.

- ## School teacher

  This has been defined in guidance issued by the DCSF and is referred to in the last section of this chapter.

- ## Teaching assistant

  Teaching assistants are also referred to as classroom assistants. They provide help and support to the school teachers, but they are not qualified as teachers.

- ## Higher level teaching assistants

  These are experienced teaching assistants who have demonstrated to the Teacher Training Agency that they have the necessary skills and experience and meet the agreed national professional standards through one of the higher level teaching assistants assessment and training programmes that are available across the country.

- ## Vertical or mixed grouping

  This is where a school organises classes which have more than one year group in the same class. Such arrangements will not normally merge pupils from more than one key stage.

- ## The Dedicated School Grant

  This is the name given to funds allocated by the government each year to Local Education Authorities (LEAs) to help them provide educational facilities in their area. It is up to each LEA to decide how that grant is shared between the schools in their area.

QUICK LIST
1 Have you checked the published admission number of the school?
2 Do you understand what a class size appeal is?
3 Do your circumstances come under one of the exceptions to class size legislation?
4 Do your circumstances come under one or other of the two grounds on which an appeal can be successful?
5 Have you found out how many teachers are employed at the school?
6 Did the admission authority make a mistake in dealing with your application?
7 Was the decision unreasonable?

What is a class size appeal?

In 1999, the government decided that it would not be appropriate for pupils aged five, six and seven (Key Stage 1) to be taught in classes of more than 30 children unless there is more than one qualified teacher present. What this means is that, irrespective of the size of the classroom, the admission authority will base its case on the published admission number for the school being 30, or a multiple of 30. Appeals against the refusal to offer a place are commonly known as 'class size appeals'. For pupils older than the age of seven, there is no legal limit to the size of the class, but LEAs may use local guidelines.

At the same time the government also limited the grounds on which an appeal could be successful. This is why it is important to understand the issues involved because if an admission authority can persuade an appeal panel that the hearing should be considered as a class size appeal, then your chances of success will be greatly reduced because there are only two grounds on which an appeal can be successful (see below).

A class size appeal is where the admission authority claims that if the published admission number is exceeded, that the school will have to employ another teacher and/or provide additional accommodation so that the legal limit of 30 pupils to one teacher is not exceeded; these are referred to in legislation as 'qualifying measures'. If, at the appeal, the panel accepts that if the published admission number is exceeded, the school will have to take 'qualifying measures', there are only two grounds on which an appeal can be successful:

1. That the admission authority made a mistake in dealing with your application and that if the mistake had not been made, a place would have been offered; or

2. That the decision which the admission authority took was unreasonable.

It may well be that you feel that you have very good reasons for your child to attend a particular school or there are special, or even exceptional, reasons why your child should attend the school. But unless your appeal comes under one of the two grounds referred to above, regretfully, it will be unsuccessful. In fact, there may well be situations where an appeal panel would allow an appeal if it was dealt with as a normal prejudice appeal, where the panel is not bound by anything, but it will fail as a class size appeal because of the restrictions imposed by legislation and the Codes on School Admissions and Appeals.

Has the admission authority made a mistake?

Usually, if a mistake has been made, this can be fairly easy for the appeal panel to determine. In these circumstances the only decision the panel has to make is whether the mistake resulted in a place being denied. The appeal panel will look at the published admission criteria and decide if it was correctly applied in your case.

Case Study 1 illustrates that it is not sufficient to demonstrate that a mistake has been made. You also have to show that the mistake resulted in a place being denied.

CASE STUDY 1

Mr and Mrs X applied to a one-form entry primary school but their application was not successful. Mr and Mrs X lodged an appeal when it was discovered that the admission authority had made a mistake in measuring the distance Mr and Mrs X lived from the school. However, when the distance was correctly measured it was discovered that there were still 32 children that lived nearer to the school. In the circumstances the appeal was not successful, even though a mistake had been made.

A mistake could mean, as in the example above, that the distance was incorrectly measured or it could mean that the admission authority did not take into consideration a sibling at the school. If the school is a voluntary aided church school, it could mean that the commitment requirement has been misinterpreted or the admission criteria have not been applied correctly.

Was the decision unreasonable?

This is a subjective assessment the appeal panel will need to make, but it is much more restrictive than you may think. What this ground actually means is 'was the decision that the admission authority took unreasonable' based on the information that the authority had when it took its original decision? This is why it is important that you submit all the information you can with the original application form.

At an appeal, you can introduce fresh information which was not available to the admission authority when it made its original decision, but such fresh information is subject to two requirements which will be considered by the appeal panel. The first requirement is whether the fresh information could have been made available when the admission authority made its original decision. This could be an existing medical condition or some other information or circumstances that have not occurred since the decision was made. For example, say you did not reveal an existing medical condition because you felt that you would secure a place at the school without the need to disclose it. Such a medical condition would need to have existed at the time of the application and not be discovered afterwards. A medical condition that was diagnosed after the closing date for applications would not meet this requirement.

The second requirement is that the fresh information must be persuasive. This is much more difficult to quantify because it will be a subjective decision by the appeal panel. The courts have determined that 'persuasive', in this context, is a very high threshold and it is unlikely that many circumstances will meet this threshold. However, in order for an appeal to be successful, the fresh information must satisfy both requirements.

The new Code on School Admission Appeals is seeking to make it even more difficult to win an appeal under this ground. Most infant school decisions on applications will be issued after 1 March 2008 and therefore will be subject to more limited grounds on which an appeal can be successful. The new Code is seeking to prevent the introduction of fresh information at an appeal so that the appeal panel's decision is based on the information which the admission authority had when it made its decision. According to the Code, the panel should review the admission authority's decision in the light of the material available at the time when it made its decision. Exceptionally, a panel may consider material which would have been available to the admission authority if it had acted reasonably (e.g. if a parent had provided the information with his application, but the admission authority had lost it). In addition, the panel can also consider evidence submitted by the parents to show what their circumstances were at the time the decision was made in order to support their claim that no reasonable admission authority would have made that decision. It will be a matter of time to see how the courts interpret these provisions in the new Code.

Case Study 2 illustrates that you have to meet two conditions identified by the courts to show that information not disclosed to the admission authority is both persuasive and also could have been available when the original decision was made.

CASE STUDY 2

Ms X applied to a school and did not disclose any special circumstances in her application and she lived too far away to secure a place on distance. Ms X appealed. As part of the appeal, Ms X stated that since the application had been submitted she had discovered that her daughter's father, from whom she was separated, had been arrested and charged with child pornography offences and was prevented from seeing his daughter unless it was supervised. Ms X had found out that such an investigation had been ongoing for some time and although she did not know anything about the offences, these had occurred some time ago and the police investigation had been ongoing before the closing date for applications.

Ms X stated that had she known of this information at the time, she would have disclosed such information on her application form. The appeal panel decided that the information could have been made available to the admission authority because it was known to the police before the closing date for applications.

In addition, because the father was not allowed unsupervised contact with his daughter, this meant that he would not be able to pick her up from school and this meant that her grandmother would have to pick her up instead. Her grandmother was disabled and could only walk short distances, and only to the school which was the subject of the appeal and not to the allocated school.

In the light of this fresh information, the admission authority confirmed that if it had been made aware of this information, it would have placed the applicant in the admission category of exceptional reasons to attend the school, which would have resulted in a place being offered. The appeal panel decided that the fresh information was persuasive. The panel decided that the appeal met both of the circumstances described by the courts and the appeal was successful.

Case Study 3 illustrates that even if there are exceptional reasons to attend a school, this does not necessarily result in an appeal being successful.

CASE STUDY 3

Ms Y applied to a school but her application was not successful. Ms Y appealed. As part of her appeal Ms Y confirmed that she worked in child protection and potentially could come across parents she was involved with as part of her work if her daughter attended the allocated school. She said that she had deliberately avoided schools when she expressed her preferences where this situation was likely to arise. She had not disclosed this information on her application form because she thought that she would secure a place at the school as she lived closer to the school than the last successful applicant last year (she had found this information in the LEA's admissions booklet). This situation was in existence before the closing date and met the first requirement that it could have been made available on the application form.

In addition, the admission authority admitted that if this information had been made available to it, it would have allocated the child to the top priority of exceptional reasons, which would have resulted in a place being offered. However, the child's birthday was not until August and she did not legally need to be in school until the following academic year (the term following the child's fifth birthday). In this case the appeal panel did not accept that the issues were persuasive, as Ms Y did not meet the second requirement. As a result, the appeal was not successful.

What these two case studies illustrate is that in order for an appeal to be successful, the appeal needs to meet both requirements and meeting one will not be sufficient to win an appeal.

Is it, or is it not, a class size appeal?

In relation to class size appeals, appeal panels must take into consideration not only the situation in reception, but also the effect on the class in Years 1 and 2. There are a number of different scenarios which will be dealt with in turn.

Schools with one-form entry

If there is only one form of entry at the school, it should be clear as to which type of appeal you will have to face. There are many schools that admit one class with an admission number of 30. If this is the case, the admission authority will argue that it will have to take qualifying measures if the published admission number is exceeded.

There are many village schools with an admission number of 20 or 25. If the school operates vertical or mixed grouping, where it mixes the classes of different age groups, it is possible that even without an admission number of 30 the admission authority may still argue class size prejudice. For example, say the admission number for the school is 20 but the school organises the pupils in two classes of 30 over the first three-year groups. In this example, one class comprises 20 pupils from reception and ten pupils from Year 1, and the other class comprises the remaining pupils from Year 1 and 20 pupils from Year 2. In this example, the governors could argue class size prejudice because any increase in numbers could require the school to take qualifying measures. However, if the admission number was 14, the admission authority would not be able to argue class size prejudice since, whatever internal arrangements the school operates, it will not arrive at 30 per class. In this example, the admission authority could argue normal prejudice (see Chapter 5), but not class size prejudice.

As a general rule of thumb, if the published admission number results in a class of 30 or a multiple of 30, then the admission authority is likely to argue class size prejudice.

Schools with two or more forms of entry

The same principle applies here. If the published admission number is a multiple of 30 (e.g. 60, 90 or 120), then the admission authority will argue class size prejudice. However, if the number is different, then class size prejudice will not normally apply.

An example quoted in the Special Report of the Ombudsman published in 2004 is a published admission number of 85. The admission authority argues that this is a class size appeal because there are three classrooms and it is not possible to place more pupils in the class of 25 because of the size of the accommodation. Any additional admissions will have to go into one of the classes of 30, thereby requiring the school to employ an additional teacher. This is not a class size appeal.

Several examples of what is and what is not a class size appeal is included in the Special Report of the Ombudsman, published in 2004. You can obtain a copy of the report at the Ombudsman's website at www.lgo.org.uk.

CASE STUDY 4

A school has an admission number of 55. The reception group is organised into one class of 30 and one class of 25 (the latter being in a small room). The admission authority says that an additional child could not be put in the class of 25 because of the capacity of the room, so the child would have to be added to the class of 30, and that would require qualifying measures to be taken.

This is not a case of infant class size prejudice. An additional child would not necessarily have to be added to the class of 30, as the appeal panel may believe that he could be added to the class of 25. In this example, an addition to the class of 25 would not require the admission authority to take qualifying measures because a class of 26 does not breach the statutory class size limit of 30. The admission authority could, however, argue normal prejudice.

CASE STUDY 5

A reception class has 28 pupils. The admission authority says that its policy is that no class should exceed 28 pupils with one teacher, and the school would have to supply an additional teacher if a class exceeded 28. It says that the employment of an additional teacher is a 'qualifying measure' under the infant class size prejudice arrangements and the school would have to employ an additional teacher if more than 28 children were admitted.

This is not a case of class size prejudice. Having a class of 29 with one teacher would not breach the statutory class size limit and the school would not have to employ an additional teacher to comply with the law.

CASE STUDY 6

A school has an admission limit of 30. The reception class has 31 pupils and has two teachers. This is because the admission authority found that it had denied a place to a child in error, so it added the child to the class and employed an additional teacher. A parent appeals and argues that this is not a class size prejudice appeal because the admission of his child would not mean that qualifying measures would have to be taken, as the additional teacher was already being employed.

This is, in fact, a case of class size prejudice. The employment of the additional teacher is a temporary measure, which the authority chose to take and it was not intended to be permanent. So, at some suitable point when one child leaves, the class would revert to having one teacher. This situation is covered in the Code of Practice on School Appeals.

What about multiple birth children?

Almost inevitably, those parents with twins or triplets will come across the situation where they apply for a place in reception and one or two children are accepted and one or two are not. The guidance given to admission authorities is that if there is not a class size issue, all pupils are accepted, even if it means breaching the published admission number. However, there is no provision or exemption for circumstances where a school is allowed to admit pupils which result in a class of more than 30 children being taught by one school teacher. Parents are then placed in a very difficult situation. Whatever the situation, the published admission arrangements should explain what will happen in such cases.

It is surprising the number of incidents that occur where twins and triplets apply for places and fall either side of the cut-off point, which then, potentially, causes a problem for the parents. It is up to each admission authority to decide how such applications should be dealt with, but the guidance is that children should not be split up unless it would result in the class size legislation being breached. The admission arrangements should explain how an authority will deal with such applications if the application of the admission criteria means that one child is offered a place and not the other(s). In the absence of an explanation, common sense should prevail, which would normally mean that all multiple birth children should be offered places, even if this means exceeding the published admission number, except in the case of class size legislation; here the admission arrangements should explain how an admission authority should determine which child to admit. The general advice is that the admission authority should approach the parents to see which child should be offered the place or maybe secure places at an alternative school where they can be all accommodated.

CASE STUDY 7

Mr and Mrs X applied for their twins to attend the local church school, but only one twin was offered a place. Mr and Mrs X appealed. The basis of their appeal was that the school's admission arrangements did not have any provision for twins. The school had simply offered the place to the first application that had been looked at and it had not discussed the position with the parents or asked them which twin to make an offer to. In the circumstances, the appeal panel decided that the actions of the admission authority had amounted to a mistake in the application of its admission criteria and it offered a place to the other twin. The appeal was successful.

Guidance issued by the Department for Children, Schools and Families (DCSF)

The DCSF has issued a guidance note on class size appeals to try to clarify a number of misconceptions about a range of different issues that frequently occur. This guidance is set out below.

Section 122 of the Education Act 2002 and the Education (School Teachers' Prescribed Qualifications, etc.) Order 2003 has sought to define what is regarded as a school teacher. A school teacher has been defined as follows:

- A head teacher

- Qualified teachers

- Overseas trained teachers

- Instructors with special qualifications or experience

- Staff on an employment-based teacher training scheme

- Graduate teachers

- Registered teachers

- Student teachers

- Teacher trainees who have yet not passed the skills test

The guidance note also clarifies who is not regarded as a school teacher. The following are not classed as school teachers:

- Teaching assistants

- Higher level teaching assistants

- Other support staff

However, support staff, including teaching assistants and higher level teaching assistants, may carry out 'specified work', which can include delivering lessons to pupils, within certain circumstances. These circumstances are as follows:

- The head teacher must be satisfied with the support staff's skills, expertise and experience to carry out such work;

- The work carried out must be to assist or support the work of the 'school teacher'; and

- He must be subject to the direction and supervision of a 'school teacher'.

Supervision does not mean that the teacher must be alongside the teaching assistant or higher level teaching assistant, but the teacher is able to ensure that the member of the support staff is effectively teaching the class.

So what does this all mean in practice? Within all school budgets there is provision for teachers to spend up to ten per cent of their time on what is referred to as planning, preparation and assessment time (often referred to as 'PPA' time). Therefore, although schools with infant classes must have sufficient school teachers to be able to teach its pupils in groups of 30 or less, support staff can 'teach' classes, providing that they meet all the above criteria when teachers are not available because of 'PPA' time.

At a class size appeal, the admission authority may argue that any additional admissions will require it to employ another teacher. If a school is a one-form entry primary school with seven classes, and the school employs seven teachers, then it is very likely that the admission authority will be able to convince an appeal panel that it is a class size appeal. If, on the other hand, the school employs ten full-time teachers, this situation will be more difficult to justify, even if an allowance is made for 'PPA' time, which, in this example, would be equivalent of 0.7 of a teacher (which is 0.1 multiplied by seven).

The admission authority must convince the appeal panel that it is a class size appeal; it must not be assumed that it is.

CASE STUDY 8

I attended an appeal and, as part of his introductory remarks, the appeal panel Chair stated that the appeal would be dealt with as a class size appeal. I did not challenge this because the parent attended two appeals and her other appeal was successful. However, in my view, this is a ground to challenge the decision with the Ombudsman because it was clear that the Chair had already made his mind up about its being a class size appeal without hearing the evidence.

The appeal panel will decide if it is a class size prejudice appeal after hearing the evidence. If the Chair's opening remarks suggest that a decision has already been taken before the evidence has been presented, then this could be a ground to make a complaint if the appeal is not successful. If you raise this at the appeal, you run the risk of the appeal being aborted there and then and you being granted another appeal. This may take some time to organise and it may cause a further period of anxiety and uncertainty for you.

The DCSF has also produced a list which is described as myth busters and common misconceptions about the class size duty. These are described as follows:

Myth 1: A child can be admitted to a faith school as a permitted exception if there is no other school of that faith within a reasonable distance.

No. The regulations refer to there being no other schools with places available which provide a 'suitable education', within a reasonable distance of the child's home. This definition does not mean particular types of school, but is described as 'efficient full-time education suitable to his age, ability and aptitude and any special education needs he may have'. A child should not be admitted as a permitted exception under this category unless the local authority has first given its approval.

Comment – While this is the advice to admission authorities, it is up to an appeal panel to consider this information and it may not agree with it. Also, a reasonable distance is not defined in the Code of Practice and it is open to local interpretation. An appeal panel will need to decide what a reasonable distance is; the panel may go along with the statutory walking distance, which is two miles for children under the age of eight. However, it may consider access to public services and also the topography of the area (i.e. how hilly it is) and it may decide that a shorter distance is an unreasonable distance. There is nothing to stop you trying to convince the appeal panel that the distance to the allocated school is an unreasonable distance. You can also argue that the ethos of the school is not suitable if there is no school of the same faith as you within a reasonable distance.

Myth 2: If a class size exceeds 30, the school can meet the class size duty by putting another adult in to support the teacher.

Not necessarily. The teacher must be a 'school teacher', as described above.

Comment – Despite the guidance issued by the DCSF, there still seems to be some doubt about this, so you should question and challenge the admission authority. Find out how many teachers are employed at the school and how many support staff are able to teach under supervision.

Myth 3: Any child admitted outside the normal admissions round can be treated as an exception to the class size limit.

No. Only those listed in the Code of Practice on School Admissions.

Comment – This is clear and there are no grounds for interpretation.

Myth 4: The class size limit does not apply to mixed nursery/reception or Year 2/3 classes.

This is not necessarily true. The statutory limit applies to classes where the majority of children will reach the ages of five, six or seven within the academic year. So, if the majority of children within a class will be aged five, six or seven by the end of the academic year, the class must comply with the statutory limit.

Comment – The situation described will usually apply to small village schools with a small published admission number which therefore operate with mixed or vertical grouped classes. Whether class size legislation applies will depend on the number admitted. You will need to look at the pupil numbers very carefully and also the number of classes and teachers.

Myth 5: Twins or multiple birth children are 'permitted exceptions' and must be admitted.

No. Admission authorities can choose to give these children priority within their published admission arrangements. But if they do not, it is not unreasonable to refuse admission to a child (e.g. one can be offered the 30th and last place, but the other can be ranked 31st against the school's published admission criteria).

Comment – Twins and multiple birth children are not 'permitted exceptions', but the admission authority's published admission arrangements should describe how such places are allocated. In the absence of such a description, you, or the appeal panel, are entitled to take a different view and you could challenge the fact that the admission arrangements have not been correctly applied. If you can convince an appeal panel that the admission arrangements have not been correctly adhered to, you can win an appeal on the basis that a mistake has been made by the admission authority.

Myth 6: Extra funding is available to ensure that the school complies with the class size limit.

Separate funds were originally put aside to help schools reorganise to meet class size limits (e.g. to create additional classrooms and to employ additional teachers). However, funding to help local authorities meet the class size limit is now included within the Dedicated Schools Grant allocations. Local authorities can choose to include in their funding formula, in consultation with their schools' forum, a factor to direct resources to schools with Key Stage 1 classes to enable them to meet the class size commitment. This means that LEAs can allocate extra resources to the more popular schools so that they can admit more pupils without exceeding the legal limit of 30 pupils per school teacher.

Comment – It is true that the government provided what was described as 'transitional arrangements', which included additional funding for the more popular schools when the class size legislation was first introduced in 1999. Many authorities will argue that this transitional funding has now ceased and is not now included in the Dedicated Schools Grant. As a result, virtually all schools will have adjusted their published admission numbers to ensure that they comply with the class size limit legislation with the obvious exception of small village schools. However, you can still challenge the figures produced by the admission authority and put forward an alternative view that an additional admission would not require the school to take qualifying measures.

Myth 7: If admitting another pupil meant that the school had to move to mixed age teaching groups to comply with class size limits, the school could refuse admission.

No. When dealing with applications for admission at normal point of entry, i.e. reception class, the school must admit up to its published admission number. For Years 1 and 2 applications, the admission authority could refuse admission if it would be necessary to employ another teacher or incur some other cost in order to comply with class size limit, but given the number of schools which have successfully adopted mixed-age teaching, it would be extremely difficult to justify this as a reason for refusing admission.

Comment – The advice here is clear. The option to move to mixed age classes is not a legitimate ground to refuse an application and therefore it can be challenged at an appeal.

Myth 8: If the admission authority says that it cannot admit an applicant without breaching the class size limit, an appeal panel cannot uphold an appeal.

No. The admission authority may put forward a case to an appeal panel, claiming that it refused admission because this would have breached the infant class size limit. But it is up to the appeal panel to determine whether this would be the case. If the panel agrees that admission would have breached the limit, it can then only uphold an appeal if the child had been refused a place in error, or if the decision to refuse admission was unreasonable, i.e. wholly irrational. But if the appeal panel finds that admission would not have resulted in the limit being breached, the appeal hearing should proceed in the same way as for a normal prejudice appeal, which is dealt with in Chapter 5.

Comment – This is sound advice. No assumptions can be made and the admission authority has to make a case. This may or may not be accepted by the appeal panel. If the panel accepts that an additional admission would require the school to take qualifying measures, then the only two grounds on which an appeal can be successful are that the admission authority made a mistake that denied a place at the school or the decision was unreasonable. You will then need to convince an appeal panel that one or other of these two grounds applies in your case. If you can, then your child will become one of the permitted exceptions to class size prejudice. If you can convince the panel that it is not a class size appeal, then the appeal will be dealt with as a normal prejudice appeal, which is covered in Chapter 5.

Myth 9: An appeal panel could uphold an appeal on the basis that the decision to refuse admission was unreasonable if it thinks that the admission criteria should have given priority to siblings.

No. The courts have defined 'unreasonable' in this context as being one which is 'perverse in the light of the admission arrangements' or 'a decision which is so outrageous in its defiance of logic or of accepted moral standards that no sensible person who had applied his mind to the question could have arrived at it'. With such a definition, it is likely that only very exceptional cases would be upheld on the basis of a decision to refuse admission being unreasonable.

Comment – It is up to each admission authority to determine its own admission criteria, providing that it is clear, fair and objective. Most admission authorities will use siblings in their criteria, but there is no legal obligation to do so. Therefore, if an admission authority decides not to include siblings, then this, in itself, is not an unreasonable decision, although you may not agree with it. It is very likely that if an appeal panel were to uphold an appeal in such circumstances, the admission authority would apply for a Judicial Review to set the decision aside as being outside the jurisdiction of the appeal panel. This is covered in more detail in Chapter 9. In effect, what would happen is that the offer of a place would be suspended pending the outcome of the Judicial Review.

Myth 10: Year 2 appeals should be automatically upheld because the children admitted would be permitted exceptions for the remainder of the academic year, if they were admitted on appeal, and the class size limit would not apply in Year 3. (It is the view of the government that there have been some successful appeals for Year 2 because the appeal panel know that the school will not have to employ an additional teacher because the legal limit does not apply in Year 3 and above.)

No. The reason that admission has been refused is because to do so would result in a breach of the class size limit. The appeal panel's job is to consider the following:

a)   Would admission have resulted in the class size exceeding 30?

b)   If so, was the decision made correctly?

c)   Was it an unreasonable decision as described in Myth 9?

Comment – While this is strictly the position, most appeal panels will be sympathetic to your circumstances and they appreciate that a positive decision will not require the admission authority to employ another teacher. It is certainly worth pursuing this at an appeal.

Myth 11: A panel should allow appeals on the basis that pupil numbers will be reduced as a result of pupil turnover at the school and the class is not likely to exceed the class size limit for a significant period of time.

No. The panel cannot know exactly what changes will occur, and it should not anticipate that other children may leave.

Comment – The panel should not anticipate what may or may not happen in the future. The panel must not assume that pupil turnover, due to children leaving the school, will result in pupil numbers returning to their former level before a successful appeal. However, there is nothing to stop you raising this as an issue. It may not win an appeal on its own, but if this reason is combined with other issues, it may be seen as persuasive by an appeal panel.

Many parents seek professional help with their appeals and an example of a professionally prepared response to an admission authority's statement, which was successful, is shown in Appendix 3. You will see that the response draws on relevant paragraphs in the Code of Practice on School Admission Appeals, which was published in 2003, and which explains what is expected in an admission authority statement. This advice has been further endorsed by the Ombudsman in his Special Report published in 2004. You will see that the response also uses the performance figures for the school, along with extracts from the most recent Ofsted inspection, to help to undermine the admission authority's statement.

CHECKLIST 6

1 Do you understand what class size prejudice is?

2 Do you understand what 'qualifying measures' are?

3 Is the published admission number 30 or is it a multiple of 30?

4 Will your appeal be treated as a class size appeal?

5 Did the admission authority make a mistake?

6 Was the decision reached unreasonable in relation to the published admission criteria?

7 Do you understand what the definition of a school teacher is?

8 What is the pupil/teacher ratio for the school (see Chapter 5)?

9 Do any of the myths apply in your case?

Chapter 7

Selective schools and sixth form appeals

You may feel that your child will flourish at a grammar school because you feel that it offers the right environment for him to develop his academic ability and potential. Although reference is made throughout this chapter to grammar schools, the issues are exactly the same as for sixth form applications.

The issues covered in this chapter are as follows:

- What are the grounds for refusal?
- Admissions not compatible with the school's admission arrangements
- Admissions that will cause prejudice to efficient education or efficient use of resources
- Sixth form appeals

Quick reference

- ### Grammar school

  A grammar school selects all its pupils by ability. A range of tests take place in October/November to assess whether applicants are suitable for a place at the school.

- ### SATS results

  This term actually refers to 'Standard Assessment Tasks', but it relates to National Curriculum tests taken at the end of each key stage.

- ### Key stage

  There are four key stages which are covered by the National Curriculum and these have been identified in Chapter 2.

QUICK LIST
1 Was the application unsuccessful because your child did not secure enough marks?

> **2** Did the school conduct an internal review of the test papers?
>
> **3** Is your child's primary school willing to support an appeal?
>
> **4** Are your child's predicted SATS scores above average and is your child suitable for a grammar school?
>
> **5** Will your child flourish in a grammar school setting?
>
> **6** Do you think that your child may struggle in a grammar school?
>
> **7** Were there any mitigating circumstances that may have affected your child's performance?

All grammar schools receive more applications than they have places available, and meeting the preferred school's admission criteria will be very important because all the available school places will be filled with first preference applications. As with other secondary schools, the admission authority is able to use whatever criteria it wishes, provided that it is clear, fair and objective.

Unfortunately, the timing of the grammar school tests (in October/November) and also the closing date for preference forms (which is also in October/November) will usually mean that you will not know how your child has performed in grammar school tests before the preference forms have to be submitted. It is critical that you consider your preferences very carefully in order for you to maximise the possibility of securing a place at the school of your choice.

CASE STUDY 1

Mr and Mrs X wanted their son to attend a grammar school so they placed it first on their preference form and then listed their local oversubscribed comprehensive school as second preference. Their son took the grammar school test and did not secure a place at the grammar school because he did not gain enough marks. The local comprehensive was filled with first preference applicants and Mr and Mrs X's son was offered a place at an underperforming local comprehensive school.

This situation arose because the parents did not know the grammar school results before they had to submit the preference form. If they had known the result of the tests before they submitted the preference form, they would have secured a place at the comprehensive that they wanted because they would have placed the comprehensive school as a first preference.

While this illustrates the difficulty and risks involved in choosing schools, this particular situation should not arise in the future, following the introduction of equal preference arrangements (see Chapter 1 for more information). The effect of this means that the order in which you rank your preferences is not as critical as it was previously under the first preference first arrangements, where an admission authority would offer places to first preference applications first before considering second and third preferences. If a school was oversubscribed with first preferences, no places would be available to second or third preference applications.

CASE STUDY 2

Mr Y's son took the grammar school test and Mr Y did not think that his son would pass it. As a result, he placed the grammar school as his third preference and the popular local catchment comprehensive school as his first preference. His son passed the test, but he did not secure a place at the grammar school because it was filled with first preference applicants. Mr Y appealed and won because he was able to convince the appeal panel that his son was suitable for a grammar school place.

What are the grounds for refusal?

There are only two grounds which can be used to refuse your application. The first reason is that your child did not do well enough in the grammar school tests. The official legal ground is that your child's admission will not be compatible with the school's admission arrangements.

The second ground is that your child's admission would prejudice efficient use of resources or efficient education; this is the same ground given to refuse applications to comprehensive schools. If this is the reason given, it will mean that your child passed the grammar school test, but there were more successful applications than places available and other pupils had a higher priority than your child when he was measured against the published admission criteria.

Admissions not compatible with the school's admission arrangements

This occurs where your child did not secure enough marks in the grammar school test in order to obtain a place at the school. If your child failed to secure a place at a school for this reason, you will be entitled to an appeal, where you will be given the opportunity to convince an appeal panel that a place should be offered. If this is the case, an appeal panel will take into consideration any issues you put forward as to why your child did not perform to his best on the day of the test. Of course, the bigger the difference between the pass mark and the mark your child obtained, the more difficult it will be to convince an appeal panel that your child is suitable for a grammar school place. To do this, you will need to explain about any issues that may have adversely affected your child's performance when he took the test. It may be that your child was ill on the day of the test. If this is the case, you will need to provide a medical report from your doctor explaining about the illness and the extent that it may have affected your child's performance. Some illnesses are more serious than others and they may have a more significant impact on your child's performance. For example, if your child had a cold on the day of the test, it is likely that this will have affected his performance, but it will be difficult to establish what that effect was, and how it was translated into marks.

There may be other reasons why your child did not perform to the best of his ability. There may have been a family incident that may have affected his performance; there may have been a bereavement of a close family member or a close relative may have been taken to hospital with a serious illness. You will need to explain in detail why this adversely affected your child's performance and provide third party support.

According to the Code of Practice, an appeal panel should not try to make an assessment of your child's ability, but it is difficult to see how the panel cannot do this and yet determine that your child is suitable for a grammar school place. In order to help the appeal panel, you should take along copies of your child's most recent school report and any other supporting information, such as a letter from the head teacher giving an objective assessment of your child's abilities. In addition, you should also take along your child's predicted SATS results, which will also provide an indication of your child's ability.

Before the appeal, some schools use an internal review for those pupils who just missed the pass mark to see if the papers were correctly marked. This is not part of the official appeal process and it will be carried out by the school. However, if such a review exists and a place is still not offered, it does make it more difficult to win a subsequent appeal because the school will be able to demonstrate that it did review the test papers. You will usually be asked to submit a statement or response for the review and sometimes you may be invited to attend the review. You will need to look through the admission arrangements for the school to see if a review is used by the school as part of its admission arrangements.

*The new Code has made reference to the internal review which is conducted by some schools. It states that where there is a local review process, the appeal panel **must not** make its own assessment of the child's ability, but it **must** consider whether the child's review was carried out in a fair, consistent and* *objective way (e.g. whether the same type of evidence was used in all cases). If there is no clear evidence that this has been done, then the appeal panel **should** consider any factors put forward by the parents. This will include any mitigating circumstances, together with any evidence submitted to support their claim that their child is of the required academic standard (e.g. school reports giving Year 5/6 SATS results or a letter of support from their current or previous school clearly indicating why the child is considered to be of grammar school ability).*

Admission authorities have discretion as to how they hold their appeals. It may be that they simply hold a grammar school appeal, as described above, and if you are successful, you may be required to attend a subsequent appeal to challenge the school's case on whether there is sufficient room at the school. Alternatively, it may form part of the grammar school appeal. Either way the appeal panel will follow the arrangements in Chapter 5.

Some grammar schools form consortiums so that the tests are exactly the same for a number of schools. In these circumstances you may need to appeal if your child did not secure a sufficient number of marks. If you can convince the appeal panel that your child is suitable for a grammar school education, you may then need to appeal for a place at a particular school. Again, the school's admission arrangements should clarify the admission and appeal process.

Admissions that will cause prejudice to efficient education or use of resources

Where the admission authority has a set pass mark and more pupils obtain the mark than there are places available, the admission authority will apply the published admission criteria to see which applications will be successful. Those applicants who are unsuccessful will be offered an appeal, which will follow the arrangements as shown in Chapter 5.

Sixth form appeals

The admission arrangements are different for sixth forms. Usually schools will require a minimum qualification before they will consider applications. If an application is rejected, it will be because your child did not meet the academic level required. This could either be the number of GCSEs or specified grades. Although it is possible that your child may have been rejected because there were more applications that met the minimum standard than there were places available, it is more likely that the reason for the rejection is because your child did not reach the minimum standard.

If the reason for the rejection is because there were more suitable applications than places available, the procedure for the appeal will be as set out in Chapter 5. If, on the other hand, your child did not meet the required academic standard, you will need to convince the appeal panel that your child is suitable for a place in the sixth form.

Many parents seek professional help with their appeals and an example of a professionally prepared response to an admission authority's statement, which was successful, is shown in Appendix 1. You will see that the response draws on relevant paragraphs in the Code of Practice on School Admission Appeals, which was published in 2003, and which explains what is expected in an admission authority statement. This advice has been further endorsed by the Ombudsman in his Special Report published in 2004. You will see that the response also uses the performance figures for the school, along with extracts from the most recent Ofsted inspection, to help to undermine the admission authority's statement.

CHECKLIST 7

1. Do you understand what constitutes a grammar school appeal?
2. Did your child obtain sufficient marks for a grammar school?
3. If so, have you followed the guidance in Chapters 5 and 8?
4. Did your child not gain sufficient marks to secure a place at the school?
5. Were there any mitigating circumstances?
6. Was your child ill on the day of the test and do you have a letter from your doctor?
7. Will the primary school support your appeal?
8. What are your child's predicted SATS results?
9. Do you have a copy of last year's school report?
10. Do you feel that your child will be suitable for a grammar school?
11. Has your child the academic ability and potential to succeed in a grammar school?
12. Did the admission authority inform you of your child's scores in its decision letter? If so, has your child missed the pass mark by more than five per cent? If the answer is yes, it will not be easy to convince an appeal panel that he will be suitable for a grammar school place.

Chapter 8

Preparing your case

The contents of this chapter will show you how to prepare your case for an appeal and also how to challenge the admission authority's case. There are two distinct elements to preparing your case. Firstly, there is the admission authority's case which you can challenge, and, secondly, there is your case and the personal reasons why you would like a place for your child at your preferred school.

The issues covered in this chapter are as follows:

- The admission authority's case
- Why was the application not successful?
- Additional admissions that will cause prejudice
- Responding to the admission authority's statement
- Preparing your statement

Quick reference

- ### Admissions committee
  This is often the group of people delegated by the governing body of the school in voluntary aided and foundation schools and academies who consider and make recommendations to the governing body about which applications to accept. For community schools, this function is carried out by officers of the Local Education Authority (LEA).

- ### Priest, vicar or minister of religion
  This is the person in your faith who you ask to complete a religious commitment form for voluntary aided schools with a religious ethos.

- ### Prejudice
  This is the term used by admission authorities to determine the point at which any additional admissions will cause problems for the school.

- ### Admission authority's statement
  This is the written submission made to the appeal panel by the admission authority.

- School Organisation Plan

  This is a five-year plan prepared by the LEA that sets out the policies and practices in relation to the schools in its administrative area. The plan will also include current and projected pupil numbers and capacities of the schools, along with any plans to respond to any increasing or decreasing demand for places. A copy of the plan is usually on the LEA's website or a hard copy can be obtained from the authority.

QUICK LIST

1 Do you know why your application was not successful?

2 Have you received the admission authority's statement explaining why the school cannot accommodate any more pupils?

3 Have you looked at the school's performance figures and most recent Ofsted report?

4 Have you checked the school's net capacity?

5 Do you know what the net capacity range for the school is?

6 Why do you want your child to go to the school?

7 For a voluntary aided school, have you obtained a letter of support from your minister of religion?

8 Have you obtained any letters of support for your appeal?

9 Have you sought any professional help for your appeal?

The admission authority's case

The admission authority is required to send you its statement at least seven days (five working days) before the appeal. There is no requirement to send you the statement so that you receive it seven days before the appeal, so it is possible that you may not receive it until five days before the appeal. In these circumstances, you will have to consider either whether you have sufficient time to respond to the statement or whether you should seek an adjournment in order to allow more time for you to prepare for the appeal. Usually the admission authority will send the statement to you through the post, but it can email it, if required,

The new Code on School Admission Appeals has now changed the timetable for decisions issued either on or after 1 March 2008. The Code now requires the Clerk to the Appeal Panel to send you the appeal papers, which will include

the admission authority's statement and papers which you have submitted, at least seven working days before the appeal hearing, which does not include the date of the appeal or the day on which the papers were despatched. This means that the Clerk should send you the appeal papers nine working days before the hearing.

The different types of appeal have been described in previous chapters, but the basis of the admission authority's appeal remains the same; it will have to explain in detail why your application was refused and also explain why, in its view, an additional admission will cause prejudice, whether it is normal prejudice (see Chapter 5) or class size prejudice (see Chapter 6).

The quality of the statement will vary. I have seen some statements that amount to no more than a few sentences to some that amount to 15 or 16 pages. This is really from one extreme to the other. Curiously enough, the Code of Practice on School Admission Appeals leaves it to the admission authority to decide what information to include, but it does give guidance as to the minimum information that should be included and the Special Report of the Ombudsman gives further general guidance. The Code can be found on the Department for Children, Schools and Families (DCSF) website and the Special Report is available on the Ombudsman's website (see Appendix 9 for details). Either way, there should be enough information to enable an appeal panel to make a decision on prejudice. The guidance provided in the Code is set out in Chapter 4.

Why was the application not successful?

If the school is oversubscribed, the admission authority will have to apply the published admission criteria to decide which applications will be successful. It is important for the appeal panel to be able to decide if the published admission criteria have been correctly applied in your child's case when the decision was taken to refuse your application. When you are looking through the admission authority's statement, you should be able to see the reason given as to why your application was not successful. However, sometimes admission authorities do not include an explanation in their statements. If this is the case, it is possible that the presenting officer may expand on this at the appeal hearing and if he does not, this may give you grounds to make a complaint if the appeal is unsuccessful.

Some admission authority's statements make no reference to why your application was not successful and they simply seek to convince an appeal panel that the school cannot accommodate more pupils. If this is the case, what should you do? I feel that the best advice is to draw the appeal panel's attention to this oversight and to say that you find it difficult to see how the panel can decide if the admission arrangements have been correctly applied in the absence of this information. The admission authority may provide this information at the hearing, but this will illustrate that there are some flaws in the admission authority's case. You can then use this to start to undermine its case.

If, on the other hand, the admission authority explains why the application was not successful, you will need to look at this very carefully. Usually the reason will be that you live too far away from the school and, if this is the case, you will need to check how much further you live from the school than the last successful applicant; the closer you are, the easier it is to challenge the figures. The statement should confirm the distance measured for the last successful applicant and the distance that you live from the school. This is the most common reason given for community schools.

If, however, you have applied to a voluntary aided church school, it may be the application of the commitment requirement that will be in question. The Code of Practice on School Admission Appeals requires any admission criteria to be objective and not subjective. Look very carefully at how the commitment requirement has been assessed and by whom. If the form that has to be completed requires any form of interpretation by either the priest, vicar or minister of religion, and his response is interpreted by the governors, the assessment of commitment is subjective and can be challenged.

In voluntary aided schools, often the trust deed for the school (which is the legal document which establishes the school) means that priority is given to parents living in certain parishes. This is quite common and there is absolutely nothing wrong with this. However, where some schools fall down is where the parish priest or vicar sits on the committee or panel that makes recommendations to the governors on which applications to approve, and he also takes an active part in the admission arrangements by signing forms for applicants which confirm religious commitment. If this occurs, it is a breach of the principles of natural justice because a person cannot make decisions on applications in which he has taken some part in completing. This may well render the arrangements as invalid.

So how can you find out who sits on the admissions committee or panel and who are the governors? Usually this information is included on either the school's website or in the governors' annual report. If the information is not available there, then write to the school and ask for it. If you find out that the vicar or priest does sit on the admissions committee or panel, this is another ground for challenging the validity of the decision. I am not questioning the integrity of such people, but by pointing out that such practices go against the principles of natural justice, you will make the appeal panel take a look at this matter very carefully and reach a decision.

In truth, there are a number of grounds where the decision can be challenged because administrative processes are fallible and so are people. Often this can be down to inexperience or ignorance, but many schools will be very careful how they operate their arrangements and will also take it personally if such decisions are challenged. However, they must appreciate that it is not personal and you are simply exercising your statutory rights. Every appeal and parents' individual circumstances are unique and it is not possible to cover every eventuality that may arise, but the vast majority of circumstances fall into the issues covered in this chapter.

Additional admissions that will cause prejudice

The Code of Practice on School Admission Appeals states that the obligation rests with the admission authority to demonstrate that an additional admission will cause prejudice. This can be normal prejudice, covered in Chapter 5, or class size prejudice, covered in Chapter 6. So how will the admission authority seek to do this? As mentioned previously, the standard of the statement can, and does, vary considerably. In simple terms, the shorter the statement, the easier it is to challenge.

The minimum requirements for statements are included in paragraph 4.28 of the Code of Practice, issued in 2003, and paragraph 2.19 of the Code issued in 2007, and also the Special Report of the Ombudsman. These Codes can be found on the DCSF website and the Special Report is available on the Ombudsman's website (see Appendix 9 for details). Statements submitted by the admission authorities will often fail to provide the minimum necessary information to convince the appeal panel that an additional pupil can be admitted without causing problems for the school. Details of the minimum requirements are described in Chapter 4.

Responding to the admission authority's statement

How do you attempt to challenge the admission authority's case? First of all, do not be intimidated into not challenging the authority's statement. The authority will not take it personally and it will appreciate that you have every right to challenge and question its case. When preparing a response, start from the point of view that the authority has not demonstrated prejudice and then go on to question and challenge each point raised in the statement. The statement will usually follow a similar pattern. Most authorities will use a template and will amend it each year. This is an area that can be exploited because the persons responsible for preparing the statements do not always take enough care over them and consequently they contain errors. Bearing in mind that you are only seeking one place (unless you have multiple birth children), any inconsistencies in the statement can be highlighted to demonstrate that prejudice has not been demonstrated.

Common mistakes are that the figures do not add up. If you add up the total of the year groups, it may not add up to the overall total. If it does not, what is the reason for the discrepancy? Sometimes the number of admissions in each admission criteria does not add up to the published admission number. Again, this discrepancy can be challenged. The point here is that the reason for the discrepancy is probably a typographical error, but it does start to question the integrity of other information included in the statement.

It is possible that the number of pupils at the school quoted in the statement may differ from other figures that may be published in the school's prospectus or on the school's website. Alternatively, you can check the figures on the DCSF website at www.edubase.gov.uk. This will provide details of the school population when the last census was carried out. The census is carried out in January every year and it is submitted to the DCSF by the school via the LEA, and therefore it has to be accurate at that time. The Edubase website also details the net capacity for the school. This has been described in Chapter 5. If the net capacity has not been included or it is significantly higher than the number of pupils at the school, this is a discrepancy that can be pointed out to the appeal panel. Any discrepancy in the figures can be used to your advantage and this will start to raise doubts about the accuracy of other figures. It will also cast doubts about whether one extra pupil will really cause problems for the school. If you have not already received the details about the classroom sizes, ask for them. If you have the classroom sizes and you combine this with the net capacity figures for the school, this again will help to undermine the admission authority's case, if there are any inconsistencies.

One of the other favourites to include in the statement is health and safety issues. This can be to do with either the numbers in classrooms and the potential risks involved in the case of escape should there be a fire, or the limited size of the corridors which were not built for the numbers currently at the school. In many ways these are quite legitimate concerns, but admission authorities cannot make such claims unless they are backed up by firm evidence. For example, the school may claim that increased numbers at the school have resulted in a significant increase in reported accidents. If such information has been produced, it is certainly possible that the reason for the increase is not simply down to numbers, but it may be because the method of reporting has changed or the school has been more proactive in logging such incidents. It is up to the admission authority to demonstrate that the health and safety issues are causing problems and most admission authorities will not have this information readily to hand at an appeal hearing.

Some admission authorities may claim that they are experiencing difficulties with either teacher recruitment or retention, or both. If this is the case, they must produce actual, and not simply anecdotal, evidence. It must be based on firm evidence. In general terms, if a school is popular, and therefore oversubscribed, then it is likely that it will not experience such problems.

These are examples of the most common reasons put forward by admission authorities. To challenge the admission authority, you will need to systematically go through the statement and challenge as many points as you can. Obviously, the more points you can challenge, the more likely it will be that such a challenge will be successful. In preparing a response, include extracts from the most recent Ofsted report that supports your view and also quote the school's performance figures. The details of websites that can help are as follows:

- www.dcsf.gov.uk/performancetables/
- www.ofsted.gov.uk

You may also be able to obtain interesting information in the LEA's School Organisation Plan. This plan usually covers a period of five years and includes information on each individual school concerning projected numbers for admission and other details which may contradict information in the school's statement. Details of this can usually be found on your local council's website, but if this is not the case, then contact the LEA and ask for a copy.

You will find an example of a response that was professionally prepared for a successful grammar school appeal in Appendix 1. Appendix 2 is a response for a successful secondary school appeal and Appendix 3 is a response to a successful class size appeal.

Preparing your statement

Before you see the admission authority's statement, you will be asked to submit your statement setting out your grounds for your appeal. Many parents ask me, 'What are my grounds for appeal?' and the response is quite simple. The grounds for your appeal are the reasons why you chose the school in the first place.

Parents have different reasons for selecting particular schools. You would think that some schools would be universally popular, but this is not always the case. I have come across some schools where a parent is desperately trying to secure a place there and, at the same time, other parents are trying to move their children to a different school. What this illustrates is that parents are looking for different features and facilities at schools.

However, the usual grounds for wanting a school are as follows:

- It is the closest school.
- It has a good academic record.
- You like the caring ethos of the school.
- Your child has a particular ability in the school's specialism.
- Your child has friends attending the school.
- Most of the children in your child's school are transferring to the same school.
- There are strong medical reasons why your child should attend the school.
- There are exceptional reasons why your child should attend the school.
- The school is within walking distance.
- The school runs after-school and breakfast clubs.

There may well be other grounds which you would like to include. For an appeal to be successful, you will need to support your reasons with firm evidence. For example, if you believe that there are strong medical grounds, you will need the written support of your doctor. To be convincing, the doctor's support will need to be based on a physical examination and be a proper diagnosis. He must state that it is essential that your child attends a particular school. I have seen many doctors' letters that start with 'Mrs X tells me that her son is suffering from Y, etc.' I am afraid that this type of letter does not carry much weight at all with appeal panels. It has to be much more specific.

CASE STUDY 1

Mrs X attended an appeal stating that her son suffered from asthma and he needed to attend a particular school because it was within ten minutes' walking distance from her home. She provided a letter from the doctor stating that her son suffered from a particularly serious strain of the illness, which meant that he received no warning of an imminent attack and once it was triggered he needed attention within 20 minutes, otherwise the attack could be fatal. The walking distance to the school which had been allocated was 45 minutes, which meant that her son could leave school feeling fine but would not be able to get home safely if such an attack started after he left school. In these particular circumstances the appeal panel agreed

---

that it was essential that he attended the school in question and his appeal was successful.

Illnesses, such as asthma and eczema, can be distressing, but most schools will usually be equipped to deal with them, so generally it will not be regarded as essential for your child to attend a particular school. Such illnesses will not normally be accepted as persuasive by an appeal panel, unless your grounds are supported by very strong medical evidence.

If your child has friends attending the school in question, it will be beneficial to obtain a letter from the friends' parents confirming this, because they will be able to provide mutual support for each other at school. It is a well-known fact that transferring schools can be an exciting time, but it can also be an anxious one and the presence of close friends can help to ease the transition.

If you feel that there are exceptional grounds for your child to attend the school, this must be supported by a third party, whether it is a medical practitioner, social worker, psychologist or any other professional. This does not mean that if such support is not produced, the appeal panel will not believe you, but panel members are trained to treat uncorroborated evidence with caution.

Many parents want their children to attend the closest school because, generally, it will be the local community school and it will enable their children to develop strong community ties which will help them in the future. Often, in these circumstances, there are also strong environmental benefits of the child's being able to walk and your not having to drive to school. If this is the case, you may be able to point out inconsistencies between local authorities' policies which may be to your advantage. You can usually find these issues out on your LEA's website.

As mentioned earlier in this book, many schools have successfully applied for specialist status but they do not reserve places in the published admission criteria for pupils with the ability or potential in that specialism. Many parents cannot understand why a school will specialise in a particular subject, but this will not be reflected in the admission criteria. It is a difficult one to answer, but schools attract extra funding for a successful specialism because the facilities provided are for the benefit of the local community and not just the school. If the school is a community school, it will be a decision of the governors to apply for the specialism. However the LEA is the admission authority for community schools and most LEAs are generally against selection. If this applies in your case, you will need to demonstrate to the appeal panel why you feel that your child would benefit

I S X

from attending the school. If, for example, the specialism is performing arts, you will need to provide details of your child's experience and also what potential he has. Therefore, if your child is learning to play an instrument, copies of certificates, proving that he has successfully passed the music examinations, will help. You may also like to submit a letter from his tutor explaining his progress. All this background information will help to persuade an appeal panel.

Although it is dangerous to generalise, I would suggest that the optimum size for a statement is between three and four pages. This will give you sufficient opportunity to be able to explain to the appeal panel why you want your child to attend the preferred school. You will, of course, be given the opportunity to expand on this at the hearing.

CHECKLIST 8

1   Have you read through the admission authority's statement and do you know how to challenge it?

2   What are the issues raised by the admission authority?

3   Can you challenge them?

4   Have you looked at the performance figures for the school?

5   Have you looked at the Ofsted report for the school?

6   Have you obtained all the supporting information for your case?

7   Have you got any professional support for your appeal?

8   Have you included all the issues why you want your child to go to the school, in order to strengthen your appeal?

9   Are there any other issues that you can ask the appeal panel to consider?

A flow chart showing the appeal process in England

The parent receives the decision from the admission authority refusing the place – the parent must be given at least ten school days to lodge an appeal

The parent lodges an appeal within the prescribed timetable set by the admission authority and receives a written acknowledgement

The parent must receive at least ten school days' notice of the date of the hearing

The parent prepares his response to the admission authority's statement

The Clerk must send a statement to the parents and panel at least nine working days before the hearing

The admission authority must supply its statement to the Clerk at least ten school days before the hearing

At least three working days before the hearing the Clerk must send to the parents the name of the Clerk and panel members, the witnesses and information reasonably requested by the parents

THE DATE OF THE HEARING

The appeal decision should be sent by the Clerk to the parents and the admission authority within five working days

Chapter 9

What to do if your appeal is unsuccessful

Unfortunately, even with the best advice available, some appeals will be unsuccessful. So if this happens to you, what options do you have? Under the Code on School Admissions you are entitled to apply and appeal each academic year. So, if nothing else, you can wait until the next academic year and apply again, and if this application is not successful, you can lodge a further appeal and hope that it will be successful.

However, if you do not want to wait until the next academic year, there are three other options. The first is to make a complaint to the Local Government Ombudsman; the second is to apply for a Judicial Review; and the third is referred to as a 'material change of circumstances'.

The issues covered in this chapter are as follows:

- Making a complaint to the Local Government Ombudsman
- What constitutes maladministration?
- Applying for a Judicial Review
- A material change of circumstances

Quick reference

- ### The Local Government Ombudsman

  This is the government-sponsored office that has the power to investigate complaints about a range of services provided by the local authority. The Local Government Ombudsman (LGO) can investigate complaints made by parents about a school admission appeal. The LGO can recommend that you are offered a fresh appeal if it finds that the original appeal was unfair due to maladministration that caused injustice. If the appeal is deemed to be so unfair that an appeal panel would have been expected to allow it, the recommendation can be the offer of a place at the school in question. A complaint will be investigated by an investigator working for the LGO.

- ## Maladministration

  This is deemed to be an administrative fault (or faults) in the way that an appeal was handled. If it is acknowledged that such fault (or faults) also caused injustice, the LGO can recommend a fresh appeal or a place at the school.

- ## A Judicial Review

  This is where a parent feels that an appeal was unfair and he applies to the High Court for such a decision to be set aside. In the first instance, an approach is made through a solicitor to assess the likelihood of success. The cost of such action will run into thousands of pounds.

- ## Material change of circumstances

  If an application was refused and your own, or your child's, circumstances have changed, you can apply to have your application redetermined by the admission authority. If the admission authority agrees that there has been a change in circumstances, but it still fails to offer your child a place, you will be entitled to another appeal. The same situation applies if the school's circumstances have changed. Unfortunately, there is no appeal if the admission authority does not agree that there has been a material change of circumstances. Examples of a change in circumstances would be either a change of address or the diagnosis of a serious medical condition.

QUICK LIST

1. Have you checked the decision letter from the appeal panel to see if there was a breach of the Code of Practice?

2. Do you feel that your appeal was not a fair hearing and were there any breaches of the Code of Practice?

3. Have you spoken to the LGO about lodging a possible complaint?

4. Have you spoken to a solicitor about applying for a Judicial Review?

5. Has there been a material change of circumstances since the appeal?

Making a complaint to the Local Government Ombudsman

If your appeal was not successful, and you feel that it was dealt with unfairly, you can make a complaint to the LGO. Your complaint will be investigated and what the investigator will be looking for is maladministration that caused injustice. What this means is, 'Was there any administrative flaw in the way that your appeal was handled which caused injustice?' If this is found, there are a couple of recommendations that can be put to the admission authority. The more common recommendation is a fresh hearing, but in the more extreme cases the LGO can recommend that a place be offered if it is believed that the appeal was so flawed that the appeal panel would have offered a place. It is possible that the LGO may find maladministration, but if it is not considered that this resulted in injustice, a fresh hearing will not be recommended. Of course, it is also possible that maladministration will not be found.

It goes without saying that every parent will be disappointed if an appeal is not successful, but this does not necessarily mean that the appeal was conducted unfairly. A complaint to the LGO will only be successful if there was maladministration that caused injustice.

What constitutes maladministration?

In some ways this is a difficult question to answer, but a look through previous investigations will give you some indication. A selection of summaries of previous investigations is set out in Appendix 4. You can also download summaries from the Ombudsman's website at www.lgo.org.uk. However, what the LGO will look at is a failure in the process and procedure, rather than the decision itself. Even if the LGO disagrees with the decision, it cannot interfere with the decision unless it finds maladministration that caused injustice.

The LGO has defined where a fresh appeal would be appropriate. The circumstances are as follows:

- If there was some flaw in the appeal procedure and it is not clear what the outcome would have been if the appeal had been considered correctly; or

- If the constitution of the appeal panel was unlawful or otherwise improper (whether or not it seemed that the result of the appeal may have been different), and such a flaw was so fundamental that there could not be any confidence that the appeal was fair and independent.

Surprisingly, a common fault that frequently occurs is where the representative of the admission authority is present with the appeal panel without the parents being present. The Code of Practice is quite clear that at no time should either side, that is the admission authority or the parents, be left alone with the appeal panel without the other side. If this occurs, this is maladministration.

Another common fault is where there is no representative from the admission authority present at the appeal. This is also maladministration because the Code of Practice on School Admission Appeals makes it clear that the representative of the admission authority must be prepared to answer detailed questions about the authority's statement and, obviously, he will be unable to do this if he is not present. Maladministration may also occur if the appeal panel takes into consideration something that it should not have or, alternatively, it does not take into consideration something that it should have.

If the admission authority does not give you sufficient notice of the appeal, as prescribed in the Code of Practice on School Admission Appeals, without having asked you to waive such a notice, then this will be maladministration. The same applies if the admission authority does not send you its statement within the prescribed time. These issues are covered in Chapter 4.

In fact, there are a range of issues that could amount to maladministration and such complaints will be investigated by the LGO. There will be no cost to you if you make a complaint to the LGO and it is an inexpensive way to determine your complaint. But remember that the LGO will only investigate if you believe that your appeal was unfair; it will not investigate simply because you disagree with the decision.

Applying for a Judicial Review

Alternatively, you can apply for a Judicial Review. You will initially need to consult a solicitor who will be able to advise you on the likely success of such a review. However, like the LGO, the High Court cannot overturn a decision of an appeal panel, but it can set the decision aside and order a fresh hearing. If you do apply for a Judicial Review, this could turn out to be quite costly with the bill running into several thousand pounds. There is little difference in the two, with the exception that the LGO can only make recommendations which most admission authorities will accept, but the LGO can recommend that a place be offered which a Judicial Review could not; all that would happen here is that a decision could be set aside and a fresh hearing ordered.

A material change of circumstances

You are normally only entitled to one appeal per academic year. However, if there has been a material change of circumstances, this could trigger a second appeal. The Code of Practice defines a material change of circumstances as follows:

> 4.83 Although parents who have appealed unsuccessfully can reapply for a place at the same school in a later academic year, and they have a right of appeal if they are unsuccessful, some parents may also seek to reapply in the same academic year. Unless there are significant and material changes in the circumstances of the parent, child or school, which are relevant to a further application, the admission authority may decide not to reach a fresh decision (or determination) in relation to such applications. Common examples of changes in circumstances since the time the original application was made would be medical reasons, or that the family has moved house. Where the admission authority has refused to consider another application for the same year group, no fresh appeal can be made. However, if its policy is not to consider repeat applications in the same academic year, unless there has been a change of circumstances relevant to the application, this policy must be clearly stated in the published admission arrangements.
>
> *The Code of Practice on School Admission Appeals 2003*

What this section of the Code means is that you will be able to apply for your application to be redetermined or a fresh decision made on the basis of a material change of circumstances and if the admission authority agrees that there has been a material change, but it still fails to offer a place, this will trigger another appeal. However, if the admission authority explains that, as a matter of policy, it does not consider repeat applications, unless there has been a change in circumstances, this must be set out clearly in the admission arrangements published by the admission authority.

If the admission authority accepts that there has been a material change of circumstances but it still fails to offer a place, this will trigger a second appeal. It is recommended that if a second appeal is awarded, the panel that considers the second appeal should be different from the first panel.

CHECKLIST 9

1   Do you feel that you received an unfair hearing which was unsuccessful and you wish to make a complaint?

2   Have you considered the issues that you want to raise with the LGO?

3   Do you believe that these issues are inconsistent with the Code of Practice?

4   Do you believe that the issues are not just maladministration, but also caused injustice?

5   Do you know how to make a complaint to the LGO?

6   Do you want to apply for a Judicial Review?

7   Have you spoken to a solicitor to discuss your case and the likelihood of a successful challenge?

8   Has there been a material change of circumstances since the appeal?

9   Have you contacted the LEA to see if it will consider redetermining your application in the light of the fresh information?

Chapter 10

Choosing a school in Scotland

If you are applying for a school in Scotland, many principles that are used are similar to those in England. However, there are some significant differences. The admission process will be described, followed by Chapter 11, which outlines how the Local Education Authority (LEA) deals with your application, and then Chapter 12, which deals with the appeal arrangements.

The following issues are covered by this chapter:

- How to decide which school you would like your child to attend
- What should you do if you want your child to attend the designated school?
- What should you do if you want your child to attend a school other than the designated school?
- When do you make your request?
- The choice of schools for children under the age of five
- Changing schools
- Taking into account your child's views
- What are the choices available to pupils over the age of 16?
- What is the school leaving age?
- What about schools run by another LEA?
- What does the law say about travelling to and from school?
- The right to send your child to your local designated school

Quick reference

- ### The Local Education Authority (LEA)
  The LEA is the local government body responsible for providing education for pupils of school age in a particular administrative area.

- ## Admission criteria

  When there are more applicants than there are school places available, the LEA uses principles and rules known as admission criteria to determine which of its applicants can be offered a school place. In simple terms, admission criteria are practical, objective measures, such as the distance between an applicant's home and the school, whether or not the applicant already has siblings at the school, or if the applicant can demonstrate the necessary religious affiliation, in the case of a faith school. All LEAs are required to ensure that their admission criteria are explained clearly.

- ## Siblings

  These are usually brothers and sisters of the same family living at the same address. However, this term may include any children living at the same address. The published admission criteria will define siblings.

- ## Catchment areas

  Catchment areas (often referred to as 'zones') are established before applications are sought from parents and they do not necessarily give priority to children living closest to the school. However, living in a catchment area will not guarantee you a place at a school. No admission criteria can give such a guarantee.

- ## Local designated school

  This is the school which has been chosen by the LEA for your child to attend, based on where you live. It will usually be the school which is also your catchment school.

- ## Statutory walking distance

  The statutory walking distance is two miles (3.2 kilometres) for children aged under eight, and three miles (4.8 kilometres) for children aged eight and over.

QUICK LIST

1. Have you obtained a copy of the prospectus of the school that you are interested in?

2. Have you studied the admission criteria for your preferred school (or schools)? You can obtain the criteria from the LEA in which the school is located.

3. Have you checked to see how well you meet the admission criteria?

4   Have you researched the school (or schools) that you are considering?

5   Have you visited your preferred school (or schools) and looked around to see what you think?

6   Have you spoken to parents whose children already attend the school (or schools) of your choice?

7   Have you spoken to pupils already attending the school (or schools) of your choice?

8   Have you talked to teachers at the school (or schools)?

9   Have you listened to your child, to see what he thinks about the school (or schools)?

10   Have you used this book to assess your chances of making a successful admission application or admission appeal?

11   **Have you made sure that you have sent your application in on time?**

You will need to approach the school concerned to obtain a copy of the prospectus, which will contain valuable information about the school. This will include details of examination results and budgeted running costs of the school; the school's policies on children with additional needs; and the school's policies on the development of spiritual, moral, social and cultural values.

If a school receives more applications than places, admission criteria will be used to determine which applications will be successful. Admission criteria, in general, have been discussed in Chapter 2. The admissions Code in England defines admission criteria that are considered to be lawful and unlawful. Although the admission criteria are not defined as such in Scotland, the general principles still apply in that admission criteria must be clear, fair and objective and if they are not, this may enable you to challenge any decisions that have been made on the basis of fairness.

How to decide which school you would like your child to attend

You have a right to express a preference as to which school your child attends at both primary and secondary level, and it is the LEA's duty to meet this wherever possible. The vast majority of LEAs use catchment areas (also referred to as 'zones') to determine places and children will usually attend their catchment school. The LEA will normally suggest that your child attends the local school designated by it and it may well be that you are happy for this to happen. However, the LEA should advise you of your right to choose a different school and provide details of where you can find out information about that school. You may decide to change school at any time and the information provided here applies equally whether your child is changing school along with other children, when joining a primary or secondary school, or at any other time.

There are a number of important considerations that you will need to take into account. These are as follows:

- Find out all you can about the school which the LEA has determined as your local designated school. You are strongly advised to contact the school so that you can look around the school and speak to the head teacher. This will provide valuable information to help you make up your mind. Schools will usually make arrangements for parents to view the school so that they can assess whether it meets their requirements.

- Schools will usually advertise in the local paper about arrangements for parents to view the school.

- If you want to consider a school other than your designated school, contact your LEA, which should be able to provide details of how you can arrange a visit to the school concerned.

- LEAs are required to publish certain information about schools that come within their jurisdiction. This information is available free of charge to anyone who requests it and you should make sure that you obtain copies of this information to help you make a decision. LEAs will produce a guidance note or booklet, which is usually available on their websites or as a hard copy. The information will include such details as the number and names of the schools coming within their jurisdiction; the admission criteria to be used if there are more applications than places; and details about the admission arrangements and also any appeal arrangements.

It is helpful to establish in advance whether your application is likely to be successful. You can do this by finding out what happened in previous years and therefore make an assessment as to whether your application will be successful or not. You can contact the LEA about the school concerned and request information about the admissions for the last five years, just in case there have been some abnormal years where the usual pattern of admissions did not occur. You will also need to ask the LEA whether there has been any significant change in the admission criteria in recent years, which may have affected the allocation of places.

In Scotland there appears to be a general presumption that your child will attend your local designated school and in the vast majority of cases this is what will happen. It is only when you decide that this would not be appropriate that you will need to consider other issues. These other issues will now be discussed.

What should you do if you want your child to attend the designated school?

If you are content to send your child to the school designated by the LEA, then all you will normally need to do is to enrol him by the advertised date. However, some LEAs may ask you to let them know if your child will be attending the school designated by them or to enrol by a certain date. Check with your LEA to see what it expects you to do.

What should you do if you want your child to attend a school other than the designated school?

You must tell your LEA what you want to do and you must put it in writing. Some authorities may provide forms to be completed, but if not, a letter to the LEA will suffice. The minimum information that you must provide is discussed in the section below entitled 'When do you make your request?' You should contact your LEA to see if there is a time limit for notifying it of the details of the school that you want. If the LEA has set a time limit, this does not mean that if you notify it after the date you will not secure a place at the school, but it is less likely if the school receives more applications than places available. Once your written request has been received, the LEA will offer a place at the school of your choice, unless all the available places have been taken or there are other special circumstances. These issues will be discussed later under the section on when an LEA can refuse a school place (see Chapter 11).

If you would like the LEA to consider more than one preference, then you must indicate what your first preference is because the LEA is only obliged to consider your first choice. You are not required to give reasons for your choice, but it may be helpful if you do. It is possible that the reasons may help the LEA in reaching a decision.

When do you make your request?

If your child is due to start primary school in August, or he is due to transfer to secondary school, then normally your LEA will provide information in the preceding December, January or February about choosing a particular school. The LEA will normally send you a letter and place advertisements in the local press. If you are expecting a letter and do not receive one by the end of February, then contact your LEA and find out what the position is. In addition, the head teacher, of either your local designated school or the school that you are interested in, will be able to advise you if there is a date when your request has to be received.

If, however, you have decided by February which school you would like your child to attend, you can write to your LEA and let it know which school you have chosen. All that the law requires is for you to send details of your name and address, the name of your child and the name of the school. In addition, it may be helpful to also include the name of his existing school and the stage of his education.

The choice of schools for children under the age of five

You may want your child to start primary school before the compulsory school age. This is defined as children who are five years of age when they start school in August or who will become five years old before the following March. If you would like your child to start school before this, then you will need to contact your LEA to see what arrangements it has in place for assessing your child's ability. If the LEA agrees that it would be appropriate for him to start school before he reaches school age, because of his aptitude or ability, it will provide a school place for him at one of its schools. However, you do not have a statutory right for your child to start school early, but the LEA may be able to allocate a place at a particular school. If the LEA is not able to allocate a place, there is no right of appeal.

Changing schools

You have a right to express a preference for your child to attend a particular school at any time up until your child reaches the school leaving age of 16. After the age of 16, pupils may opt to stay on at school to take Higher Grade and Advanced Higher qualifications, usually at the same school. Alternatively, these qualifications can also be undertaken at college. Note that admission to colleges is outside the scope of this book.

There are many reasons why you may feel that your child would benefit from a change of schools. If this is the case, you should discuss this, in the first place, with your child's present head teacher or class/guidance teacher to see if anything can be done before you go down the route of changing schools. If you have explored all of the other options and you decide that the only way forward is to change schools, you can ask for a place at an alternative school. You do not have to wait until the beginning of the next academic year and you can make such a request at any time. Of course, if you feel that moving school is the only option, bear in mind that changing schools can be very unsettling for your child and it can possibly damage his education, so you should only consider this option after very careful consideration. It is recognised that changing schools can be a very traumatic time for children and therefore it should not be entered into lightly.

It is possible that the LEA could refuse a request if it considers that your child has already moved schools too much and another move could be seen as damaging. However, there are only limited grounds on which the LEA can refuse a request and if this happens, there is an appeal process. Both of these issues will be discussed in Chapter 12.

Taking into account your child's views

It is universally accepted that all parents will want the best for their children and this also includes the best education. This desire is underpinned in Scotland by the Children (Scotland) Act 1995, which sets out your parental responsibility to safeguard and promote your child's health, development and welfare. The Act also recognises your child's rights to have his views taken into consideration when any major decisions are being taken that will affect his development and welfare. Naturally, choosing a school is a very important decision and your child may have his own views that he would like to be considered. The LEA will take such views into consideration, but the responsibility lies with you, as his parent, until he reaches the age of 16.

What are the choices available to pupils over the age of 16?

Once your child reaches the age of 16, he, and not you, may choose which school to go to. If your child wants to change schools, he will need to write to the LEA to say so. If there is a difference of opinion between you and your child, the LEA will act in accordance with your child's wishes and not yours.

What is the school leaving age?

The age at which your child can leave school lawfully will depend on when his birthday falls in the year. If your child's 16th birthday falls on or between 1 March and 30 September, he can decide either to leave school or to ask for another school from 31 May of that year. However, if your child's 16th birthday falls either on or between 1 October and the last day of February, he can decide to leave, or he can ask for another school in December. If you are unsure, either check with the LEA or the school, which should be able to provide advice.

What about schools run by another LEA?

It is possible that you may ask for a place at a school run by another LEA. This often occurs when you live close to the administrative boundary of more than one LEA. If this is the case and you feel that your child would benefit from attending a school in the adjoining LEA area, you should write to the LEA that manages the particular school you are interested in and not your own LEA.

What does the law say about travelling to and from school?

The law is quite clear here. If your child attends a school suggested by the LEA and the school is further than the statutory walking distance, then the LEA must make arrangements to get your child to school. If, on the other hand, you choose to send your child to an alternative school, the LEA is relieved of its obligation to provide a school bus or pass, or any other help with transport. Although the LEA may be relieved of its legal responsibility, this does not necessarily mean that the LEA will not provide any help, so it may be worth checking with the LEA to find out the position. If the LEA decides not to provide any help, you will have to decide very carefully how your child will get to school.

The statutory walking distance is two miles (3.2 kilometres) for children aged under eight, and three miles (4.8 kilometres) for children aged eight and over.

The right to send your child to your local designated school

After considering all of the options available, you may decide that you would prefer to send your child to the school designated by the LEA, but you may be concerned that there is no longer any room for him. Normally, there should be no difficulty in your child either starting at your local designated primary school or transferring to your designated secondary school. Your LEA is able to reserve places in schools for children who may move into the catchment area of the school during the school year of admission or transfer. The LEA cannot keep places open indefinitely. The

LEA has an obligation to consider the demand for places in the area and decide whether to reserve places at the school.

If you move into a catchment area in the middle of your child's schooling, and the designated school is very popular, you may find that the school is full and that there are no places available. If this is the case, you may have to wait until a child leaves which will create a vacancy for your child. If this happens, the LEA will arrange for your child to attend an alternative school in the meantime. It is important, if you are moving into an area, that you contact the LEA as soon as possible, so that you can consider and determine what options are available.

CHECKLIST 10

1 Have you obtained a copy of the school's prospectus?

2 Do you understand how places will be allocated if there are more applications than available school places?

3 Having studied the published admission criteria for last year's admissions, is it your opinion that your child will be allocated a place in your preferred school?

4 Have you attended your preferred school (or schools) and spoken to the staff and the students?

5 Having consulted the current year's admission criteria, is your choice of school realistic and reasonable?

6 Have you obtained from the LEA details of successful admissions for the last five years?

7 Have you found out from the LEA whether the admission criteria have been amended recently?

8 Have you obtained any advice you have received from the LEA or from the school in writing, and if so, have you kept this information to hand?

9 Have you obtained all the documentation to support your admission application?

10 Have you checked to make sure that you have enclosed **all** of the necessary information with the application form?

11 Have you ensured that your application was submitted on time?

12 Have you checked to ensure that your application was received by the admission authority?

A summary of school admissions in Scotland

1. Get the admissions booklet from the Local Education Authority

2. **DECIDE WHAT YOUR PRIORITIES ARE FOR YOUR CHILD**

3. Decide which schools best meet those priorities and go to the open evenings

4. Talk to the teachers and pupils to get their views about the school

5. Assess the facilities at the school to see if they meet your expectations

6. Look through the most recent HM Inspectorate report and the performance figures for the school

7. **LOOK AT THE ADMISSION CRITERIA FOR THE SCHOOL AND ASSESS YOUR CHANCES OF SUCCESS**

8. Check to see if you would have secured a place at the school in the last five years, based on the admission criteria

9. List your preferences in order with the one that offers the best chance of success at the top

10. **MAKE SURE THAT THE APPLICATION IS SUBMITTED TO THE ADMISSION AUTHORITY BY 15 MARCH FOR THOSE CHILDREN STARTING OR TRANSFERRING IN THE FOLLOWING SEPTEMBER**

Chapter 11

Scotland: The LEA's response to your request

This chapter covers what action the Local Education Authority (LEA) will take when it considers your request for a place at a school in Scotland. The issues covered in this chapter are as follows:

- What happens when the LEA receives your request?
- How quickly does the LEA have to reply?
- What should you do if your request is turned down?
- When can an LEA refuse a place in a school?
- What will happen if there are more requests for a school than there are available places?

QUICK LIST

1 Has your request been received on time?

2 Has the LEA replied within the prescribed timetable?

3 What was the reason given for the LEA refusing your application?

4 Were there more applications than places at the school?

5 Did the LEA apply admission criteria to determine successful applications?

What happens when the LEA receives your request?

So what does the LEA have to do when it receives your written request for a place at a school? It must:

- let you know within a few days that there will be a place for your child at the school of your choice or tell you who will decide whether there is a place for your child (the timeframe of when the LEA will advise you of the formal decision is discussed in the paragraph below.);

- tell you whether you will have the chance to talk about your wishes to the person who will make the decision, or whether you should write to him;

- tell you the name of the person you should contact if you have any questions about how your request is being handled;

- send you details about what the law says about the reasons why your request may have to be refused;

- tell you when your request will be treated as having been turned down;

- tell you about your right to appeal against refusal.

How quickly does the LEA have to reply?

If you want your child to start at the school of your choice at the beginning of the school year in August, and your letter reaches the LEA by 15 March in that year, you must be given an answer by 30 April. You can ask for a school place before this, but it is unlikely that you will receive a response any earlier. If you do not receive a response from the LEA by 30 April, your request is deemed to have been refused and this will trigger an appeal. Details of how to appeal are dealt with in Chapter 12.

You are strongly recommended to submit your request before 15 March because, otherwise, you may not get the school you want. If you do ask for a place after 15 March, the LEA has two months from the receipt of your letter of request in which to make a decision, but by that time all of the available places at the school of your choice may well have been filled.

If you want your child to change schools in the middle of the school year, the LEA has two months to provide an answer. If your letter of request is received after 15 March, or if you want a place for your child in the middle of a school year and you do not receive a written response from the LEA within two months, your request will be deemed to have been refused and this will trigger an appeal.

What should you do if your request is turned down?

Unfortunately, there will be circumstances where the LEA is not able to offer you a place at the school of your choice. If this is the case, the LEA must tell you in writing exactly why it is unable to offer you a place at the school. This should be included in the decision letter which you should receive on or before 30 April. The reason that is given must be one of the reasons allowed in law. These will be discussed in the following section. If you do not accept or understand the reason given, contact the person who wrote to you and seek a further explanation.

If your child cannot attend the school of your choice, has the LEA told you which school your child can attend instead? The LEA will normally let you know which school has been allocated when it advises you that your child has not secured a place at the school of your choice. If it has not suggested an alternative school, contact the LEA and find out what your options are. Do you agree that your child should attend the school suggested by the LEA? If you agree, then tell the LEA. If, on the other hand, you do not agree, is there another school that would be your second choice? If there is, ask the LEA in writing if your child can attend this alternative school. If you feel strongly that your child should attend your first choice school, you may want to appeal against the LEA's decision.

When can an LEA refuse a place in a school?

Once you have chosen a school and have told the LEA in writing, the reasons the LEA can use to refuse your request are defined in law. These reasons are as follows:

- If, to do so, the LEA would have to employ an additional teacher or spend a lot of money (e.g. where it would have to provide an additional classroom).

- If your child's education would suffer from a change in school.

- If education in the school that you want would not be suitable to the age, ability or aptitude of your child. This may apply if you want your child to be admitted to a stage of education for which your child is not ready, or to a school which cannot meet your child's needs.

- If the LEA thinks that your child can only be provided for in the school you want at the expense of other pupils' education.

- If the school you want has been provided specifically for children with special educational needs and the LEA thinks that your child does not need the special equipment or specially trained staff it has provided in that school.

- If your child has been troublesome at school. If your child has been excluded from a school, the LEA is not bound to readmit him. If your child has been in constant trouble, and you ask that he be moved to another school, the LEA can refuse to provide a place if it thinks that he would be likely to disturb the order and discipline in that school, or the educational well-being of pupils attending the school. The LEA may suggest another school that is better able to cope with your child.

- If you want your daughter to attend a boys' school or your son to attend a girls' school.

- If accepting the request would prevent the LEA reserving a place at the school for a child likely to move into the area of the school in-year.

- If accepting a request would make it necessary for the LEA to create an additional class or employ an additional teacher at a future stage of your child's primary education.

The exact wording for the reasons is set out in Appendix 7.

What will happen if there are more requests for a school than there are available places?

It is possible that a school may not have enough places available to satisfy all the requests that it receives. If this is the case, all LEAs must produce guidelines that will determine the priority (or admission criteria) given to all applicants. The guidelines will normally give priority to children living within the catchment area of the school. Preference may also be given to applicants with siblings already at the school. Guidelines may also cover schools where a child can study a particular subject or take a course that is not available at his local school. It is possible that guidelines issued by a LEA may apply to all schools within its administrative area or only to certain schools. If you are not sure what the guidelines are, you should contact your local LEA's education office for further details. In most cases hard copies of the guidelines will be available or can be downloaded from the LEA's website.

There is an obligation placed on LEAs to advertise any proposed changes in their guidelines, so that you and other interested people can let the LEA know your views.

CHECKLIST 11	
1	Was your placing request received on time by the LEA?
2	Did the LEA respond to your request within two months?
3	What were the reasons given for the refusal?
4	Has the LEA offered an alternative school?
5	Is the alternative school acceptable?
6	Do you think that you have grounds for an appeal?

Chapter 12

Scotland: How to appeal

The contents of this chapter will show you how you can appeal and what you need to do in order to be successful. The issues covered in this chapter are as follows:

- Appeal committees
- Deciding whether to appeal
- How often can you appeal?
- Can any refusal be appealed?
- When can you appeal?
- How to appeal
- Deciding how to make your case
- Making your case in writing
- So how do you make your case?
- Arranging the hearing
- Hearing several appeals at once
- So what happens at the hearing?
- How long will it be before you receive the decision?
- What happens if the committee does not give a decision or does not arrange a hearing?
- Appealing to the Sheriff

Quick reference

- Sheriff Court

  For legal purposes, Scotland is split into six regions called Sheriffdoms. Each Sheriffdom has a Sheriff Principal, who, in addition to hearing appeals in civil matters, has responsibility for the conduct of the courts. The Sheriff Court will consider appeals against decisions of appeal committees.

- Appeal committees

  This is the group of people appointed to hear your appeal and which will comprise councillors and local people.

- Special educational needs

  These are children who have been identified to need additional support. The level of support will depend on the extent of their needs. Children with special educational needs who have statements are usually offered school places irrespective of school numbers, but children with special needs who do not have statements do not usually get priority in the admission process.

QUICK LIST

1 Do you understand the make-up of appeal committees?

2 Do you understand the questions you should ask yourself before deciding to appeal?

3 Do you understand the reasons that a school can give for refusing a place at a school?

4 Do you understand the circumstances when it is not possible to appeal against a decision of the local LEA?

5 Do you know the timeframe when an appeal can be lodged?

6 What information do you need to provide on your appeal form or letter to the LEA lodging an appeal?

7 Do you know what will happen at the appeal hearing?

8 Can you bring along anyone to support you at the appeal?

9 When will you receive the decision of the appeal committee?

10 What are your rights of appeal against the appeal committee's decision?

Appeal committees

If you wish to challenge the LEA's refusal to offer you a place at the school of your choice, you can appeal against the decision. If this is the case, the LEA must set up an appeal committee to consider your request for a place at the school of your choice. Each appeal committee is made up of no more than seven people. Persons that are eligible to sit on committees are councillors or local people, such as teachers or parents. However, nobody who has considered your original request can be a member of an appeal committee. In addition, nobody can be a member of the committee if he is a parent of a pupil at the school of your choice, or the school the LEA has suggested, or if he is a teacher at either school.

The committee will be led by a person, the Chair, who is appointed by the LEA and he will be someone who has accumulated a significant amount of experience in appeals and thus has the knowledge to be able to fulfil this role. The committee will be assisted by a Clerk, who will be impartial and thus able to give any party to the appeal advice or guidance, either to do with process and procedure or evidence.

After the appeal committee has heard the appeal, it must decide whether to allow or dismiss it. If the committee decides to refuse your appeal, it must say whether the members of the committee agree that there was a good reason for refusing your choice of school (one of the reasons permitted by law); and it was right to refuse your request. If the appeal committee decides that the reason given to refuse a place was lawful, but nevertheless it feels that your child should be offered a place at the school, the LEA must do so. The decision of the appeal committee is binding on the LEA.

Deciding whether to appeal

It is natural that if your request has been refused, you will be disappointed. However, before you appeal you will need to decide whether it is worth appealing, because you will not win an appeal simply because you are disappointed. You will need to have good reasons for your appeal and to ask the appeal committee to review the decision. Before you decide to appeal, you should ask yourself a number of questions:

- Do you agree with what the LEA has said? If you do, there is little point in appealing.

- Are the reasons given by the LEA for refusing your request allowable in law? The legislation will be discussed later in the chapter, but most of the allowable reasons are subjective judgements and, as such, they can be challenged using information that is publicly available.

- Have the LEA's guidelines been followed by the person who decided that your child could not secure a place because there was no room? It is, of course, possible that the person making the decision made a mistake; he may have used the wrong address, or not recognised a sibling connection. If there is any doubt, ask for clarification of the information.

How often can you appeal?

Normally, you will only be entitled to appeal once per academic year for each of your children.

If you have been unsuccessful with your first choice school, then you will be entitled to appeal, and you can consider making a second choice for an alternative school. Assuming that you want to make a second choice, you need to take into consideration that your second choice may be turned down and if this occurs, you will have to decide whether your appeal is likely to be more successful with your first or second choice. This is because, normally, you will not be allowed to appeal for both schools. I believe that the system is unfair because if you have more than one school in mind, you have to make a further choice and it is unlikely that you will be in possession of all the facts when you are asked to make such a difficult decision.

Decisions on appeal, whether to an appeal committee or the Sheriff Court, are based on precedent. What this means is that if the circumstances of your appeal are identical to a previous appeal, which was successful, then your appeal should be successful too. If it was not, then, exceptionally, you may make a second appeal. In this circumstance, the LEA must review the decision and it must tell you, in writing, the outcome of that review. If the LEA fails to reverse the decision concerning your child, you may appeal.

Although this seems logical in some respects, how will you, as a parent, be able to find out if the decision on your appeal differs from a previous decision because, by their very nature, such information is confidential? There has been a number of cases where parents have believed that the circumstances of their appeal have been identical to another, but this has not always proved to be the case. If you feel that your circumstances warrant a second appeal, then the best course of action is to speak to an expert on school admissions or a solicitor to see if there is scope to challenge the decision.

Can any refusal be appealed?

The simple answer is no. You cannot appeal against the refusal of a place in a nursery school. If you applied for a place at a nursery school and the LEA said that it cannot offer a place in a particular nursery school, its decision is final. The same also applies if you have asked for a place in a primary school for your child and he is under school age.

If your child has been identified as having special educational needs, you have the same right of appeal on a placing request as any other parent.

There are, however, differences in the procedure. A separate guide for parents of children with special educational needs is available, and you can ask your local LEA or the Scottish Executive Education Department for a copy. The function of special educational needs appeals is outside the scope of this book.

When can you appeal?

If you want to appeal against a decision not to allow your child to attend the school of your choice, you must inform the appeal committee no later than 28 days from the date on which either:

- your request is deemed to have been refused by the LEA because no response has been received by 30 April; or

- you receive a letter from the LEA refusing a place at the school of your choice (if the letter is received before the date on which your request would be deemed to be unsuccessful).

It is important that you consider your decision to appeal quickly. If you do not tell the appeal committee within the prescribed timetable allowed by law, you may lose your right to appeal. The LEA will advise you as to how you can lodge an appeal, either by completing an appeal form provided by the LEA or by appealing by letter.

How to appeal

The letter from the LEA will explain about your right of appeal and where to write to if you decide to appeal. Your letter lodging an appeal should include the following:

- Your name and address.
- The name of your child.
- The name of the school of your choice.
- The date of the LEA's letter of refusal.
- A statement that you wish to refer the LEA's decision to the appeal committee.

There is no need to say why the LEA refused your request, because the LEA will tell the appeal committee. It may well be that the LEA will provide an appeal form for you to complete.

Deciding how to make your case

The appeal committee will arrange the date, time and place for your appeal and it will advise you accordingly. However, before the hearing takes place you will have to decide how you want to tell the appeal committee about your reasons for appealing. So what are the options?

- You can go to the hearing and speak to the appeal committee yourself.

- You can take up to three people with you and, if you wish, you can ask one of those people to speak for you. This can be either a friend, relative or someone professional, either an expert or a solicitor.

- If you are unable to attend, you can ask someone else to attend in your place and speak for you.

- You can put your arguments in writing beforehand.

- You can put your arguments in writing, even if you also want to attend and speak yourself, or ask someone else to speak for you.

It is not essential that you do any of these things. However, if the appeal committee does not receive any written arguments from you, and if you or no one attends the hearing on your behalf, the appeal committee will consider the information given to it by the LEA and then reach a decision. This is a very important decision for you and therefore I would strongly urge you to attend the hearing because you will be able to explain in more detail about the reasons why you want your child to attend the school. If the appeal committee has any questions, you will be able to answer them. If you do not attend the appeal, those questions will remain unanswered and this may prejudice the decision.

Making your case in writing

When you are deciding whether to put your arguments in writing, it is important to consider if there is anything you want to say that you have not already told the LEA about. If there is, it is best to put it down in writing for the appeal committee and the LEA and send them both copies. If you say something to the committee that the LEA has not heard before, the appeal committee would have to give the LEA time to think about the new information and this may delay the committee's decision.

It is best to start thinking about whether you want to put your arguments in writing as soon as possible after you have told the appeal committee that you want to refer the LEA's decision to it. The reason for this is that you are required to send any written arguments to the appeal committee and the

LEA ten days before the hearing. So do not wait until you know the date of the hearing, otherwise you may not have sufficient time to properly consider your written submission. Any written information the LEA intends to send to the committee will be copied to you at least ten days before the hearing.

The issues discussed in the previous paragraph are covered by what is known as the 'principles of natural justice'. What this means is that both sides to the appeal are given the opportunity to present their own case and to be able to question the other side's case. In order to do this, they must be given a proper opportunity to consider and respond to the other side's case. If each side is not given proper opportunity, then the appeal committee will have to decide whether to continue with the appeal or whether to adjourn to enable the party, who has not had time to consider fresh information, to be able to consider and respond to it.

So how do you make your case?

This will very much depend on what reason (or reasons) the LEA gives for refusing your choice. Let us then look at the reasons that may be given:

- **The school would have to employ an additional teacher or spend a lot of money (e.g. it would have to provide an additional classroom).**

  The LEA will have to explain why it feels that it would have to employ an additional teacher or provide an additional classroom. This may depend on the size of the classrooms and the number of pupils in the class. You will need to find out how many pupils there are on roll at the school, and how many pupils there will be in the year group in question. You will also need to find out if, and how many, places are being kept back for pupils moving into the area and how realistic this figure is and what it is based on. For example, how many places have been reserved for the last five years and how many places were filled? You will be able to find out this information by asking the LEA prior to the appeal hearing. You will also need to establish the pupil/teacher ratio (see Chapter 5) and how this compares with other schools, both locally and nationally.

  You will need to find out the size of the classrooms and why it is not possible to accommodate one more pupil without causing problems for the school. You will also need to find out the performance record of the school and how the school has performed over the last four years. You can approach the school and ask for this information, and if it is unwilling or unable to provide this information, you can approach your local authority. Details of all local authorities are listed in Appendix 8. In addition, you should also look at the most recent inspection report from the HM Inspectorate of Education in Scotland to see what it has to say about the school. Its website is www.hmie.gov.uk.

You should be able to find out all of this information from the LEA and, depending on what the answers are, you can use this information to undermine the LEA's case.

- **Your child's education would suffer from a change of school.**

This reason is unlikely to be used when your child is starting primary school or when he is transferring to secondary school. This is a very subjective judgement and, as such, it can be challenged. Who has assessed that your child's education will suffer? What are the reasons for making such an assessment? The only time that it is likely to be used is if your child has changed schools too often in the past and he may be unsettled by a further move. However, you obviously feel that a change will be beneficial and it may be as a result of a house move, which means that attending the existing school is no longer suitable. In any event, if this reason has been given, the LEA will need to explain exactly why it has formed this opinion. You will need to explore this reason so that you can challenge it.

- **Education in the school you have chosen would not be suitable to the age, ability or aptitude of your child.**

This may apply if you want your child to be admitted to a stage of education for which your child is not yet ready, or to a school which cannot meet your child's needs. I would suggest that this reason is seldom used. However, if it is, you will need to demonstrate that the school would be suitable for your child. It is a subjective judgement, again, and therefore it can be challenged, so you will need to support any claims with supporting evidence. Such evidence may include, for example, school reports or independent evidence from an educational psychologist confirming your child's academic ability or potential and that the school allocated would not be appropriate for your child.

- **The LEA thinks that your child can only be provided for in the school you want at the expense of the other pupils' education.**

This is almost the reverse of the second ground referred to above. Again, it is a subjective judgement and it can be challenged. What evidence has the LEA provided to demonstrate that your child's admission will have the effect anticipated? You will be able to use all the information that is referred to in the first ground above to show that your child's admission will not have the effect that the LEA has suggested.

- **The school that you have chosen has been provided specifically for children with special needs, and the LEA thinks that your child does not need the special equipment or specially trained staff that it has provided in that school.**

Presumably, if this reason has been given, you believe that your child has special needs, which is a view not shared by the LEA. If this is the case, you will need to provide an independent report or assessment to demonstrate that your child has special needs and would therefore benefit from attendance at the school.

- **Your child has been very troublesome at school.**

As mentioned in Chapter 11, if your child has been excluded from a school, the LEA is not bound to readmit him. This is a little more difficult because if your child has had problems at school, it may be necessary to try to establish why this has happened and whether there are any underlying issues that may need to be addressed. Bear in mind that the LEA will be trying to provide help and to do what is best for all concerned. There may well be very good reasons why you selected a particular school and you will need to explain why you feel that the school in question will be best for your child.

- **You want your daughter to attend a boys' school, or your son to attend a girls' school.**

If this is the case, no appeal will be successful.

- **Accepting the request would prevent the LEA from reserving a place at the school for a child likely to move into the area of the school in-year.**

If this reason has been given, you will need to find out how many places have been reserved and how many pupils have moved into the area in the last five years. Of course, this is only an indication and it is by no means a certainty. If you can show that the number of reserved places is unreasonable, bearing in mind the number of pupils that have moved into the area on average in the last five years, you may be able to convince the appeal committee to allow your appeal. You will be able to find this information out from the LEA. If, for example, ten places have historically been reserved and only five places have been needed, this might illustrate that the number of places being reserved is unreasonable.

- **Accepting the request would make it necessary for the LEA to create an additional class or employ an additional teacher at a future stage of your child's primary education.**

  The same issues apply as for the first reason above. You will need to obtain the same information to challenge the case put forward by the LEA – all of which should be available from your local LEA.

Arranging the hearing

After you have lodged your appeal, you should receive an acknowledgement within approximately seven days. It may take up to two weeks for the committee to inform you of the date, time and venue for the hearing. The hearing should take place about two weeks later.

In the section entitled 'When can you appeal?' it was explained that you have 28 days in which to lodge an appeal, either from the date you receive the decision or the application is deemed to be refused. The LEA then has a period of 28 days in which to arrange the appeal (this period may be longer for multiple appeals). This means that for individual appeals the maximum period from receiving the decision to appeal is 56 days or eight weeks. However, assuming that all parents do not wait until day 28 before submitting an appeal and that the LEA do not wait until day 28 before arranging the appeal, this means that, on average, you will have about five weeks in which to prepare for your appeal and you will have to send any written submissions ten days before the hearing to the committee and the LEA. You may be asked to agree to a hearing and you are given less than two weeks' notice so that your hearing fits in with others being arranged by the committee. You do not have to agree to this if you require the full two weeks so that you can prepare for the appeal.

If you want to attend the hearing but the date is not convenient for you, you can ask the committee to fix another date. However, the committee may not agree to this if the date fixed is convenient for other parents or for other committee members themselves. If the hearing has to proceed and you cannot attend, you may want to ask someone else to speak for you. In order to try to avoid this, you could advise the committee of dates when you will not be available when you lodge the appeal.

If your appeal has not been heard within two months of receipt by the LEA, the appeal is deemed to have been refused, which will trigger an appeal to the Sheriff's Office. See section below entitled 'What happens if the committee does not give a decision or does not arrange a hearing?' for more details.

Hearing several appeals at once

If the committee receives a number of appeals for the same school and the reason given for refusal is the same, the committee may want to hear all the appeals together. If this is the case, it may affect the way that your appeal is handled. It may affect your hearing in two ways:

1. Normally your hearing must be held within 28 days after the committee receives your letter of appeal. If it wants to hear your appeal with other parents, it may take longer than 28 days.

2. If some parents appeal after the date of your hearing has been set, the committee may postpone your hearing and fix a later date so it can hear all the appeals together.

If the committee hears several appeals together, you have a right to ask the committee to let you speak to it without the other parents and their friends being present. You should be invited by the Chair of the appeal committee if you would like the chance to do this, and if you do, he will ask the other parents to leave the room while you speak.

So what happens at the hearing?

At the beginning of the hearing the Chair of the committee will explain how the appeal will be conducted. This will normally be as follows:

- The person speaking for the LEA will explain why your request was refused and other people may be asked to speak in support of what the LEA has said.

- You, or the person speaking for you, can ask questions.

- You, or the person speaking for you, can explain to the appeal committee why you think that your child should be awarded a place at the school and why you think that the LEA should not have refused it. You can also ask people to speak in support of what you have said. The guidance issued by the Scottish Executive does not define who can, or cannot, speak for you and therefore you can ask whoever you want. This could be a friend or maybe even a parent of a child already at the school. If you have written down your reasons and sent them in to the appeal committee and the LEA beforehand, you may not wish to say anything, but instead rely on your written submission. However, I feel that you should explain to the committee why you want a place at the school because the appeal committee will be able to understand why you are appealing and why the LEA was wrong to refuse your choice.

- The person speaking for the LEA may ask questions of you, and any of your witnesses. Anyone who attends the appeal and contributes to the hearing is liable to be questioned by the LEA in order to clarify any issues which have been raised and remain unclear.

- The person speaking for the LEA will sum up his reasons.

- You, or the person speaking for you, may sum up your reasons for the appeal.

If you want to give the committee any paper at the hearing, the person speaking for the LEA should also see it and be able to copy it. If the LEA gives the appeal committee any new paper, you can ask to see a copy of it too. If, at the hearing, the LEA says anything new to the committee which you regard as being important and you want time to be able to consider and respond to it, you can ask the committee to adjourn to another occasion to enable you to properly consider it. However, the committee does not have to agree to this if it does not accept that the new information is important. Similarly, if you say anything at the hearing that the LEA did not know about, it too can seek an adjournment subject to the same provisions. However, to avoid this happening, it is best to include everything in your written statement which you will have sent to the committee and the LEA ten days before the hearing.

Apart from the people speaking for you and for the LEA, only a limited number of people may attend the hearing. These may include councillors, or their officials in charge of schools, or people appointed to see that appeal committees operate fairly. Members of the public are not entitled to attend.

How long will it be before you receive the decision?

This will depend, to a large extent, on whether the appeal committee decides to adjourn because substantial new information has been produced at the hearing or because the committees want you, or the LEA, to provide more information. However, the committee must send you its decision within 14 days of the end of the hearing, whenever that is. The decision must be sent to you in writing and it must include the reasons for the decision. If the committee agrees with the LEA, and dismisses your appeal, it must advise you of a further right of appeal to the Sheriff.

If, on the other hand, the committee disagrees with the LEA and says that the LEA was wrong to have refused your request, the LEA must let your child have a place in the school that you asked for.

What happens if the committee does not give a decision or does not arrange a hearing?

If the appeal committee does not:

- hold a hearing within two months of receiving your letter saying that you want to appeal;
- fix a date for the hearing to continue within 14 days of adjourning a hearing; or
- send you its decision and its reasons for it within 14 days of ending a hearing;

the LEA's decision to refuse your request remains, but you can then lodge a further appeal to the Sheriff in the same way as if the appeal committee had agreed with the LEA's decision. In these circumstances the appeal committee is deemed to have dismissed your appeal.

Appealing to the Sheriff

If the appeal committee agrees with the LEA's decision and dismisses your appeal, and you feel strongly that your child should attend the school of your choice, you can appeal to the Sheriff against the appeal committee's decision. If you want to lodge an appeal, you must lodge a summary application with the Sheriff Clerk. This application can be obtained from the Sheriff Clerk's office and it allows you to explain the grounds for your appeal. It is described as an initial writ, which is legal jargon to describe the format on which the information regarding your appeal is to be submitted. You can contact the Sheriff Clerk's office for more information or you can look at the court's website at www.scotcourts.gov.uk/sheriff/index.asp. You must lodge an appeal within 28 days of receiving the appeal panel's decision or within 28 days of the relevant deadline described in the previous section.

A summary application must be in the prescribed form of an initial writ (described above) for which a court fee would be payable. Normal court procedures will be observed. You may consider it desirable to consult a solicitor, either at this early stage or at some later stage. A late appeal, made after 28 days, may be accepted if there is good reason for it. The way that the courts operate, like most courts, can be complicated to the untrained observer and therefore if you feel that you have a good case, then you are urged to consult a local solicitor who will be able to assist you with the process. The Sheriff Clerk's address and telephone number will normally appear in the telephone directory under 'Sheriff Court'.

If you do appeal, the Sheriff will have to decide whether the reasons given by the LEA for refusing your application were lawful and therefore constitute grounds for an appeal. If not, he will overturn the LEA's decision and your child must be admitted to the school of your choice. However, even if the Sheriff decides that the reasons given by the LEA were lawful, the Sheriff will consider whether your request should still be accepted. You can submit reasons as to why your child should be admitted to the school in question and these will constitute the grounds for your appeal. In most cases the reasons given will be the same as were considered by the appeal committee.

The Sheriff's decision may be subject to a Judicial Review, at your, or the LEA's, request. This will usually occur if it is felt that the court decision was in some way flawed, to such an extent that the outcome was not just. A Judicial Review is a process where a court decision can be reviewed by a higher court. You may feel that it is appropriate to seek legal advice before proceeding further.

CHECKLIST 12

1 Do you understand how an appeal committee operates?

2 Have you prepared your submission and provided third party support for your appeal?

3 What are the reasons given as to why the LEA has refused your application?

4 Have you received and considered the LEA's case?

5 Have you prepared any questions to be asked of the LEA at the appeal?

6 Will you need anyone to represent you at the appeal?

7 Will you be taking any witnesses to the appeal?

8 Have you received the appeal committee's decision within the prescribed period?

9 Do you wish to appeal against the appeal committee's decision?

10 Do you understand the reasons on which an appeal can be made to the Sheriff's Court?

A flow chart showing the appeal process in Scotland

The parent receives the decision from the admission authority refusing the place – the parent must be given at least 28 school days to lodge an appeal

→

The parent lodges an appeal within the prescribed timetable set by the admission authority and receives an acknowledgement

→

The parent must receive at least two weeks' notice of the date of the hearing, unless the parent agrees to a shorter period

→

The admission authority must supply its statement at least ten days before the hearing

→

The parent must send his statement to the admission authority at least ten days before the hearing

→

The parent prepares his response to the admission authority's statement

→

THE DATE OF THE HEARING

→

The appeal decision should be sent by the Clerk to the parents and the admission authority within 14 days of the hearing

→

The parent considers whether to appeal to the Sheriff Clerk's office

Chapter 13

Choosing a school in Wales

The National Assembly for Wales assumed the powers of the Secretary of State for Wales for school admission arrangements in May 1999. The Welsh Assembly published a Code of Practice in April 1999, which sets out, in some detail, the requirements for school admissions and appeals. Much of the principles used in school admissions are based on the arrangements in England, but there are now some significant differences as the arrangement evolves. All references in this chapter to the Code of Practice refer to the Welsh Code.

There are many similarities between the English and Welsh admission systems. As the advice about securing a place at the school of your choice is the same, please refer to the guidance covered in Chapter 1.

The issues covered in this chapter are as follows:

- What are the aims and objectives of admission policies and practices?
- Making admissions easier for parents
- Primary schools
- Interviews
- Waiting lists
- Fees
- The withdrawal of school places
- Powers of direction
- Taking account of parental preference
- Admission (oversubscription) criteria
- Infant class sizes
- Partial selection
- Banding
- Priority on the basis of aptitude
- Pupils with special educational needs but not statements
- Pupils with challenging behaviour

- Applying for a place at a school of your choice

Quick reference

- ## Welsh medium schools

  This is where the National Curriculum is taught in a Welsh-speaking setting. Parents will have a choice as to whether their children are taught in a Welsh- or English-speaking school. The Welsh Assembly is considering widening the opportunities for children to be taught in a Welsh-speaking school or setting.

QUICK LIST
1   Have you obtained a copy of the admissions booklet, which deals with school admissions? If more than one Local Education Authority (LEA) is involved, obtain all the admissions booklets. This is important because you will find the admission criteria for your preferred school (or schools) in the admissions booklet. You will need this information to complete your admission application.
2   Have you studied the admission criteria for your preferred school (or schools)?
3   Have you checked to see how well you meet the admission criteria?
4   Have you researched the school (or schools) that you are considering?
5   Have you looked at the school's (or schools') prospectus (or prospectuses)?
6   Have you visited your preferred school (or schools) and have you looked around to see what you think?
7   Have you spoken to parents whose children already attend the school (or schools) of your choice?
8   Have you spoken to pupils already attending the school (or schools) of your choice?
9   Have you talked to teachers at the school (or schools)?
10   Have you listened to your child, to see what he thinks about the school (or schools)?
11   Have you used this book to assess your chances of making a successful admission application or admission appeal?
12   **Have you made sure that you have sent your application in on time?**

What are the aims and objectives of admission policies and practices?

Much of the aims and objectives are enshrined in the School Standards and Framework Act 1998. The key objectives are to ensure that any admission arrangements work for the benefit of all parents and children and that they should be as simple as possible for parents to understand. They should also be easy to use and to help parents to be able to make sound decisions about their child's education. In order to do this, admission criteria should be clear, fair and objective for all children including those with special educational needs or those with disabilities. In addition, admission criteria should also enable parents to express a preference for a school of their choice and facilitate those preferences to the maximum extent possible.

Making admissions easier for parents

When you apply for a school place for your child, the local admission arrangements should be clear, fair and objective and give your child a reasonable chance of securing a place at the school of your choice. To do this, you should be provided with as much information as possible to enable you to make a reasonable choice and also for you to be able to assess the likely chances of a successful application. Of course, if you are unsuccessful, you are given the statutory right of an appeal to an independent appeal panel.

School governing bodies are under an obligation to publish information about their schools and LEAs are under an obligation to publish information about the admission arrangements for all maintained schools in their area. Most, if not all, authorities will publish a single booklet that gives all the relevant information about all the schools in their area.

The Code on School Admissions suggests that the information provided should be in both English and Welsh and also in other commonly used languages, so you can understand what is needed when you are applying for a school place. The information should give details of any timescales and deadlines for the submission of applications, and also the admission criteria that will be used to determine applications, should more be received for a particular school than there are places available. Such information should also include the number of successful applications in previous years, together with the criteria under which they were accepted.

The Welsh Assembly believes that a school's performance is also important when deciding which schools to choose, along with any school inspection reports, and these should be available if you would like to look at them before making your choices. If you have access to the internet, this information is available and details of websites are given in Appendix 9. If you do not have access to the internet, information can be obtained from your LEA. The contact phone numbers for the LEA are also set out in Appendix 8.

The Code on School Admissions suggests that LEAs should operate co-ordinated schemes, wherever possible, as this will ensure that all opportunities are dealt with equally, and common timetables, deadlines for applications and notification dates will help to ease any anxiety you may have. This means that LEAs will co-ordinate admissions within their authority to ensure, wherever possible, that parents receive at least one offer of a place and other parents will not receive multiple offers. The co-ordinated scheme will explain about the admission arrangements that will be used to deal with applications as and when they are received. It will also set out the process by which the LEA will communicate with other admission authorities and vice versa. If you need to find out more, you can request a copy of the co-ordinated scheme from the LEA where you live.

Religious and denominational schools may require further information than maintained schools in order to establish religious commitment. A supplementary form, which can be obtained from the school, can be used to obtain such information.

You should be given at least six weeks within which to make up your mind about school places and this time should be used for you to find out as much information as you need to help you make your final decisions. There is not a prescribed date for the submission of applications which applies throughout Wales, but you should receive at least six weeks' notice from the publication of the admission arrangements, which for secondary schools is from the beginning of the autumn term in September until the closing date for applications, which will usually be in the latter part of October or the early part of November. For primary schools, the closing dates for applications will usually be later; these may well be December, January or even February. The LEA's admissions booklet will explain the timetables.

Primary schools

Your child does not need to start school until the term following his fifth birthday. The date that your child reaches the compulsory school age is determined by the Secretary of State or the Welsh Assembly, and for the autumn term (commencing in September) it is 31 August; the spring term (commencing in January) is 31 December; and for the summer term (commencing in April) is 31 March.

Some admission authorities provide primary school places for children before they reach the compulsory school age. If you are offered such a place but you choose to defer your child's entry until he has reached the compulsory school age, the admission authority may agree to this request, provided that the place is taken up during the same academic year. If this is the case, the place is not available for another child to take up, even though it may appear that there is a place at the school.

Interviews

Admission authorities, or governing bodies, should not interview you, or your child, as part of the published admission arrangements. However, if you are applying to a religious-based school, it is currently permissible for an interview to be conducted in order to assess religious commitment. A governing body of a school can also conduct an interview so that it can assess your child's suitability for a boarding school place. The prospectus published by the school where the governing body is the admission authority will explain about the admission arrangements, including interviews. There are only a few public schools offering boarding school places with most being in the private sector, and thus outside the scope of this book. The school prospectus will also define the eligibility for such places.

Interviews, other than for boarding school places, have now been banned in England for pupils starting school from September 2008 and it is likely that the Welsh Assembly will adopt similar provisions in the foreseeable future. However, even if interviews are held, they must still be clear, fair and objective, and if they are not, this may well be grounds for an appeal for unsuccessful applications.

Waiting lists

Admission authorities are not obliged to operate waiting lists but, where they do, they must operate in exactly the same way as the published admission criteria. If they do not, then this could be grounds for an appeal or a complaint to the Local Government Ombudsman for Wales (LGO), which deals with complaints about appeal panels.

Fees

Admission authorities are not entitled to levy any fees whatsoever in relation to the admission process. Voluntary contributions could be seen as disguised fees and should be discouraged.

The withdrawal of school places

There are only limited grounds when a school place can be withdrawn. These grounds are either where a place was offered on the basis of fraudulent information provided by the parent or where a parent has not responded to an offer within a reasonable time. A reasonable time has not been defined in Welsh legislation, but a period of 14 days is used in England and this can be helpful as a yardstick. However, if a place has not been accepted by the parent within the timeframe set by the admission authority, it is suggested that a further letter should be sent to the parents explaining that if the place is not accepted by a certain date then the place will be withdrawn. This is to allow for the fact that the parents did not receive the original letter because, for example, they were away at the time. Where a place has been withdrawn, the parent is entitled to an appeal.

Even where a place was obtained fraudulently, it is unlikely to be withdrawn if the child has already started school. However, if you can show that you were denied a place because of a fraudulent application, then this could be a ground for a successful appeal.

Powers of direction

The LEA can direct a school to admit a child where the child has been permanently excluded from, or refused admission to, every school which provides education within a reasonable distance from the child's home. However, reasonable distance is not defined and this could be open to interpretation and possibly challenged. The governing body of the school concerned can challenge this decision and it can refer the matter to the Welsh Assembly for determination. However, the LEA cannot make such a determination if it would result in the class size regulations being breached for classes which are subject to the statutory infant class size limit. This is dealt with later in this chapter.

Taking account of parental preference

Admission authorities must make provision within their published admission arrangements to enable you to express a preference (or preferences) as to where you would like your child to be educated. You can express up to three preferences. Presently, first preference first systems (see Chapter 2) do not apply universally across Wales, but it is possible that when new Codes are published that these arrangements may be replaced with equal preference systems (see Chapter 1). Where you express such a preference, the admission authority must offer you a place, unless to do so would cause, what is referred to as, prejudice to either efficient education or efficient use of resources. What this means is that the admission of your child will cause problems for the school. This is the reason most often used by admission authorities and it will be used when the number of applications exceeds the number of places available at the school and the admission authority believes that any additional admissions will cause problems for the school. This is linked to the net capacity for the school, which will be discussed later in this chapter.

However, there are a number of other reasons:

- If the school in question has a religious-based ethos and you do not meet the religious commitment requirements. Such schools will be either voluntary aided or foundation schools.

- Where your child has been permanently excluded from two or more schools and one of the exclusions took place after 1 September 1997. If this is the case, you lose the right to express a preference for a period of two years after the date of the last exclusion.

- Where admission would be incompatible with co-ordinated admission arrangements covering two or more maintained schools, which have been approved by the Secretary of State or the Welsh Assembly (this refers to selected schools, where schools allocate places on ability). The co-ordinated arrangements are established by the LEA and they set out how applications will be dealt with to ensure fairness to all applicants.

- Where an admission would result in the class size legislation being breached for infant classes (see page 169).

When considering applications to year groups other than the normal year of admission, admission authorities will not normally be able to prove prejudice while the number of children at the school remains below the published admission number for that year group. A partially selective school, where some places are allocated on the basis of ability or aptitude, and a school which operates a banding arrangement must admit up to its published admission number and it cannot keep places open if it does not have sufficient applicants of the required standard.

Admission (oversubscription) criteria

If a school receives more applications than places, the admission authority must apply published admission criteria to decide which pupils will be admitted. The oversubscription criteria must set out clearly how and when such criteria will be used. The admission authority has considerable discretion in deciding which admission criteria to use, provided that it is clear, fair and objective. The most commonly used admission criteria are the distance from school, siblings, and special medical or other exceptional reasons for your child to attend a school. However, in each case the admission authority must explain how the criteria will be applied. For example, if a distance factor is used, how will it operate? From which points at the school and the home will the distance be measured? Is the measurement accurate? Is it a computer-based programme and is it reliable? For a more detailed examination of possible admission criteria, please refer to Chapter 2. The Code applicable in England goes much further than the current Welsh Code; hence some criteria have been determined as unlawful in England. This is not the case in Wales but similar principles will still apply. It is still necessary for any admission criteria to be clear, fair and objective and if its not, there may be grounds to challenge it.

Many admission authorities will operate what is known as 'catchment areas'. A catchment area is drawn up before applications are sought and children living in the area will be given priority if there are more applications than places available. What has become known as the Rotherham judgment, where the High Court was asked to make a judgment on the lawfulness of a catchment area, has confirmed that there is nothing wrong, in principle, with having catchment areas as part of the oversubscription criteria which gives priority to local children. However, living in a catchment area cannot guarantee a place at a school.

In addition, what is referred to as the Greenwich judgment, where the High Court was asked to make a judgment on the lawfulness of giving priority to children who live in the administrative area of the LEA, means that it is unlawful to give priority to children simply because they live in the administrative area of the LEA. Applications from parents living outside the administrative area must be considered on an equal basis.

If a sibling is one of the criteria, what is the definition of a sibling? A sibling is not as easy to define as it was some years ago. Does it, for example, include half-brothers and half-sisters, or other children living in the same household? The LEA will have to define what will be recognised as siblings. The new English Code states that a sibling can only be taken into consideration if he will still be attending the school when the younger sibling starts. There is no such provision in the Welsh Code at present, bur this may change in the future.

If an authority has special medical or exceptional reasons to attend a school as one of its criteria, it will need to have an objective way to assess such applications; otherwise, it will be subjective and therefore subject to challenge. It will also have to define what is meant by special medical or exceptional reasons.

Voluntary aided and foundation schools which give priority to members of a particular faith must publish how such a priority will be tested. In addition, the published arrangements must also state what support is needed from the family's priest, minister or other religious leader, and how it will be used.

In addition, admission authorities must ensure that admission criteria comply with other legislation, such as sex and race discrimination, so that they are not unlawful.

All of these admission criteria are discussed more fully in Chapter 2.

Infant class sizes

Legislation was introduced in 1999 which limited the size of classes in reception and Years 1 and 2 to 30, unless there is more than one qualified teacher present. There are only four exceptions where classes can exceed 30, and these are as follows:

1. Where a child moves into an area outside the normal admissions round and there is no other school which would provide suitable education within a reasonable distance of his home.

2. Where a child's parents want Welsh medium education (a Welsh-speaking school) and there is no other school which would provide suitable education within a reasonable distance of his home.

3. Where a child receives a statement of special educational needs naming the school, or a pupil with a statement which names a particular school moves into the area, with each case being outside the normal admissions round.

4. Where the admission authority made a mistake and denied a place which otherwise would have been offered, or where a child is offered a place as a result of a successful appeal.

The four exceptions only apply for the remainder of the academic year in which the child is admitted and if there is no change in the following academic year, the admission authority must take steps to ensure that the statutory class size limit is not breached.

A child that has a statement of special educational needs will be treated as an exception for any time that he is in an infant class in a mainstream school. This also applies to secondary schools as children with statement of special educational needs will always be admitted.

Partial selection

Only two schools in Wales use partial selection as part of their admission arrangements. This is where there is provision in the school's admission arrangements that allow some places to be determined by a process of selection. Such partial selection has been allowed to continue by virtue of section 100 of the School Standards and Framework Act 1998, provided that there is no increase in the proportion of pupils selected or there is no change in the basis of selection. The selection can continue, provided that other admission authorities do not object or the Welsh Assembly has determined against such objections.

Banding

Grammar schools select high ability pupils. Comprehensive schools are non-selective and are described as all ability schools. However, schools can use their admission arrangements to enable them to allocate places that ensure a proportionate spread of children with different abilities. Banding systems are seen as good practice, provided that they are fair and objective and not used as a means of unlawfully admitting a disproportionate number of pupils with higher ability.

What will normally happen is that prospective applicants will be tested (usually during October/November) and placed in one of usually three, four or five bands. If a school operates three bands, it may allocate the bands as follows:

Band 1   Pupils achieving 75 per cent and above

Band 2   Pupils achieving between 25 and 75 per cent

Band 3   Pupils achieving below 25 per cent

The school will then allocate places according to each ability band. Say the school has 160 places available. It will allocate 40 places (25 per cent) to Band 1; 80 places (50 per cent) to Band 2; and 40 places (25 per cent) to Band 3.

However, schools that operate a banding system must not apply any other tests once applicants are allocated to bands. Also, the banding will only operate if the school receives more applications than places available. If there are fewer applicants than available places, all of the applications will be successful. In addition, schools must not give priority within bands according to the scores of the tests. If there are more applicants in a band than there are places available, the school must use the published admission criteria in order to determine which applicants will be successful. For more information on how the banding system operates, please refer to Chapter 2.

Priority on the basis of aptitude

The School Standards and Framework Act 1998 allows schools to admit up to ten per cent of their intake on the basis of ability in one of the specialisms. These specialisms are as follows:

- Physical education or sport
- Performing arts
- The visual arts
- Modern foreign languages
- Design and technology, and information technology (IT)

If a school specialises in more than one specialism, the overall limit is still no more than ten per cent of the total of pupils to be admitted.

Pupils with special educational needs but not statements

Children who have been diagnosed with special educational needs, but do not have statements, must be treated in exactly the same way as children that do not have special educational needs. It is unlawful for a school to refuse admission because a child has special educational needs. If your child has a statement, there is a special procedure for dealing with this which is outside the scope of this book. However, you will need to contact the Special Educational Needs Tribunal; the website of the Tribunal is www.sendist.gov.uk.

Pupils with challenging behaviour

An admission authority cannot refuse to admit a child because of his challenging behaviour. If, after admission, a child exhibits such behaviour, he can be excluded, either for a fixed period or permanently, provided that the admission authority has followed the school's published disciplinary policy. If a child is permanently excluded once, it will remain on his school record and the parents will still be able to express a preference as to where he continues his education. However, if the child has been permanently excluded twice, then the parent will lose the right to express a preference for a period of two years from the date of the last permanent exclusion.

Applying for a place at a school of your choice

Having read through the various issues above you will now be in a position to decide which school you would like your child to be educated. The process through which you will have to go is the same as in England and is covered in Chapter 1.

CHECKLIST 13

1   Have you obtained a copy of the LEA's admissions booklet?

2   Are you interested in applying to a community school (also called a 'state' school), for which the LEA is the admission authority?

3   Are you interested in applying to a voluntary aided school or foundation school, for which the governing body is the admission authority?

4   Have you obtained the prospectus (or prospectuses) for the school (or schools) that interest you?

5   Do you understand how places will be allocated if there are more applications than available school places?

6   Having studied the published admission criteria for last year's admission (which can be obtained from the LEA), is it your opinion that your child will be allocated a place in your preferred school?

7   Have you attended your preferred school's (or schools') open evening (or evenings), and spoken to the staff and the students?

8   Having consulted the current year's admission criteria, is your choice of school realistic and reasonable?

9   Do you understand how the equal preference system will operate should it be used by the admission authority? This is described on page 14.

10 Have you obtained details of successful admissions for the last five years? This can be obtained from the LEA.

11 Have the admission criteria been amended recently? You can obtain this information from the LEA.

12 Have you obtained any advice you have received from the LEA or from the school in writing and, if so, have you kept this information to hand?

---

13 If you are applying to a grammar school, have you arranged for your child to sit the entrance tests?

14 If you are applying to a faith school, are you certain that you can demonstrate your religious affiliation?

15 If you are applying to a faith school, have you asked your parish priest or minister of religion for a letter of support?

16 Have you obtained all the documentation to support your admission application?

17 Have you checked to make sure that you have enclosed **all** of the necessary information with the application form?

18 Have you ensured that your application was submitted on time?

19 Have you checked to ensure that your application was received by the admission authority?

A summary of school admissions in Wales

1. Get the admissions booklet from the Local Education Authority

2. **DECIDE WHAT YOUR PRIORITIES ARE FOR YOUR CHILD**

3. Decide which schools best meet those priorities and go to the open evenings

4. Talk to the teachers and pupils to get their views about the school

5. Assess the facilities at the school to see if they meet your expectations

6. Look through the most recent Estyn report and the performance figures for the school

7. **LOOK AT THE ADMISSION CRITERIA FOR THE SCHOOL AND ASSESS YOUR CHANCES OF SUCCESS**

8. Check to see if you would have secured a place at the school in the last five years, based on the admission criteria

9. List your preferences in order with the one that offers the best chance of success at the top

10. **MAKE SURE THAT THE PREFERENCE FORM IS SUBMITTED BY THE DEADLINE SET BY THE ADMISSION AUTHORITY**

Chapter 14

Wales: How to appeal

The Welsh Assembly has produced a Code of Practice on School Admission Appeals that gives guidance on how the appeal process should operate. The Code was published under section 84 of the School Standards and Framework Act 1998.

The issues covered in this chapter are as follows:

- The aims and objectives of the appeal process
- What does the law say about admission appeals?
- The powers of appeal panels
- Other Acts of Parliament
- The constitution of appeal panels
- The right of appeal
- Notice to be given by you that you intend to appeal
- Notice given to you of the date of the appeal hearing
- Information about the appeal
- The admission/appeal timetable
- 'Rising fives'
- The venue for the appeal and accommodation requirements
- The interests of panel members
- The lobbying of panel members
- The Clerk to the Appeal Panel
- The role of the Chair
- The panel members
- The appellants
- The presenting officer
- The admission authority's case
- The right of representation
- The evidence and witnesses

- The appeal hearing
- Matters to be taken into consideration by the appeal panel
- The record of proceedings
- The decisions of appeal panels
- Notification of the decision
- Further appeals
- Complaints

Quick reference

- **Estyn**

  This is the official inspectorate in Wales and it operates in the same way as Ofsted in England.

- **Public Services Ombudsman**

  This is the Welsh equivalent to the Local Government Ombudsman (LGO) in England. The powers which they have are predominantly the same.

QUICK LIST

1 Do you understand the make-up of appeal panels?

2 Do you understand the questions you should ask yourself before deciding to appeal? These questions may include:

   a) Do I believe that the admission authority has made a mistake with my application?

   b) Do I believe that the decision was unreasonable?

   c) Does my child have any exceptional reasons to attend the school?

   d) Are there any issues that were not disclosed on the application form to the admission authority?

3 Do you understand the reasons that can be given for your child being refused a place at a school?

4 Do you know the timeframe when an appeal can be lodged?

5 Do you know how to prepare your case?

6 What information do you need to provide on your appeal form?

7 Do you know what will happen at the appeal hearing?

8	Can you bring along anyone to support you at the appeal?
9	When will you receive the decision of the appeal panel?
10	What are your rights against the appeal panel's decision?
11	Did you receive a fair hearing?

The aims and objectives of the appeal process

The intention is that the appeal process provides a simple, straightforward and accessible system to enable you to appeal against a decision of an admission authority to refuse a place for your child at the school of your choice. However, the system should work for the benefit of all concerned, including you, your child, the admission authorities and the schools themselves.

It is important that the appeal system is not only independent and impartial, but also seen as such. The basic objectives of the appeal process are to:

- provide an independent, impartial but informal forum for parents and the admission authority concerned to present their cases respectively and to be confident that they will be given a fair hearing;

- ensure that appeal panels weigh up all of the evidence presented to them carefully and objectively before reaching a final decision on the appeal;

- operate within the requirements of education legislation, and also have regard to the implications of other legislation, such as the Sex Discrimination Act 1975, the Race Relations Act 1976, the Disability Discrimination Act 1995, and the Human Rights Act 1998. Appeal panels carry out a judicial function and must apply the principles of natural justice;

- have regard to all relevant guidelines in conducting appeal arrangements including the three Codes on School Admission, School Admission Appeals and Children with Special Educational Needs (this Code deals with admissions for children with special educational needs. Only children with a statement of educational needs will be given priority in the admission arrangements; other children with lesser special educational needs will not be given priority simply because of the nature of their needs. If your child has special needs, you should contact your Local Education Authority (LEA) to discuss how you should proceed);

- provide a system which is clear, consistent and easy to understand for everyone involved; and

- make workable the class size legislation (see Chapter 13).

What does the law say about admission appeals?

Admission authorities are defined under section 88 of the School Standards and Framework Act 1998. The LEA is the admission authority for community or voluntary controlled schools, unless this has been delegated to the governors by the LEA. However, if this is the case, the LEA is still responsible for arranging admission appeals. In the case of voluntary aided and foundation schools, the governors are the admission authority. Voluntary aided schools are mainly religious or 'faith' schools. The governing body employs the staff and sets the admission criteria. The school's land and buildings are normally owned by a charity and the governing body contributes to building and maintenance costs. Voluntary controlled schools are similar to voluntary aided schools but are run by the LEA. Like voluntary aided schools, the school's land and buildings are normally owned by a charity who may appoint some governors.

The admission authority must make arrangements to enable you to appeal against any decision made as to which school your child is to be educated. In theory, you could appeal against the school which has been allocated and if you win your appeal, the LEA must allocate you another school. In practice, most, if not all, parents will appeal for the school which they have chosen and, at the same time, explain the reasons why the allocated school is not appropriate.

The only circumstances when you would not be entitled to an appeal are where your child has been permanently excluded twice and the second exclusion was after 1 September 1997. In these circumstances you will lose the right of appeal for a period of two years from the date of the second exclusion and your child will have to attend the school where he is allocated.

The Code confirms that if you have expressed a preference for more than one school, then you can appeal for all of those schools. The Code suggests that, where a single LEA is the admission authority for all of your preferences, one appeal panel should determine them all. The Code also suggests that one appeal panel should hear appeals for the same school. In theory, this means that one appeal panel should hear all the appeals for all schools. It has been accepted that this is not possible and, in the circumstances, different panels can hear appeals for different schools.

There is another reason. If you are unable to persuade an appeal panel that your first preference appeal should be successful, then it is, in my view, extremely unlikely that you will be able to persuade the same appeal panel to allow an appeal for a second or third preference school. If this is the case, then I would push to have separate appeals. The other advantage is that you may learn things at the first appeal that you could usefully use at a second appeal, but you could not do this if all of the appeals are heard at the same time.

However, the Code says that an appeal panel should not take into consideration the fact that you may have other appeals pending, but it can be told if you have already attended a successful appeal; for example, if you have had a successful appeal for a second or third preference school but you still want to appeal for a first preference school.

The powers of appeal panels

The responsibility of appeal panels is to consider your appeal in the context of the published admission arrangements for the school of your choice and to decide if the appeal should be successful. The appeal panel does not have any powers to listen to complaints or objections on the wider aspects of local admission policies and practices; these are matters for the Welsh Assembly. If an appeal is successful, the decision is binding on the admission authority, whether this is the LEA or the governors of the school.

If you feel, in any way, that the appeal was not handled in accordance with the guidance issued in the Code or any other supplementary guidance, you can make a complaint to the Public Services Ombudsman. The Public Services Ombudsman will investigate complaints about process and procedural issues, but not simply because you disagree with the decision. The Welsh Assembly has no power to investigate complaints or decisions of appeal panels. Appeal panel members should receive training and the lack of it may well lead to procedural flaws that the Public Services Ombudsman can investigate. Such flaws may well include the failure to follow the guidance in the Codes of Practice and also the failure to properly consider any issues which may be raised at an appeal. Panel members will receive training on the Codes and any other relevant legislation, and also their behaviour and conduct in an appeal hearing.

Other Acts of Parliament

When considering appeals, panel members must also be aware of the implications of other legislation including the Sex Discrimination Act 1975; the Race Relations Act 1976 and the Disability Discrimination Act 1995 amongst others. More details on this legislation can be found in Chapter 4.

The constitution of appeal panels

The Code of Practice sets out clearly how appeal panels should be constituted. The Code provides for panels of either three or five members. In practice, most panels will comprise three members, as admission authorities find it difficult to recruit people to sit on panels because it is a voluntary function.

There are two categories of people that can sit on an appeal panel; one category is laypersons and the other category is persons experienced in education. Anyone can be a layperson, provided that they have had no practical experience in a paid capacity in a school. Therefore, governors and voluntary helpers would be eligible. The person experienced in education will usually be a serving, or retired, head or deputy head teacher.

However, the Code also disqualifies certain people from sitting on a panel. These are as follows:

- Any member of the LEA, or the governing body of the school which is the subject of the appeal;

- Anyone, other than a teacher, employed by the LEA or the governing body;

- Anyone where doubts may be raised about their impartiality. This would include anyone who has, or ever has had, any connection with the LEA or the school, or with any employee of the LEA or the governing body, except a teacher. Being a teacher does not disqualify the person automatically, unless there is anything else that may call into question his impartiality; and

- No one can be a panel member if they were involved with making the original decision.

The right of appeal

You must be given the right to appeal against any decision by the admission authority to refuse your child a place at a school of your choice. The authority must give details of the reason why the application was unsuccessful and also details of how to appeal.

Notice to be given by you that you intend to appeal

If you have been refused a place at the school of your choice, you must lodge your appeal within the prescribed period set by the admission authority. This period must not be less than 14 days (ten working days) from the date of notification. If you submit an appeal after the deadline, the admission authority should not unreasonably refuse to accept it. If a late appeal is accepted, it should be heard at the same time, or as soon as possible after any other appeals for the same school. Wherever possible, the appeal panel should be the same.

Notice given to you of the date of the appeal hearing

You should be given at least 14 days' notice (ten working days) of the date of your appeal hearing, unless you have agreed to waive this notice period. If you have agreed to a shorter period, you should confirm this in writing to the Clerk to the Appeal Panel (see page 183 for a description of the Clerk's role). Before you agree to a shorter period, do make sure that you are fully prepared and that your appeal will not be compromised by such an agreement.

Information about the appeal

The admission authority should provide some guidance notes explaining about the appeal process and what you should expect at an appeal. You should be advised that you have a right to appear in person at an appeal, or to send a representative to appear either with you or in place of you, if you are not able to attend.

If it is not clear whether the appeal will be conducted as a normal prejudice appeal or a class size appeal, you should be asked to prepare for both; the definitions of these have been described in Chapters 5 and 6. It will be the appeal panel which ultimately decides if it is a normal prejudice or class size prejudice appeal, after it has heard the various arguments by both parties.

The admission/appeal timetable

It is important, wherever possible, that one appeal panel should hear the appeals for a particular school. Therefore, admission authorities are encouraged to organise appeals so that holiday periods are avoided. It is recommended that appeals for secondary schools are heard before the summer break.

'Rising fives'

The Code on School Admission Appeals provides that, where admission authorities allow children to join the reception class at different times, they should try to ensure that all appeals are dealt with at the same time.

The venue for the appeal and accommodation requirements

The Code states that in order to ensure that appeal panels are seen to be independent, it would not be wise to hold an appeal at the school in question and it is better to hold the appeal at a neutral venue.

In cases where appeals have been held at the school, the Public Services Ombudsman has not considered that this amounts to maladministration, unless there have been some other significant faults with the appeal.

In order to demonstrate that the appeal is independent, the Code suggests that when considering the venue, there is sufficient room to allow both parties, and their representative or advisor, to have separate discussions, and arrangements should be made to ensure that the hearing is not interrupted. In addition, the location should be a place where there is unlikely to be disturbance by external noise and people waiting outside should not be able to hear the discussions inside.

One of the features of the appeal process is that the appeal should be as informal as possible and the room layout should ensure structure, comfort and informality. Refreshments should be available and name plates for the panel and the Clerk should be provided.

One of the other issues is that the admission authority should ensure that there is enough time for the appeal to be heard. This has been the subject of many complaints to the Public Services Ombudsman, where some authorities only allow ten or 15 minutes for each appeal. In most cases this will not be sufficient and if you are not given time to say all that you want, without repeating yourself, then this will be regarded as maladministration.

The interests of panel members

Earlier the book has outlined who is disqualified from sitting on an appeal panel. There are circumstances where, although someone is not disqualified, it would not be appropriate for them to sit on a panel. The admission authority should always be sure to avoid bias, or the appearance of bias. Anyone who is closely related to, or involved with, you should not sit on a panel. Equally, anyone with similar connections with the admission authority should not sit on the panel.

When panel members receive the appeal papers they are required to disclose any such relationships to the Clerk so that a decision can be taken on whether they should be replaced. Equally, you should be advised of the names of the panel members in advance so that if you too have any concerns, these can be raised with the Clerk. There is no timetable for when you should receive this information. Sometimes such a relationship may not be known until the hearing itself. If this is the case, both parties should be asked if they have any objection to the appeal proceeding and if they do, the appeal should be deferred until a fresh panel can be found.

The lobbying of panel members

Panel members are encouraged not to get involved in discussions with parents before an appeal because this would not be appropriate. Do not try to contact a panel member because this may invalidate your appeal. Similarly, the same applies to the admission authority. If you are in any doubt, raise this with the Clerk, who is completely independent and thus able to give advice to all parties.

The Clerk to the Appeal Panel

Every panel will have the services of a Clerk. The Clerk plays a very important role because he is able to give advice and guidance to all parties. He can also give advice about the process and procedure, and he can inform you of when the panel is reaching a decision on the appeal. The Clerk is not a member of the appeal panel, but he will be present throughout and he will also convey the panel's decision to you and the admission authority.

Clerks should not deal with school admissions as part of their normal employment, and LEAs and governors should look outside their own staff for people that have the relevant experience in the conduct of enquiries or disciplinary hearings. It is important for the Clerk to have a good understanding of the Codes of Practice and also legislation and guidance issued in relation to appeals.

The Clerk's key tasks are to:

- explain the basic procedures to appellants and to deal with any questions they may have;
- ensure that all the relevant facts are presented;
- determine the order in which the appeal is conducted (usually the admission authority will put its case first, but this is a discretion exercised by the panel);
- record the proceedings, decisions and reasons for the decision; and
- notify all parties of the panel's decision.

The Clerk should be able to provide an independent source on procedure and evidence. If you are unrepresented or appear to be experiencing difficulty in presenting your case, the Clerk may tactfully intervene to assist you or the panel with the procedure. This will enable you to ensure that all the issues you want to raise will be presented, and that factual matters which are not in dispute are clearly identified. If the panel withdraws in order to reach its decision, the Clerk will remain with the panel to give advice on procedure or the law.

The role of the Chair

Like the Clerk, the Chair plays a very important role in directing the proceedings and his ability to control the hearing fairly and firmly is essential. It would be helpful if the Chair has experience as a magistrate, committee chair, senior union official or the like. The Chair should aim to put you at ease and to ensure that the appeal is conducted in a structured, but informal, way. He should introduce all the people at the hearing and also explain the role of the Clerk. The Chair should also explain that the panel is independent and its decision will be binding on the admission authority. The Chair should conclude the hearing by asking you if you have had the opportunity to say all that you want to say. The Chair should not ask you if you have had a fair hearing because you may be inclined to say 'yes', which may well go against you if you subsequently lose the appeal and you wish to take it further.

The panel members

The panel members should be aware of the order of the proceedings and they should also take an active part in questioning both you and the presenting officer for the admission authority. They must not be seen to favour either one side or the other and they must be conscious of the need to be seen to be acting independently of the admission authority or the school's governing body.

The appellants

You must prepare yourself beforehand and you should have been given guidance by the admission authority. The admission authority is required to provide you with any information which you reasonably ask to enable you to prepare your case or to challenge the admission authority's case.

It is generally recognised that appearing as an appellant may well be a daunting one and this should be borne in mind all the time. In fact, no matter how informal a hearing is, you may well be intimidated by it. Most parents describe the experience as very stressful and they feel very nervous at the hearing. This is quite natural because you will no doubt feel that the outcome of the appeal will depend, to a large extent, on how you present your case at the hearing. This is why preparation is the key because I believe that knowledge breeds confidence and there is much more information and guidance available now to help you through this difficult time.

The appeal panel should be courteous and sensitive in your treatment, but, at the same time, you should expect to be questioned about your case, and the presenting officer for the admission authority is also entitled to question you.

The presenting officer

The presenting officer represents the admission authority and he will present the case on the authority's behalf. He must present the case as clearly as possible, giving all the relevant information. However, the officer should be prepared to answer detailed questions about the authority's case and questions about the school and its admission arrangements.

The admission authority's case

At least seven days (five working days) before the hearing, the admission authority should supply the Clerk with the following documents which should be circulated to you and the panel members:

- A written statement summarising how the admission arrangements for the school apply to your application, with any relevant background information;

- A written statement summarising the reasons for the decision with full supporting information that prejudice would arise from the admission of your child; and

- Copies of any information or documents which are to be put to the panel at the hearing, including anything that you have submitted.

The grounds under which the appeal is to be considered should also be explained to you. If it is not clear, then you should be asked to prepare for either case, that is a normal prejudice (see Chapter 5) or class size prejudice (see Chapter 6) appeal.

It should also be explained that there is no statutory deadline for you to submit information. However, you should submit any information that you want to be considered as soon as you can, otherwise you run the risk that the admission authority may seek an adjournment in order to consider and respond to any fresh information.

There should be no grounds for the admission authority to raise substantial information at the appeal which is not included in its statement. However, this may not apply to you, since you may have only been sent the authority's case seven days before the hearing.

The right of representation

Appeal panels must give you the opportunity to appear in person at the appeal and make oral representations. You should always be encouraged to appear in person and it is important to arrange a time and place that facilitates this. If it is not possible to attend, you may request an alternative date, but if there are multiple appeals for the school, this may not always be possible.

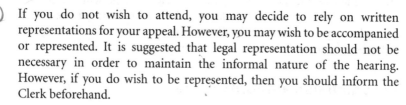

If you do not wish to attend, you may decide to rely on written representations for your appeal. However, you may wish to be accompanied or represented. It is suggested that legal representation should not be necessary in order to maintain the informal nature of the hearing. However, if you do wish to be represented, then you should inform the Clerk beforehand.

The evidence and witnesses

It is entirely up to you how you organise and present your appeal. However, it is unlikely that you will need to call witnesses, but if you wish to, this will be a matter for the appeal panel to decide. If the panel decides to allow a witness to give evidence, it will also decide if it is appropriate for the witness to remain in the appeal after giving evidence. An example might include a professional who you have invited along to support your appeal. Such a witness may be a social worker, educational psychologist or employer who will be able to explain about your child's circumstances in more detail than you are able to yourself.

The appeal hearing

The order of the hearing is at the discretion of the appeal panel, but it usually will follow the following format:

- The case for the admission authority.
- Questioning by you.
- Your case.
- Questioning by the admission authority.

- Summing up by the admission authority.
- Summing up by you.

The panel members can ask questions at any time.

Matters to be taken into consideration by the appeal panel

Having heard all the evidence, the panel will need to decide if the admission arrangements were properly applied and that the admission authority was correct to refuse your application. In other words, did the admission authority offer places to pupils that had a better claim to a place than you when they were set against the admission criteria.

If the panel decides that you were incorrectly denied a place, the appeal panel will offer you a place at the school, even if this decision results in the class size being exceeded. If the panel decides that the admission criteria were correctly applied, it will then have to decide if an additional admission will cause prejudice. If the appeal relates to Years 3 to 11, this will be classed as normal prejudice. This being the case, the panel is not bound by anything and it will consider each appeal on its own merits.

The panel will have to decide if the published admission number is the optimum number and to go beyond this will cause problems. If the panel decides that the school can accommodate your child without causing problems to the school, the panel will offer you a place. If the panel decides that an admission above the published number will cause problems, it will go on to consider the personal reasons that you have put forward and it will have to decide if the issues that you have presented are more compelling than the reasons put forward by the admission authority. In practice, what the panel will do is balance the issues put forward by both sides. If the panel feels that your reasons are stronger than those put forward by the admission authority, it will allow your appeal. If it feels that they are not, it will dismiss your appeal.

If there is more than one appeal, the panel will need to follow a different process. First of all, it will have to decide if the admission criteria were applied correctly in each case; this is the same as for individual appeals. However, the panel will then need to consider if the school can accommodate any more pupils without causing problems. If it considers that the school can accommodate more pupils, the panel will have to decide how many. Having decided this, the panel will have to decide which appeals will be successful. The panel will do this by considering the admission criteria and, importantly, the reasons put forward by the parents at the appeals. It will then rank the appeals in order and allow appeals up to the number the panel has decided the school can accommodate. After this, the panel will see if any other appeals should be allowed where the reasons put forward outweigh the problems that will be caused to the school.

If the appeal relates to reception and Years 1 and 2, the panel will have to decide if it is to be treated as a class size appeal. If it decides that it is not, then the panel will follow the procedure explained above. If the panel decides that it is a class size appeal, then the panel will have to decide if the admission authority made a mistake in dealing with your application and if it did, that decision denied a place at the school of your choice. If the panel decides that the admission authority made a mistake that denied a place, the panel will allow your appeal.

If the panel decides that no mistake was made, it will have to decide if the decision taken by the admission authority was unreasonable, bearing in mind the information that the authority had when it took the original decision. The panel can take into account fresh information that was not available when the authority took the original decision, but it must be persuasive and it could have been available when the original decision was taken. Fresh matters that have occurred since the original decision was taken will not be taken into consideration.

To see how to prepare your case and challenge the admission authority's case, please see Chapter 5 for normal prejudice appeals; Chapter 6 for class size appeals; and Chapter 8 for preparing your case. The process is exactly the same as in England.

The record of proceedings

The Clerk should take notes during the hearing, including the voting and decisions, in such a way as the appeal panel requires. Such documents are the property of the appeal panel and they will not normally be released, but if a complaint is made to the Public Services Ombudsman, the practice now is that copies are normally supplied.

The decisions of appeal panels

The decision of appeal panels is binding on admission authorities. Panels are encouraged to reach a unanimous decision, but a majority decision will suffice.

Notification of the decision

The Clerk should write to you soon after the decisions have been taken and advise you of the outcome. The decision letter should provide full reasons why the panel reached the decision that it did. There is an expectation that you should receive the decision within five working days of your appeal. However, where there are multiple appeals this may not be possible.

Further appeals

You will not normally be permitted to appeal again within the same academic year, unless you can demonstrate a material change in circumstances. Examples of a change of circumstances are moving home and medical reasons that have arisen since the original decision was taken. If the admission authority accepts that there has been a material change of circumstances but it fails to offer a school place, this will trigger an immediate appeal.

Complaints

If you feel that you did not receive a fair hearing, you can contact the Public Services Ombudsman for Wales at the following address:

1 Ffordd yr Hen Gae
Pencoed CF35 5LJ

Tel: 01656 641 150

CHECKLIST 14

1 Did you receive at least ten working days' notice of the appeal?

2 Was the admission authority's statement sent to you at least five working days before the appeal?

3 Are you prepared to waive this if not?

4 Did you receive a guidance note from the admission authority?

5 Have you made a list of the persons you want to contact because you would like them to support your case?

6 Have you started to make a list of the issues that you want to raise at the appeal?

7 Do you know what type of appeal to expect?

8 Do you understand the role of the Clerk?

9 Do you understand the role of the presenting officer?

10 Do you understand what should be included in the authority's statement?

11 Do you know if your appeal will be dealt with as an individual appeal or as multiple appeals?

12 Do you understand the principles of natural justice?

13 Do you feel that you need to be represented?

14 Do you feel confident about representing yourself?

15 Have you obtained all of the supporting documentation for your appeal?

A flow chart showing the appeal process in Wales

The parent receives the decision from the admission authority refusing the place – the parent must be given at least ten school days to lodge an appeal

The parent lodges an appeal within the prescribed timetable set by the admission authority and receives a written acknowledgement

The parent must receive at least ten school days' notice of the date of the hearing

The parent prepares his response to the admission authority's statement

The Clerk must send a statement to the parents and panel at least five working days before the hearing

The admission authority must supply its statement to the Clerk at least seven days (five working days) before the hearing

The Clerk must send to the parents the name of the Clerk and panel members, the witnesses and information reasonably requested by the parents

THE DATE OF THE HEARING

The appeal decision should be sent by the Clerk to the parents and the admission authority within five working days

Appendix 1

Appeal statement for a grammar school

Appeal for Lorena Yeasts, aged 11, for a place in year 7

Paragraph 4.28 of the Code of Practice on School Admission Appeals refers to the preparation of a written statement which summarises how the admission arrangements for the school apply to the parents' application and a written statement which summarises the reasons for the decision; for instance, full supporting information that prejudice to the provision of efficient education or use of resources would arise from the admission of the child concerned. A statement referring to accommodation, class sizes and capacity should be supported by factual information. Evidence can be produced in the form of photographs or a video, as well as layout plans of a building.

Paragraph 4.61 states that it is not enough for the admission authority to show that the admission number has been reached; it should also demonstrate what prejudice would be caused by the additional admission.

The following guidance is issued by the Local Government Ombudsman (LGO) in his Special Report dated March 2004.

The content of the authority's statement must be adequate. The Appeals Code gives good guidance on this point. We would like to highlight some points and add some supplementary points as follows:

- The document must explain, with full supporting information, why the admission authority considers that the admission of an additional child (or children) would cause prejudice to efficient education or the efficient use of resources.

- The document must demonstrate the nature of the prejudice (that is, specifically what harm would be caused by additional admissions).

- The information should include how the year group will be organised and the size of the classes (because, for example, there would be a significant difference in how a parent would need to approach the appeal, depending whether the intake of, say, 240 children would be organised in eight classes of 30 or nine classes of 26/27).

- If classes are small, some reference should be made to the reason for that (e.g. that the classrooms are small).

- In respect of the school appealed for, there should be a statement of the breakdown of successful admissions (that is, how many were admitted under each criterion).

- The document for each individual parent should explain why the child was refused a place, with relevant supporting information (e.g. if the distance from home to school is the explanation, there should be information about what this is and what is the furthest distance from home to school for children accepted under the distance criterion).

- There should be sufficient information to enable the parents to reach a proper view on whether the admission criteria were correctly applied, and for parents to be able to prepare any questions and points that they want to put.

The above details set out what the admission authority should submit in its statement to the appeal panel in order to demonstrate that prejudice will be caused by Lorena's admission. We will demonstrate below that the school has not, in our view, demonstrated prejudice to either efficient education or use of resources and it has not produced any evidence to substantiate the claims being made.

We will start by dealing with the admission arrangements. First of all, we would like to acknowledge that it is a very difficult exercise that the school has in ensuring that the arrangements are properly complied with and that all applicants have been dealt with fairly. However, we do feel that there have been a number of unfortunate incidents that have conspired to put Lorena in a less fortuitous position than other candidates.

We acknowledge the scores that she achieved in the original tests. However, according to the original letter from the school dated 30 March 2007, Lorena's confirmed scores were 117 for verbal reasoning, 22 for Maths and 14 for the essay, giving a total of 153 marks. Yet, after we appealed, the figure quoted in the school's statement to the appeal panel says that the mark for the essay was 12 and not 14. It also confirms that, following a re-mark, Lorena's verbal reasoning paper was adjusted to 116 and, following the re-mark of the Maths paper, her score was adjusted to 27. This gave her a total score of 155, which put her in the borderline zone.

What this does show, in this particular case, is how critical one mark is between a place being offered and not. The statement confirms that those candidates who achieved a score of 155 to 158 had their books scrutinised. However, because of the fault with the marking of the Maths test, Lorena's books were not scrutinised because her original score was outside this zone. But, of course, since the error had been discovered, and her marks adjusted, Lorena's score brought her within the range where her books would have been scrutinised, but this has not happened. We believe that this situation has unfairly discriminated against her.

You will also see that in the statement the governors have stated that three applicants, who scored below 158, were offered places because of exceptionally high verbal reasoning scores. We would respectfully point out that, because of the marks available for the three tests, a considerable weighting is already given to the outcome of the verbal reasoning test, since it accounts for 140 marks out of a possible 210, equivalent to 66 per cent. We would also point out that nowhere in the admission criteria or supporting documentation does it say that those pupils who achieve an exceptional score in this test would, in effect, be given priority, even through the total score did not achieve the cut-off score of 158.

In addition, we do find it puzzling that School B does not cover algebra in the curriculum when it is clear that it forms a significant part of the Maths paper and that if Lorena had achieved an extra mark, she would have qualified for a place at the school. We, therefore, feel that these events have conspired to place Lorena at a distinct disadvantage compared to other pupils.

We now look at the school itself. The net capacity for the school is 764 and the number of pupils on roll is quoted as 754, which is ten below the capacity. We also note that the published admission number is 145 and yet the school has offered 152 places. In our view, this renders the arguments put forward about the school meaningless, since the school has voluntarily exceeded the published admission number and, presumably, it would not have done this if it was not satisfied that the school could not cope with these numbers. The school refers to six classes of 25/26. We would argue that Lorena's admission would not cause these figures to be exceeded, since if there were six classes of 26, the number on roll would be 156 and therefore we do not consider that the school has demonstrated that her admission will cause prejudice. Her admission would be consistent with the recommendations of the Working

Party (established by the school to consider the optimum size of classes) in that classes would not exceed 26, and indeed there would be three classes of 25 and three classes of 26.

We will now look at the performance of the school. We will, first of all, look at the performance for Key Stage 3.

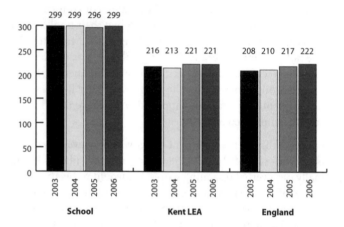

This shows that the results for the school are quite outstanding. The scores are for the three core subjects of English, Maths and Science and the percentage of pupils that achieve the expected level or better. Therefore, the maximum score would be 300. As can be seen, the scores for the school range from 296 to 299. All these scores are substantially better than the local and national averages.

We will now look at the Key Stage 4 figures.

5+A*-C (and equivalent) including English and Maths GCSEs

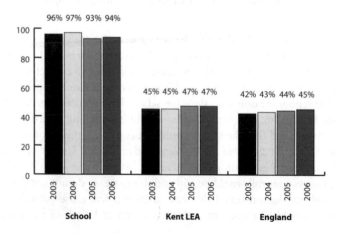

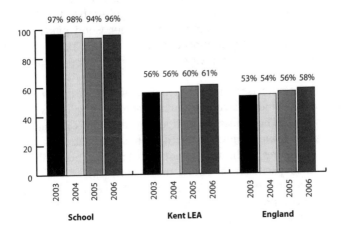

5+A*-C (and equivalent)

Again, these are quite outstanding results. There is nothing here to suggest that Lorena's admission will cause any problems for the school.

Let us see what an independent assessment provides. Ofsted provides an independent assessment of a range of educational issues so we will look and see what it has to say. The last inspection was carried out in March 2003.

HOW GOOD THE SCHOOL IS

This is a distinctive school with many strengths; some of which are outstanding. It has a very well-defined ethos, which enables many of its pupils and students to achieve very high standards, both academically and personally. Results in National Curriculum tests, and in GCSE and GCE examinations, are consistently well above average, although a minority of pupils underachieve. The overall quality of teaching is good. The head teacher leads the school very effectively, in conjunction with the senior staff, and their leadership and management are good overall. The provision for boarding is very good. The school gives good value for money.

HOW THE SCHOOL HAS IMPROVED SINCE ITS LAST INSPECTION

The school was last inspected in 1997. The overall improvement has been good. In relation to the key issues, the head teacher has initiated effective procedures to monitor and evaluate teaching and learning. Curriculum shortcomings have been well addressed, although there are still some shortcomings for information and communication technology and design and technology. Standards have improved overall, as evidenced in the results and the quality of teaching, and in the roles of subject leaders. The school recognises that it still needs to improve the use of assessment data further. Good plans exist for improving the accommodation and there is good potential in the overall management and governance for further improvement.

These are brief extracts from the last report. However, we do not accept that the school has demonstrated that Lorena's admission will cause problems for the school. The evidence provided by the admission authority is unsubstantiated and is not supported by the information in the DCSF performance figures, or the most recent Ofsted report. The numbers on roll are below the capacity for the school and, in any event, Lorena's admission will not exceed the recommended 25/26 pupils per class. The school has already exceeded the published number, which, in our view, invalidates the school's arguments.

Nevertheless, we believe that there are strong and compelling reasons for Lorena to attend the school and we, therefore, invite the panel to allow this appeal.

Appendix 2

Appeal statement for a secondary school

Appeal for Ben Pither

Paragraph 4.28 of the Code of Practice on School Admission Appeals refers to the preparation of a written statement which summarises how the admission arrangements for the school apply to the parents' application and a written statement which summarises the reasons for the decision; for instance, full supporting information that prejudice to the provision of efficient education or use of resources would arise from the admission of the child concerned. A statement referring to accommodation, class sizes and capacity should be supported by factual information. Evidence can be produced in the form of photographs or a video, as well as layout plans of a building.

Paragraph 4.61 states that it is not enough for the admission authority to show that the admission number has been reached; it should also demonstrate what prejudice would be caused by the additional admission.

The following guidance is issued by the Local Government Ombudsman (LGO) in his Special Report dated March 2004.

> The content of the authority's statement must be adequate. The Appeals Code gives good guidance on this point. We would like to highlight some points and add some supplementary points as follows:
>
> - The document must explain, with full supporting information, why the admission authority considers that the admission of an additional child (or children) would cause prejudice to efficient education or the efficient use of resources.

- The document must demonstrate the nature of the prejudice (that is, specifically what harm would be caused by additional admissions).

- The information should include how the year group will be organised and the size of the classes (because, for example, there would be a significant difference in how a parent would need to approach the appeal, depending whether the intake of, say, 240 children would be organised in eight classes of 30 or nine classes of 26/27).

- If classes are small, some reference should be made to the reason for that (e.g. that the classrooms are small).

- In respect of the school appealed for, there should be a statement of the breakdown of successful admissions (that is, how many were admitted under each criterion).

- The document for each individual parent should explain why the child was refused a place, with relevant supporting information (e.g. if the distance from home to school is the explanation, there should be information about what this is and what is the furthest distance from home to school for children accepted under the distance criterion).

- There should be sufficient information to enable the parents to reach a proper view on whether the admission criteria were correctly applied, and for parents to be able to prepare any questions and points that they want to put.

The above details set out what the admission authority should submit in its statement to the appeal panel in order to demonstrate that prejudice will be caused by Ben's admission. We believe that the admission authority has failed to do this. We will show below that the school has not, in our view, produced any evidence to substantiate the claims being made.

The net capacity for the school is 1,080. We do not know the number of pupils on roll since the admission authority has not provided this information in its statement. Neither do we know the numbers in each of the different year groups because, again, this information is not included in the admission authority's statement. However, we do know that in January 2006 there were 1,068 pupils on roll, as this figure is mentioned in the statistics provided by the Department for Children, Schools and Families (DCSF).

However, we note from the figures, provided by the school in the net capacity calculations, that the maximum number of work places, according to the measurements within the school, is 1,175, which would accommodate an intake of 235 pupils per year. The ten per cent range, allowed in the net capacity calculations, that produces the minimum number of work places is simply a mathematical calculation by multiplying the maximum number by 90 per cent. Therefore, it is fair to say that the more accurate figure based on actual room sizes is the maximum figure. The net capacity range for the school is 1,175 to 1,058. While we acknowledge that the admission authority can determine the net capacity as anywhere within the net capacity range, in this case the agreed net capacity is at the lower end of the range.

We note that the school has adopted a figure of 1,080 and the school has sought to justify this number in relation to set sizes. However, we note that the school provides for eight forms of entry, which result in classes of 27. In addition, the school claims that the basic classrooms in Maths, English, French and Humanities are small. However, we would point out that of the 28 classrooms so designated, only five are below the size required for 27 pupils; and, in fact, most are large enough to accommodate 30 pupils. So we find this statement grossly misleading.

The school claims that there are 31 out of 58 teaching rooms that are only adequate for 30 pupils or fewer. This suggests that the other classrooms are large enough to accommodate more than 30 pupils. We would respectfully point out that Ben's admission would not cause any class to exceed 30. In fact, his admission would result in only one class increasing to 28, which is well within the maximum figures provided by both the school, in its statement, and in the net capacity figures attached to it.

We will now look at the performance of the school. We will look first at the figures for Key Stage 3.

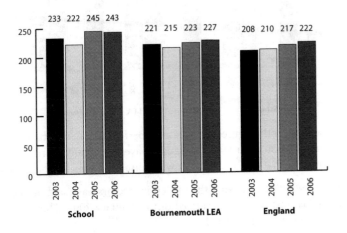

As can be seen, the figures are significantly better than both the local and national averages. This does not suggest that the numbers on roll, nor Ben's admission, is likely to compromise this result.

We will now look at the GCSE results.

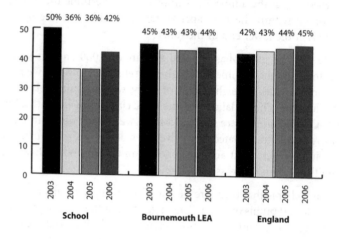

5+A*-C (and equivalent) including English and Maths GCSEs

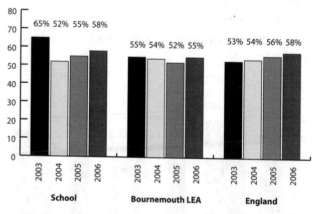

5+A*-C (and equivalent)

As can be seen by the figures, the school is performing better than the local average and it is on a par with the national average. Again, there is nothing here to suggest that Ben's admission will cause problems for the school.

We will now look to see what the Ofsted inspectors have said on their last visit. The last inspection was carried out in January 2003. The number of pupils on roll at the time was 1,068.

INFORMATION ABOUT THE SCHOOL

School A is a foundation secondary modern school for boys aged 11 to 16 years. This oversubscribed school has 1,068 pupils on roll. This is about the same size as for secondary schools nationally and about the same size as at the last inspection. The attainment of the pupils on entry to the school was below the national average for the current Years 8 to 11 and this is not unexpected in a secondary modern school operating within a selective system. Since 1999, the attainment on entry has improved greatly each year and, for the Year 7 in 2002, was broadly in line with the national average. 150 pupils have been identified as having special educational needs by the school and this figure, as a percentage, is broadly in line with the national average. Two pupils have been provided with statements of special educational needs by the Local Education Authority (LEA); as a percentage, this figure is well below the national average. The number of pupils with statements of special educational needs has declined since the last inspection, in line with the LEA's policy of devolution of much of the special educational needs funding to schools. The number of pupils who have mother tongues not believed to be English is 32 and, as a percentage, this figure is broadly in line with national figures. No pupils have been identified as asylum seekers or refugees. The number of pupils eligible for free school meals is 98 and, as a percentage, this figure is broadly in line with the national average. The school serves much of the area of Bournemouth, and the family circumstances of the pupils are in line with those nationally. The school has applied for specialist business college status.

What the school does well

- Standards at GCSE in Art and Design, Design and Technology, Drama, English Language and English Literature, Information and Communication Technology (ICT) and Religious Education (RE) were well above the national average in 2002.
- The achievement of pupils is very good.
- The quality of teaching and learning is very good.
- The personal development of the pupils is very good, as are their attitudes and behaviour.
- Leadership and management are very good. The leadership of the head teacher is excellent.
- Financial planning and management are excellent.
- The school's care and welfare for the pupils is very good.

- The range of extra-curricular activities is very good.

What could be improved?

- Attainment in Science in Years 10 and 11, which is below that of English and Maths.

TEACHING AND LEARNING

Teaching of pupils in Years 7–9 and Years 10–11

The quality of teaching and learning is very good overall and contributes significantly to the very good achievement of pupils. The teaching is excellent in Art and Design and it is very good in English, Design and Technology, Music, ICT and RE (in Years 10 and 11), and in GCSE courses for physical education and dance. Most teachers have a very good knowledge and understanding of their subjects. They have very high expectations. Their management of pupils is very good. They make very good use of resources. Literacy across the curriculum is taught well, while numeracy across the curriculum is taught satisfactorily. The teaching in the school meets the needs of the majority of pupils well. The needs of higher attaining pupils are not always met. Pupils acquire skills very well and demonstrate considerable intellectual, physical and creative efforts. They work very productively, showing a very great deal of interest. They have a very good knowledge of how well they are learning. The quality of teaching and learning in the extra-curricular activities contributes very well to the standards the pupils attain in many subjects.

HOW WELL THE SCHOOL IS LED AND MANAGED

Aspect	Comment
Leadership and management by the head teacher and other key staff.	Leadership and management are very good. The head teacher provides excellent leadership. There is a very clear vision of the school's educational priorities, linked very closely to maintaining very high standards.
How well the governors fulfil their responsibilities.	The governors fulfil their responsibilities well.
The school's evaluation of its performance.	The school evaluates its performance very well. Principles of competition and comparison in obtaining services and resources are very well applied.

The strategic use of resources.	There is very good strategic use of resources. Financial planning and management are excellent.

There is considerable attention to detail and the rigorous implementation of school procedures. The impact of the monitoring and evaluation roles of middle managers is not always consistent. Staffing is good overall. **The accommodation is good, as are the learning resources available.**

The absence figures for the school are 8.6 per cent and this means that, each and every day, there are 46 pupils who are not present. This is in addition to those not present due to school trips and examination leave.

The figures above show that the school performs significantly better than the local and national averages and there is nothing in the school's statement to suggest that Ben's admission will cause any problems for the school. Therefore, we do not accept that the school has demonstrated that Ben's admission will cause problems for the school. The evidence provided by the admission authority is unsubstantiated and is not supported by the information in the DCSF performance figures, or the most recent Ofsted report. The numbers on roll are significantly below the capacity for the school. We therefore invite the appeal panel to allow this appeal.

Appendix 3

Appeal statement for a class size appeal

Appeal for Trisha Johns

Paragraph 4.28 of the Code of Practice on School Admission Appeals refers to the preparation of a written statement which summarises how the admission arrangements for the school apply to the parents' application and a written statement which summarises the reasons for the decision; for instance, full supporting information that prejudice to the provision of efficient education or use of resources would arise from the admission of the child concerned. A statement referring to accommodation, class sizes and capacity should be supported by factual information. Evidence can be produced in the form of photographs or a video, as well as layout plans of a building.

Paragraph 4.61 states that it is not enough for the admission authority to show that the admission number has been reached; it should also demonstrate what prejudice would be caused by the additional admission.

The following guidance is issued by the Local Government Ombudsman (LGO) in his Special Report dated March 2004.

> The content of the authority's statement must be adequate. The Appeals Code gives good guidance on this point. We would like to highlight some points and add some supplementary points as follows:
>
> - The document must explain, with full supporting information, why the admission authority considers that the admission of an additional child (or children) would cause prejudice to efficient education or the efficient use of resources.
>
> - The document must demonstrate the nature of the prejudice

- (that is, specifically what harm would be caused by additional admissions).

- The information should include how the year group will be organised and the size of the classes (because, for example, there would be a significant difference in how a parent would need to approach the appeal, depending whether the intake of, say, 240 children would be organised in eight classes of 30 or nine classes of 26/27).

- If classes are small, some reference should be made to the reason for that (e.g. that the classrooms are small).

- In respect of the school appealed for, there should be a statement of the breakdown of successful admissions (that is, how many were admitted under each criterion).

- The document for each individual parent should explain why the child was refused a place, with relevant supporting information (e.g. if the distance from home to school is the explanation, there should be information about what this is and what is the furthest distance from home to school for children accepted under the distance criterion).

- There should be sufficient information to enable the parents to reach a proper view on whether the admission criteria were correctly applied, and for parents to be able to prepare any questions and points that they want to put.

The above details set out what the admission authority should submit in its statement to the appeal panel in order to demonstrate that prejudice will be caused by Trisha's admission. We will demonstrate below that the school has not produced any evidence to substantiate the claims being made.

We will deal with the prejudice issues first. We note the legislative requirements and reliance placed on them by the school. We acknowledge that the published capacity for the school is 210 places and we are informed that there are 29 pupils in reception, 30 pupils in Years 1 to 5 and 35 pupils in Year 6. The school has explained that, to admit Trisha, the school will have to employ another teacher. However, no information has been given by the school on the numbers of teachers currently being employed by the school and no information has been given about the pupil/teacher ratio. In the circumstances the school is assuming that because the school operates a one-form entry, that any additional admissions above 30 will require the school to employ an additional teacher without producing any information to support the claim being made. The very strong assumption made is that any admission will require the employment of an additional teacher so that the statutory requirements are not breached.

The school goes on to explain the implications of recruiting another teacher and the implications on the school's resources should this be the case. However, the school has not given any information on how many teachers the school currently employs and the pupil/teacher ratio to verify the claim being made. Therefore, in the absence of this information, we would argue that the school has not demonstrated that Trisha's admission will require qualifying measures. Equally, the school has not provided any plans of the school to demonstrate that additional accommodation will be required if Trisha were to be admitted. Although reference is made to inadequately sized accommodation, the school has not said that Trisha's admission would require further accommodation and therefore we assume that this would not be an issue.

Therefore, in the absence of any evidence to the contrary, we do not believe that the school has demonstrated that Trisha's admission would require the school to employ another teacher and that this appeal should be dealt with as a class size appeal.

Under Section 122 of the Education Act 2002, and the Education (School Teachers' Prescribed Qualifications, etc.) Order 2003, a school teacher has been defined as head teachers, qualified teachers, overseas trained teachers, instructors with special qualifications or experience, staff on an employment-based teacher training scheme, graduate teachers, registered teachers, student teachers, and teacher trainees yet to pass the skills tests.

Under the Education (Specified Work and Registration) (England) Regulations 2003 support staff may carry out 'specified work', such as delivering lessons to pupils, within infant classes in certain circumstances. In practice, this means that, although a school with infant classes must have sufficient school teachers to be able to teach infants in groups of 30 or fewer per teacher, a support staff member may 'teach' infant groups when a teacher is not available (e.g. when a teacher is away from his class on his planning, preparation and assessment time (PPA)), provided that the support staff member meets the following criteria:

- The head teacher must be satisfied of the support staff's skills, expertise and experience to carry out such work;

- The work carried out must be in order to assist or support the work of a school teacher; and

- He must be subject to the direction and supervision of a school teacher (supervision does not mean that the teacher must be alongside the teaching assistant or higher level teaching assistant, etc., but he must be able to ensure that the member of support staff is effectively teaching the class).

Therefore, we do not accept that the school has demonstrated that this should be a class size appeal.

We now look at the application of the admission criteria. We note that the governors have acknowledged that Trisha had been placed as equal thirtieth, based on the distance criteria. In the circumstances, the governors accepted her twin David's application on the basis that it was the first to be considered by the governing body. It is clear from the comments in the statement that the governors were aware that there were two applications of equal merit, which the governors were unable to separate.

We have checked with a number of other admission authorities to see what the practice is elsewhere. We have found that many admission authorities do give priority to twins and exceed the published number to ensure that such children attend the same school. We have examples of practices of other admission authorities. However, we have also discovered that where other authorities have faced similar situations, these authorities approach the parents to see what they would wish to do. Given such circumstances, we would have selected Trisha because we feel that she is more vulnerable and less likely to come to terms with such a change.

In the circumstances, we believe that such an oversight constitutes a mistake in the application of the published admission criteria that otherwise would have resulted in a place being offered. We also feel, as we have explained in our earlier submission, that it is unreasonable to expect the twins to be separated at this stage in their development. We do not believe that Trisha's admission will cause prejudice to the school.

We have looked at the performance of the school, which is quite outstanding.

Pupils achieving expected level or above

	School				Hounslow LEA				England			
	2003	2004	2005	2006	2003	2004	2005	2006	2003	2004	2005	2006
	294	281	297	291	234	235	241	243	234	237	240	242

Pupils achieving above the expected level

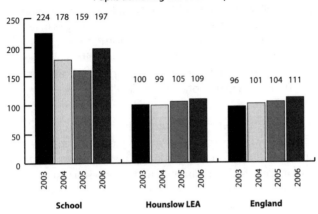

Therefore, there is no indication here that Trisha's admission will cause prejudice for the school. The above figures show the percentage of pupils that achieve the expected level or above for the three core subjects of English, Maths and Science. The maximum score is therefore 300.

We have also looked at the most recent Ofsted report, which was carried out in May 2007 when there were 244 pupils reported as being on roll. We acknowledge that this includes the nursery.

OVERALL EFFECTIVENESS OF THE SCHOOL

Grade: 2

School A is a good school with a number of outstanding features. Many of these relate to the high quality of the school's provision for promoting the personal development of its pupils. After a period of uncertainty during the year taken to appoint a new head teacher in 2006, the school is now making rapid progress improving all aspects of its provision. The parents hold this school in high regard. A good proportion of the parents returned the inspection questionnaires, and these were extremely positive in almost all areas surveyed. Many included positive comments, one of which sums up the views expressed in many others: 'Going to School A is like going home. Children love the warm family atmosphere'. Children in the nursery and reception classes are given a good start to their education. When children begin school at the age of three their attainment is above what is normally expected at this age. The school successfully builds on this good start and ensures that pupils achieve well and make good progress in all year groups. This is because pupils are taught well and the excellent curriculum provides them with a very wide range of interesting and exciting activities.

By the time pupils leave, at the end of Year 6, their attainment is consistently well above the national average in English, Maths and Science. The school's high expectations for all of its pupils in all areas of learning are evident; for example, in the excellent standard of singing. A key factor in the school's success is the excellent climate for learning in all classes. This stems from the outstanding personal development of the pupils. They behave exceptionally well in lessons, and they show a real desire to learn.

School A is a school in which every individual child really does matter. The pupils are warmly welcomed and equally valued. The school's good provision for the care, guidance and support of its pupils ensures that they feel secure. Within this provision, the quality of pastoral care is outstanding. The school provides good academic guidance for its pupils because the teachers know their pupils well. There is a clear system for checking on what individual pupils know and can do. This is relatively new, and the school recognises that it now needs to be developed.

Currently, it does not provide an overview of each pupil's progress from the foundation stage through to Year 6, nor does it incorporate the full range of subjects taught.

The driving force behind the school's success is its good leadership and management. In particular, the head teacher and her deputy make an excellent team and they provide outstanding direction for the work of the school. At present, too much of the responsibility for monitoring the day-to-day work of the school rests with the senior managers. They realise that they have to share this workload and develop the leadership skills of teaching staff with their responsibility as curriculum co-ordinators. This will help broaden the monitoring of the pupils' achievements to include all subject areas.

The school has made sound progress in addressing the single issue for improvement from its last inspection. Work to improve the outdoor provision for the foundation stage was delayed by the change in leadership, but this issue is now being tackled. The school is now very well placed to move forward on all fronts.

PERSONAL DEVELOPMENT AND WELL-BEING

Grade: 1

Pupils' outstanding spiritual, moral, social and cultural development underpins all aspects of school life. Particularly noteworthy is the excellent social development of pupils. The work of the school council not only gives pupils first-hand experiences of democracy in action, but it also enables them to help enhance the facilities that the school has to offer. For example, following representations by school council representatives, blinds have been provided in all rooms and there have been improvements in the playground equipment provided for pupils.

Pupils are bright and articulate, and extremely proud of the school. Relationships throughout the school are excellent, and pupils are generally exceptionally well behaved. One pupil commented, 'I really like the way that everyone makes you feel welcome'. The pupils also feel happy that the very rare instances of bullying are quickly and sensitively dealt with.

Attendance rates are consistently well above the national average and they illustrate the pupils' exceptionally positive attitudes towards their school. Pupils are exceptionally well prepared for the next phase of their education and for a future as life-long learners. They have an excellent understanding of the importance of healthy lifestyles, a good awareness of how to keep safe, and have high levels of competence in basic skills.

CURRICULUM AND OTHER ACTIVITIES

Grade: 1

The curriculum is very well planned to ensure that pupils have a wide range of interesting experiences. The foundation stage curriculum acknowledges the way in which young children learn. There are very good opportunities for children in the nursery to make sensible choices of activities and also to work on tasks directed by adults. In the nursery, excellent use is made of the spacious premises and good levels of staffing to ensure that children are given the very best start possible. During the morning session, children in the reception class do not have easy access to the full range of equipment available because of difficulties presented by the layout of the accommodation. However, the school compensates for this, as well as it can, by accommodating the reception children in the empty nursery classroom during the afternoon sessions. While this is an unsatisfactory situation, the school has ensured that it does not adversely affect the children's learning. The delayed project to improve the outdoor learning area is now underway.

An outstanding feature of the curriculum is the emphasis placed on music, and many pupils receive either individual or small group tuition in a wide range of musical instruments. The school is good at promoting the cultural traditions of its pupils (e.g. through the Italian club). The school ensures that visits to places of interest or visitors to the school add interest and enjoyment to pupils' learning. Pupils with learning difficulties and disabilities are given clear educational direction through their individual education plans.

LEADERSHIP AND MANAGEMENT
Grade: 2

The impact of leadership is seen in the good progress made by the pupils. The new head teacher already knows the school well. She and her deputy work well in close partnership and they make good use of the information gathered from the regular monitoring of teaching to guide the school's development. However, the leadership acknowledges that its tracking systems require further refinement.

At present, most monitoring is carried out by the head teacher and deputy. This is because many staff lack experience and training in working as subject co-ordinators and having responsibility for leading aspects of the school's work.

Governance is good. Governors carefully monitor the work of the school, they know it very well, and are good at holding it to account. An excellent feature of governance is the way in which governors ensured the smooth running of the school and the maintenance of high academic standards during the year in which the school had no permanent head teacher. The excellent deputy head teacher had a strong role to play in providing continuity and direction during this period.

Therefore, we do not accept that the school has demonstrated that Trisha's admission will cause problems for the school. The evidence provided by the admission authority is, by and large, unsubstantiated and is not supported by the information in the Department for Children, Schools and Families (DCSF) performance figures, or the most recent Ofsted report, which was only carried out a few weeks ago.

In our view, the governors have not produced any evidence to support their view that Trisha's admission will require them to employ another teacher, and therefore prejudice has not been established.

Notwithstanding this, we believe that there are compelling reasons for Trisha to attend the school and we therefore invite the panel to allow this appeal.

Appendix 4

High Court decisions and Ombudsman reports on admission criteria

In this Appendix are High Court decisions and Ombudsman reports on admission criteria. Depending on the issues raised in your appeal, you will be able to quote the outcomes of these court cases to support your appeal. As part of some headings you will see 'ex parte' referred to. The appeal panel is not in a position to take or respond to legal action and so the Local Education Authority (LEA) may act on its behalf when it is challenged by parents. This is described as acting on behalf of an interested outside party.

- **Cummings v Birkenhead Corporation (1972) Ch12**

  It was found that a policy based on catchment areas was not, in itself, unlawful. An admission authority can publish a general policy which it proposes to adopt in individual cases, provided that the policy is clearly not unreasonable, capricious or irrelevant.

- **R v the Shadow Education Committee of the London Borough of Greenwich ex parte the governors of John Ball School (1990) 154 LGRev672**

  It was found that it was illegal for a Local Education Authority (LEA) to have a policy that gives priority to pupils living within its own administrative boundaries over pupils belonging to another area.

- **R v the Royal Borough of Kingston upon Thames ex parte Kingwell (1992) 1FLR182**

  It was found that the LEA can have a reasonable policy it thinks fit, provided that it does not conflict with its duties under legislation.

- **R v the governors of the Bishop Challenor Roman Catholic Comprehensive Girls School and another ex parte Choudhury (1992) 3WLR99**

  It was found that an oversubscribed voluntary aided school was entitled to operate an admission policy intended to preserve the character of the school.

- **R v Bradford Council ex parte Ali (The Times 21/10/1993)**

  It was found that the council was entitled to take into account traditional links between a school and the areas from which it draws pupils, as well as long journeys which children living in the peripheral areas of Bradford would have to make if they could not go to their local school.

- **R v Lancashire County Council ex parte West (unreported 1994)**

  It was found that the random allocation of pupils was not unlawful.

- **R v Lancashire County Council ex parte Foster (1995) 1FCR212 (1995) ELR 33**

  It was found that the council policy of allocating Roman Catholic children in non-denominational schools only after other applications had been dealt with was deemed to be valid.

- **R v the governors of La Sainte Union Convent School ex parte T (1996) ELR 98**

  The admission criteria for the school required the pupil to be a baptised Roman Catholic and also one of both parents should be practising Roman Catholics. The governors did not accept that T fulfilled the parental requirement because she had no contact with her mother, who was a practising Catholic and her father was not a Roman Catholic.

  It was held that the parental test was met, even though T did not have any contact with her mother. It was also held that the word 'parent' had to be given its ordinary definition, which was wider than a person playing a parental role.

- **R v Wiltshire County Council ex parte Razazan (1997) ELR**

  It was held that the council policy giving lower priority to those pupils living outside the school's designated area, if the pupil had priority at a school elsewhere, was held to be valid.

- **R v Rotherham Metropolitan Borough Council ex parte Clark and others (1998) ELR 152**

  It was held that parents must be given an opportunity to express a preference for a school and also give reasons for their choice.

- **R v Sheffield City Council ex parte H (1999) ELR 511**

The council asked parents to give a reason for their preference, only if they were seeking a place at a school outside of their catchment area.

It was held that this was unlawful. The court decided that the fact that a parent could, on his own initiative, provide written reasons for his preference across the form was insufficient and unrealistic; it was insufficient because there was no space on the form for the parent to express a preference and it was unrealistic because very few parents would know of their right to be able to express reasons for a preference unless they were expressly informed about it.

- **R v Rotherham Metropolitan Borough Council ex parte Tomlinson (2000) ELR 76**

The applicants lived in Nottinghamshire, which was in the adjoining administrative council area. The parents applied to an oversubscribed school, which was outside both the catchment area and the LEA area. It was submitted that the use of a catchment area effectively meant that treating applicants equally could not be achieved.

It was held that the policy was not unlawful because if a geographical test was lawful, then so was a catchment area test.

- **R v Stockton-on-Tees Borough Council and another ex parte W (2000) ELR 93**

Six parents were unsuccessful in securing a place at their preferred school and they lost their subsequent appeals. One of the challenges at the High Court was that the council did not have a published policy about admissions outside the normal admissions round, and therefore if an application was received after the admission date, the authority would admit a child to the school for his admission area.

The application was rejected on the basis that, in the absence of a published policy, each application would be dealt with on an ad hoc basis. The absence of such a policy could not be interpreted that any application received after the closing date would result in a guaranteed place.

- **R v the independent appeal panel for Sacred Heart High School ex parte L (unreported 2001)**

This was an application to review the decision of an appeal panel dismissing the applicant's appeal. The admission criteria for the school required the applicant to place the school as first preference and also to be from a practising Roman Catholic family committed to the local community and with parish priest support.

The parish priest supported the application, but the applicant was not a Roman Catholic. At an interview, the child admitted attending church fortnightly and was unable to answer some questions about Catholicism. The application was rejected and a subsequent appeal was unsuccessful. The appeal panel was not convinced that there were compelling reasons to outweigh prejudice to the school.

It was held that there was no error in law by the appeal panel and that the panel had correctly considered the commitment to the Catholic faith. The mother was not Roman Catholic and attendance at church was fortnightly, and not weekly, as was clearly understood in the admission criteria.

- **R v the school admission appeal panel for the London Borough of Hounslow (unreported 2002)**

The admission criteria for the council gave priority to children that lived nearer to the school rather than siblings of children already at the school. It was claimed that it was unfair not to give priority to siblings. The parents argued that the policy was unlawful and unreasonable.

It was held that the policy was lawful and not unreasonable.

- **Complaint 92/B/1358**

The council operated a policy that application forms for secondary schools were sent to primary schools, which would then distribute them to parents of pupils in Year 6 via the pupils themselves. One parent did not receive a form because her child was not attending a school which the LEA knew.

The Ombudsman decided that this constituted maladministration because the council had failed in its legal duty to enable every parent to express a preference.

- **Complaint 92/B/1810**

The admission criteria for a school were as follows:

- Children whose parents have specific educational reasons which the County Council is satisfied make the school particularly suitable to meet the needs of a child.

- Children whose parents have other significant reasons for preferring the school.

The Ombudsman found that the admission criteria were not clear and consistent and, therefore, this constituted maladministration.

- **Complaint 93/C/3280**

  The admission criteria for an admission authority stated:

  'Selection made by reference to geographical factors, that is, nearness and ease of access to the preferred school in relation to other appropriate schools where there are places available; reasons put forward by parents will be taken into account at this stage, exceptional and compelling reasons for the preferred school being permitted to override geographical considerations.'

  The Ombudsman found that this constituted maladministration because the information was not clear; there were no details given as to how comparisons between applicants would be made, and there was no explanation as to how the 'nearness' and 'ease of access' would be applied.

- **Complaint 96/A/2072**

  The council had four published admission criteria and it informed the Ombudsman that the criteria were set out in priority order, but this was not clearly explained in any published material.

  The Ombudsman found maladministration because he said that it was very important that parents knew in what order places would be allocated under the various criteria.

- **Complaint 99/A/1972**

  A child attended an infant school that was traditionally a feeder school for a junior school, which was made clear in the published admission criteria. The child was refused a place at the junior school.

  Some children were refused places at junior schools despite attending the recognised feeder school because, although the junior school was their nearest school, there were alternative local junior schools which they could attend that were not options for some children who lived further away from the school.

  The Ombudsman found maladministration because priority should have been given to children attending the feeder school, which was explained in the published admission criteria. In addition, there was nothing in the published criteria which made any reference to alternative schools that children could attend being one of the criteria that would be taken into account.

- **Complaint 00/B/3593**

  One of the admission criteria that were used to determine places was distance from school. The distance was measured on a street map, but houses were not indicated on the map that was used by the admission authority.

The Ombudsman found maladministration that had caused injustice because the distance had been incorrectly measured, resulting in a place being denied. The computer generated programme relied on postcodes and not houses, and the position of the house had been incorrectly plotted.

- ### Complaint 00/B/4686

The parents applied for an out-of-catchment school and submitted their preference form before the closing date for applications. At the closing date the school was undersubscribed. However, before allocations were made, the admission authority contacted parents who had not submitted applications and, as a result, the number of applications exceeded the number of available places. The admission authority then applied the admission criterion, which was nearness to the school, and, as a result, the parent who submitted an on-time application but lived outside the catchment area was refused a place.

The Ombudsman found maladministration that caused injustice because the admission authority had not complied with its statutory duty to give parental choice in allocating school places. All on-time applications should have been dealt with before any late applications were considered and therefore the parents had been incorrectly denied a place at the school of their choice.

- ### Complaint 03/A/4304

One of the oversubscription criteria stated that applicants must have 'the highest level of church commitment', but there was no information published as to how this level of commitment would be assessed.

The Ombudsman found that this was maladministration.

- ### Complaint 05/A/2672

One of the complaints in this case involved the measurement between home and school and the measurement used as a tie break within an admission criterion.

The Ombudsman found maladministration that resulted in injustice. The tie break was described as 'the proximity of the child's house to the school, as measured on a map, with those living nearest to the school being accorded the higher priority'.

According to the admission authority, this was measured according to the council's criterion of the appropriate walking route to the main school building. The governors used the measurements from the council without any further examination. The governors said that they did not have the resources to check the distances for all the applicants, but the distance information was only needed to differentiate between applicants in the same criterion.

The council's distance measurement for applications was the distance as measured by road, using the home to school walking distance by recognised footpaths. This was not the same as the distance measurement as defined by the governors. The map provided, showing the route plotted by the computer, did not conform to the description of either the council or the governors. The route plotted was not the obvious home to school route and the final part of the route cut across one front and two back gardens to reach the school. The distance measured was approximately double the actual distance. The Ombudsman said that the parent was right to question the distance and the governors were at fault for not checking it.

• Complaint 05/B/3214

A mother complained that faults in the council's admission procedures had wrongly denied her a place at her preferred school and that an appeal panel failed to properly consider whether the admission arrangements had been correctly applied.

The Ombudsman found maladministration that caused injustice because the council had failed to take steps to overcome a computer system failure and ensure that it co-ordinated its admission arrangements with neighbouring education authorities in accordance with the published scheme. This had resulted in some parents receiving more than one offer of a school place. In addition, the council had also failed to have regard to the law and relevant Codes of Practice in the way the waiting lists operated when reallocating places.

The parent was offered a place at her preferred school and she was also awarded £500 to recognise the impact of the council's actions.

Appendix 5

High Court decisions and Ombudsman reports on the principles of natural justice

As part of one heading you will see 'ex parte' referred to. The appeal panel is not in a position to take or respond to legal action and so the Local Education Authority (LEA) may act on its behalf when it is challenged by parents. This is described as acting on behalf of an interested outside party.

- **R v the governors of St Gregory's Roman Catholic Aided School and another ex parte Roberts (1995)**

  The pupil, or the parent, was not given the opportunity to make representations to the governors. This was a breach of the principles of natural justice.

  However, there was an appeal which was properly conducted and it was held that this validated the decision of the original flawed hearing.

- **Complaint 95/B/1501**

  The parents arrived prior to the commencement of their appeal and found the appeal panel members talking to the head teacher and the governors' representative.

  The Ombudsman found that, irrespective of what discussions took place, the appearance of bias was clearly given to the parents and this was maladministration.

- **Complaint 95/C/0729**

  The deputy head, who was representing the school, was alone with the appeal panel before the parents arrived for the appeal.

The Ombudsman found that this was maladministration.

- **Complaint 96/C/1237**

The appeal committee visited the school in question and spoke to the teacher with no parent present.

The Ombudsman found maladministration.

- **Complaint 96/C/1511**

A member of an appeal panel was a governor of the school which was the subject of the appeal. The appeal panel took into consideration his experience and knowledge of the school and also details about another unsuccessful appeal by the same parents for the same child.

The Ombudsman found maladministration.

- **Complaint 96/C/1517**

Multiple appeals – a representative of the admission authority remained with the appeal panel while one set of parents left the room and another set of parents came into the room. The Chair indicated that it would only be a matter of seconds before the next set of parents arrived.

The Ombudsman found maladministration.

- **Complaint 97/A/821**

Prior to the appeals starting and before any parents were present, the Clerk gave the appeal panel information about the school's admission policy, the criteria for admission, the number of applications received, the number of places offered, the area from which pupils had been offered places on the grounds of proximity and the problems caused by the lack of school places in the borough.

The Ombudsman found maladministration because the parents that were appealing should have been allowed to hear the same information as the committee and they should have been given the opportunity to ask questions about it.

- **Complaint 98/C/1521**

An appeal panel received a briefing on the appeal without the parents being present.

The Ombudsman found maladministration.

- **Complaint 99/A/1972**

The appeal panel allowed four appeals, but it was not certain about a fifth and it decided to ask the head teacher if she would admit four or five more children. This was done in the absence of the appellants.

The Ombudsman found maladministration because it was improper for the appeal panel to discuss any issues with the head teacher without the appellants being present.

Appendix 6

Complaints to the Ombudsman, and High Court decisions generally

As part of one heading you will see 'ex parte' referred to. The appeal panel is not in a position to take or respond to legal action and so the Local Education Authority (LEA) may act on its behalf when it is challenged by parents. This is described as acting on behalf of an interested outside party.

- **Complaint 93/B/1239**

  The head teacher of a school which was the subject of an appeal wrote to the Local Education Authority (LEA). The letter could have had an important bearing on the appeal panel's decision. The letter was not put before the appeal panel and the LEA representative informed the panel that there was no record of the letter having been received.

  The Ombudsman found maladministration because it was determined that the letter had been received by the council and if it had not been lost, the appeal may have been successful.

- **Complaint 94/B/2080**

  The parents were given less than 14 days' notice of the date of the appeal hearing and were not asked to waive this period.

  The Ombudsman found maladministration.

- **Complaint 95/A/1033**

  The parents were not given any information beforehand about the way that the appeal would be conducted.

  The Ombudsman found maladministration.

- ### Complaint 95/A/4400

  The parents complained to the Ombudsman that their appeal had not been successful and that they had not received a fair hearing.

  The Ombudsman found that he could not question the merits of an appeal panel's decision without maladministration.

- ### Complaint 95/B/1501

  The admission authority allocated 15 minutes for each appeal. There was no evidence that the parents would have presented a more detailed case if more time had been allowed for their appeal.

  The Ombudsman found no maladministration. However, if there was evidence that the parents would have presented a more detailed case, if they were allowed more time, then the Ombudsman would have found maladministration.

- ### Complaint 95/C/1721

  The standard admission number for a school was 190 and the admission authority offered 217 places. There were 20 appeals heard, including the complainant whose appeal was not successful. The appeals were held in May, although in previous years the appeals had been held in July. There were two successful appeals in July, by which time only 193 places had been taken up. At the beginning of the school term, 192 pupils turned up. There were a further seven appeals of which three were successfully heard by a different panel.

  The Ombudsman found maladministration by the council because if the complainant's appeal had been heard later, it may have been successful.

- ### Complaint 95/C/2111

  There were two appeals held for the same school and for the same year group held at different times. The council did not try to reconstitute the same appeal panel to hear both appeals.

  The Ombudsman found maladministration because the council should have attempted to use the same appeal panel.

- ### Complaint 97/A/2401

  The council only held appeals four times a year and an appellant was told in October that his appeal would not be heard until the next session of appeals in March.

  The Ombudsman found maladministration because the arrangements for appeals were inflexible, which prevented the council from dealing with appeals urgently where dictated by circumstances.

- **Complaint 98/C/2730**

The standard admission number for a school was 170, but the LEA decided that the school could accommodate 207 children. The LEA admitted 206 pupils, but the appellant was not offered a place.

It transpired that the appellant already had a child at the school but, following an incident at the school, the relationship between the parent and the teachers had broken down and this had also involved the police. It appeared that the breakdown in the relationship was one of the reasons given as to why the LEA had refused the appellant a place. This was also explained at the appeal hearing and also in the decision letter from the panel.

The Ombudsman found maladministration because the reasons given by the school did not comply with the published admission criteria and the child should have been offered a place. The reason given by the LEA was not a valid reason to refuse a place at the school.

- **Complaint 99/C/1876**

The allocation of places for community schools was the responsibility of the LEA. On 25 May 1999 the head teacher of a school wrote to five parents offering their children places at the school. The head teacher had no authority to do so. On 28 May 1999, three days later, the LEA wrote to the parents concerned withdrawing the offer of those places.

The Ombudsman found maladministration because the parents ought to be able to rely on an offer made by the head teacher and the withdrawal of the offer three days later was too long; the parents' expectation of the offer of places had not been overcome because of the delay. In a similar case, where the offer of places was withdrawn the same day, it was found that the parents' expectation had been overcome (see case below).

- **R v Beatrix Potter School ex parte K (1997) ELR 468**

In this case, the head teacher of the school purported to make an offer of a place without having the authority to do so because he had misunderstood the admission criteria for the school. It was held that the offer of a place had created a legitimate expectation on which the parent and the pupil could rely. However, the offer of the place was withdrawn the same day it had been made and the High Court found that, in those circumstances, the expectation of the parent and the pupil had been overcome.

- **Complaint 99/C/4658**

An appeal panel allowed an appeal, subject to the parents, who were making the claim, submitting proof that they were moving into the priority area for the school.

The Ombudsman found that this was maladministration because an appeal panel is not allowed to attach any conditions to a successful appeal.

- ### Complaint 99/C/5295

In this case the parents sought advice from the admission authority about the likelihood of a successful application and spoke to one of the admission officers. None of the applications were successful and so the parents appealed and were surprised to find that the officer representing the admission authority was the same person who advised them on the original application. As a result, they felt at a disadvantage.

Although it was not a breach of the Code of Practice, the Ombudsman criticised the fact that the education officer who had had contact with the parents before the appeal, and had advised them on their appeal, presented the case for the school at the appeal. The Ombudsman was concerned that the parents would be unsettled by the fact that, in their minds, the officer had changed from being advisor to adversary. In addition, the officer would have had an unfair advantage because, as he had advised them on their appeal, he knew exactly how the parents would be arguing their case.

- ### Complaint 00/A/5380

The parent complained about the way her appeal was handled.

The Ombudsman found maladministration because the panel members had not received proper training and they did not have a proper understanding of their role, the tests to be applied, and the procedure to be followed. Also, there was no evidence that the admission authority had sought to ensure that the panel members were sufficiently trained.

In addition, the governors did not provide any written statement for the appeal panel and parents to consider, and the Chair of the panel was not present all the time. The panel members answered questions put by the parents and the Clerk did not keep proper records of the discussions or the decisions.

- ### Complaint 00/B/3812

The head teacher of a school was allowed to leave an appeal while it was still in progress, although he was available to be recalled if necessary.

The Ombudsman found that this was maladministration because the head teacher should have remained present throughout and this was contrary to the Code of Practice.

- **Complaint 01/A/3034**

One of the points raised was that the appeal panel members and the Clerk met the governors' Clerk over coffee before the hearings commenced. They discussed how many more pupils the school could accept and they decided that ten more pupils could be admitted. No appellant was present during this discussion.

The Ombudsman found maladministration because the panel should not have consulted the governors about the number of additional pupils to be admitted. Although the panel did not consider themselves to be bound by this figure, it was clear that the panel took the governors' view into consideration. Justice should be seen to be done and this did not happen as the parents were not present during these discussions. In addition, the governors' Clerk was also the presenting officer and he too was involved in the appeal arrangements. The Ombudsman felt that it would be preferable for an independent person to send the parents papers to do with the appeal and to advise them about the appeal procedures. This is because the appeal process needs not only to be independent but to be seen to be independent. If a member of the admission authority is involved with the appeal process then the panel's independence is compromised.

- **Complaint 01/A/8869**

One of the reasons for the complaint was that the decision to refuse a place was unreasonable since the council said that the appellant lived 1,797 metres from the school, which was more than twice the distance of the last successful applicant. This was because the council only measured roads and it did not take into account a footpath, even though it was surfaced, lit and maintained by the council.

The Ombudsman found maladministration, since the footpath met all the requirements defined in the admission criteria and it therefore should have been used by the council in measuring the home to school distance. He recommended that the parent be given a fresh appeal.

- **Complaint 01/C/3800**

The timetable for the appeals allowed only ten minutes for each appeal. The appeal panel members felt that the time was adequate and, on any occasions that the hearings overran, they were able to catch up.

The Ombudsman did not find that any injustice had occurred, but he commented that the timescale laid down was likely to generate the perception that an appeal was no more than a token gesture, bearing in mind that time should be allowed for the school's case to be fully presented and questioned, as well as the parents' cases.

- ### Complaint 01/C/6313

The appeal panel consisted of only two members.

The Ombudsman found maladministration because an appeal panel must consist of either three or five members.

- ### Complaint 02/A/3544

The parents complained that the admission criteria were not objective, as required by legislation, but were subjective, so applications were not objectively assessed. The school did not explain about how the points system operated and also it did not give proper consideration to the constitution of the appeal panel.

The Ombudsman found maladministration because the admission criteria were not objective and the head teacher and deputy head had considerable discretion as to which applications would be successful. As a result, the system was not open and transparent. In addition, the Chair of the panel had attended the school, as well as her daughter, which raised considerable doubts about her impartiality. The parents were offered a fresh appeal.

- ### Complaint 02/B/4914

The parents submitted a letter from their son's primary school as part of their submission for the appeal. The letter was returned to the parents, who were told it was council policy that such letters should not be written and, therefore, it could not be taken into account by the appeal panel. The parents complained because this was not fair and also because they were not told about such a policy.

The Ombudsman found that this was maladministration and the council offered the parents a fresh appeal.

- ### Complaint 03/A/5790

In this complaint the appellant had an unsuccessful appeal and he complained to the Ombudsman and was offered a fresh appeal. As part of his submission to the second appeal, the appellant enclosed the Ombudsman's decision letter, but the council refused to circulate it. However, the council circulated documents that it had submitted to the Ombudsman which the appellant thought was unfair.

The Ombudsman's view was quite simple. The second appeal was a fresh hearing and that both sides were entitled to submit whatever information that they wanted for the appeal panel to consider.

- **Complaint 03/A/5866**

The parent complained that the admission criteria had not been properly applied, which denied her son a place at the primary school. The parent was a practising Roman Catholic, but she did not live in the parish and she did not think that there would be 30 parents who met the first criteria, which required weekly attendance at Mass, the support of the parish priest and participation in the activities of the parish. The parent had a sibling at the school and would have qualified under the second criteria.

The Ombudsman found maladministration in that, having checked through the successful applications, only eight met the requirements of criteria one and there were places available to applicants in criteria two. As a result, the appellant should have been offered a place. The Ombudsman recommended that the school offer the appellant a place and the governors agreed.

- **Complaint 03/A/8840**

In this complaint the parent argued that she had received an unfair hearing since one of the panel members was a governor at the school where the parent's daughter had been allocated a place. At the appeal, when the parent explained that she did not want a place at the school because of poor discipline and low standards, the panel member who was the governor at the school sought to defend the school. This was clearly unacceptable and gave a strong impression that the panel was not independent.

The Ombudsman found maladministration and recommended a fresh appeal, which the council agreed.

- **Complaint 03/B/1788**

The appellant complained about the way his appeal was handled and the refusal to offer his child a place. Although a Clerk had been appointed, he was unable to attend and the Chair agreed to proceed in his absence.

The Ombudsman found that this was maladministration and a breach of the Code of Practice that required a Clerk to be present. Also, the admission criteria provided for ten points to be awarded to reflect church commitment, but the appellant's application was only awarded two points for regular attendance within the last 12 months. For the appeal, the appellant produced a second reference that confirmed his family had attended church for years and his grandfather was a founding member of the church. The appeal panel decided not to question this discrepancy and it did not challenge the number of points allocated by the admission authority.

The Ombudsman criticised the panel for not resolving this inconsistency and suggested that if a Clerk had been present, this would not have occurred. The Ombudsman recommended that the school offer the appellant a place at the school and the governors agreed.

- **Complaint 03/C/2106**

The appellant complained about the way his appeal had been handled.

The Ombudsman found maladministration and recommended that the appellant be offered a fresh appeal before a different panel. The Ombudsman was concerned about two issues. Firstly, that the appeal panel did not properly test the admission authority's case and simply seemed to accept that because the school had offered places up to the published admission number, the school was full. Some panel members were relying on information which had appeared in the local press and were not basing their decision on the evidence presented at the appeal.

Secondly, the Ombudsman was also concerned that the panel members seemed to be inhibited because they were concerned that if the appeal was successful, it would create a precedent. Panel members were reminded that panels do not create precedents and they consider each case on its own merits. The appellants were offered a fresh appeal.

- **Complaint 04/A/1909**

In this case, the appellants were refused a place at the local junior school because they failed to provide proof of residence. The application was submitted on time with the proof of address, but the proof was not received and the appellants claimed that they did not receive a follow-up letter.

The Ombudsman found that, while he accepted the need to prevent fraudulent applications, the systems should not be used to deny places from legitimate applicants. In this case, the appellants had lived at their address for eight years and their sibling already attended the school. The Ombudsman suggested that a phone call to the parents may have resolved the issue and it would have saved a lot of time spent on the investigation. He recommended that the appellant be offered a place at the junior school and the council agreed.

- ### Complaint 04/A/5213

In this case the applicant submitted a late application for a school which a sibling already attended. The admission authority did not offer a place as the school was oversubscribed. In addition, the applicant was added to the waiting list, but below all on-time applications and those applications that the authority had deemed to be on time, even though they were late.

The Ombudsman found that this was maladministration because the Code of Practice was quite clear that if the admission authority operated a waiting list, it must operate in exactly the same way as the published admission criteria, irrespective of when the application was received.

By the time this had been resolved, the applicant's son had been attending another school for some eight months and he did not want to change, so the admission authority agreed to pay £800 compensation for the additional expense incurred by the parents in attending a school which was further away than the preferred school.

- ### Complaint 04/A/7206

In this case, the appellant complained that the admission authority had refused her application on the basis that it was late. The admission authority published its admission arrangements, which provided that applications should be sent to the school in question in February. The appellant complied with these arrangements. Later that month the admission authority wrote to her explaining that the arrangements had been changed and she needed to submit a further form to the authority by the end of March. The appellant's application was received after this date and it was deemed to be a late application.

The Ombudsman found that this was maladministration. There were only limited grounds where the admission arrangements could be changed, and none applied in this case, and the new arrangements were deemed to be unlawful. Equally, the admission authority could not lawfully ignore a parent's expressed preferences which had been properly submitted. The Ombudsman accepted that if the original admission arrangements had been operated, the appellant's application would have been successful. He recommended that the authority offer the appellant a place at the school and the admission authority agreed.

- ### Complaint 04/A/10965

A parent complained that her appeal should have been successful. At the appeal it was pointed out that the published admission number for the secondary school was 145 and there was no dispute at the appeal that the number of pupils expected in Year 7 would be 140. The parent pointed out that Section 86 of the School Standards and Framework Act 1998, provided under sub-section (5), that no prejudice to efficient use of resources or efficient education could arise from the admission of pupils that did not exceed the published admission limit. If there was no prejudice, then there would be no need for the appeal panel to consider the balancing stage.

The Ombudsman pointed out that, due to the clear wording in the legislation, the appeal panel had no option but to allow the appeal. However, the panel dismissed the appeal. The Ombudsman said that this was maladministration and he recommended that the admission authority offer a place at the school, which it did.

• Complaint 04/B/6411

The appellant complained that she had not received a fair hearing. The admission number for the school was 20 and 27 applications had been received. The appellant's application was not successful and she appealed. At the appeal, the school argued that it would be a class size appeal because there were three classes of 20 and if an additional place was offered, the school would have to run another class. This was accepted by the appeal panel and the appeal was not successful.

The appellant then consulted a solicitor who stated that it should not have been treated as a class size appeal because, although there were 60 pupils at the school, each class of 20 was taught by a teacher and therefore an additional pupil would not breach the class size limit of no more then 30 pupils with one teacher. The matter was referred to the council's solicitor, who agreed, and the appellant was offered a fresh appeal which was successful. The appellant then asked the council to reimburse her legal fees, but the council refused.

The Ombudsman found that if there had not been maladministration, the appellant would not have needed to consult a solicitor and he recommended that the council reimburse her legal fees of £1,250. The council agreed.

• Complaint 04/C/2090

In this complaint the appellant complained that she had not seen a report submitted by her daughter's head teacher about her child's suitability for a grammar school place. The admission arrangements provided that the majority of places at the grammar school were offered on the basis of the 11-plus results, but a few were offered after the governors had considered a report from the pupils' primary school. The application was unsuccessful and, at the appeal, the report was not sent to the parent because it was regarded as confidential.

The Ombudsman found that this was maladministration because all parties should receive the same information at an appeal and the parent should have seen the report. However, the Ombudsman took no further action because, in his view, even if the parent had seen the report, it would not have changed the decision of the appeal panel.

Appendix 7

Lawful reasons for refusing a placing request in Scotland

The law is quite explicit about lawful reasons by the council for refusing your placing request. The details are set out in section 28A(3) of the Education (Scotland) Act 1980, as inserted by section 1 of the Education (Scotland) Act 1981, and section 28A(3A) to (3E) of the 1980 Act, as inserted by section 33 of the Education (Scotland) Act 1996, as inserted by section 44 of the Standards in Scotland's Schools etc. Act 2000. The circumstances set out in section 28A (3) are as follows:

a) If placing the child in the specified school would:

 i) make it necessary for the authority to take an additional teacher into employment;

 ii) give rise to significant expenditure on extending or, otherwise, altering the accommodation at, or facilities provided in connection with, the school;

 iii) be seriously detrimental to the continuity of the child's education;

 iv) be likely to be seriously detrimental to order and discipline in the school;

 v) be likely to be seriously detrimental to the educational well-being of pupils attending the school; or

 vi) assuming that pupil numbers remain constant, make it necessary, at the commencement of a future stage of the child's primary education, for the authority to elect to create an additional class (or an additional composite class) in the

> specified school or take an additional teacher into employment at the school;
>
> b) if the education normally provided at the specified school is not suited to the age, ability or aptitude of the child;
>
> c) if the education authority has already required the child to discontinue his attendance at the specified school;
>
> d) if, where the specified school is a special school, the child does not have special educational needs requiring the education or special facilities normally provided at that school; or
>
> e) if the specified school is a single sex school (within the meaning given to that expression by Section 26 of the Sex Discrimination Act 1975) and the child is not of the sex admitted or taken (under that section) to be admitted to the school.

Section 28A (3) goes on to say that:

> 'An education authority may place a child in the specified school notwithstanding paragraphs (a) to (e) above.'

This means that a council may agree to a request even if this would mean that the school would have to employ an additional teacher, or spend money on accommodation, or even if it thought that the move would not be very good for the child. It is not required to refuse the placing request simply because it is one of the lawful reasons for refusing such a request. This does mean, therefore, that the council does have a significant amount of discretion.

Section 28A (3A) to (3D) is worded as follows:

> '(3A) The duty, imposed by subsection (i) above [on page 239] does not apply where the acceptance of a placing request in respect of a child who is resident outside the catchment area of the specified school would prevent the education authority from retaining reserved places at the specified school or in relation to any particular stage of education at the school; but nothing in this subsection shall prevent an education authority from placing a child in the specified school.'

Section (3B) was removed by section 44 of the Standards in Scotland's Schools, etc. Act 2000.

> '(3C) In subsection (3A) above, 'reserved places' means such number of places (not exceeding such number or, as the case may be, such

percentage of places at the school or relating to the particular stage of education as may be prescribed by regulations) as are in the opinion of the education authority reasonably required to accommodate pupils likely to become resident in the catchment area of the school in the period from the time of consideration of the placing request up to and during the year from 1 August to which the placing request relates; and different numbers or, as the case may be, percentages may be prescribed under this subsection for the purpose of different cases or circumstances.

'(3D) In subsections (3A) and 3(C) above, 'catchment area' means the area from which pupils resident therein will be admitted to the school in terms of any priority based on residence in accordance with the guidelines formulated by the authority under section 28(1) (c) of this Act.'

Further useful information for admissions in Scotland

Further general information can be obtained about school admissions from the Scottish Education Office as follows:

The Scottish Executive Education Department
Victoria Quay
Edinburgh EH6 6QQ
Tel: 0131 244 4485

If your child suffers from special educational needs, you can find out additional information about choosing a school and your rights of appeal in a booklet entitled 'A Parents' Guide to Special Educational Needs', published by the Scottish Executive Education Department (the organisation's address is given above). The telephone number, however, is different. It is 0131 244 5144.

Appendix 8

How to contact your local council

England

Barking & Dagenham
020 8215 3000
www.barking-dagenham.gov.uk

Barnet
020 8359 2000
www.barnet.gov.uk

Barnsley
01226 770 770
www.barnsley.gov.uk

Bath & North East Somerset
01225 477 000
www.bathnes.gov.uk

Bedfordshire
01234 363 222
www.bedfordshire.gov.uk

Bexley
020 8303 7777
www.bexley.gov.uk

Birmingham
0121 303 8079
www.birmingham.gov.uk

Blackburn & Darwen
01254 585 585
www.blackburn.gov.uk

Blackpool
01253 477 477
www.blackpool.gov.uk

Bolton
01204 333 333
www.bolton.gov.uk

Bournemouth
01202 451 451
www.bournemouth.gov.uk

Bracknell Forest
01344 352 000
www.bracknell-forest.gov.uk

Bradford
01274 385 500
www.bradford.gov.uk

Brent
020 8937 1234
www.brent.gov.uk

Brighton & Hove
01273 290 000
www.brighton-hove.gov.uk

Bristol
0117 922 2000
www.bristol.gov.uk

Bromley
020 8464 3333
www.bromley.gov.uk

Buckinghamshire
0845 370 8090
www.buckscc.gov.uk

Bury
0161 253 5000
www.bury.gov.uk

Calderdale
0845 245 6000
www.calderdale.gov.uk

Cambridgeshire
0845 045 5200
www.cambridgeshire.gov.uk

Camden
020 7278 4444
www.camden.gov.uk

Cheshire
0845 113 3311
www.cheshire.gov.uk

City of London
020 7606 3030
www.cityoflondon.gov.uk

Cornwall
01872 322 000
www.cornwall.gov.uk

Coventry
024 7683 1622 (primary)
024 7683 1613 (secondary)
www.coventry.gov.uk

Croydon
020 8726 6400
www.croydon.gov.uk

Cumbria
01228 606 060
www.cumbria.gov.uk

Darlington
01325 380 651
www.darlington.gov.uk

Derby City
01332 293 111
www.derby.gov.uk

Derbyshire
0845 605 8058
www.derbyshire.gov.uk

Devon
0845 155 1013
www.devon.gov.uk

Doncaster
01302 734 011
www.doncaster.gov.uk

Dorset
01305 224 110
www.dorsetforyou.com

Dudley
01384 812 345
www.dudley.gov.uk

Durham
0191 383 4567
www.durham.gov.uk

Ealing
020 8825 5000
www.ealing.gov.uk

East Riding of Yorkshire
01482 393 939
www.eastriding.gov.uk

East Sussex
01273 481 000
www.eastsussex.gov.uk

Enfield
020 8379 1000
www.enfield.gov.uk

Essex
0845 603 7627
www.essexcc.gov.uk

Gateshead
0191 433 3000
www.gateshead.gov.uk

Gloucestershire
01452 425 000
www.gloucestershire.gov.uk

Greenwich
020 8854 8888
www.greenwich.gov.uk

Hackney
020 8356 3000
www.hackney.gov.uk

Halton
0151 424 2061
www.halton.gov.uk

Hammersmith & Fulham
020 8748 3020
www.lbhf.gov.uk

Hampshire
0845 603 5638
www.hants.gov.uk

Haringey
020 8489 0000
www.haringey.gov.uk

Harrow
020 8863 5611
www.harrow.gov.uk

Hartlepool
01429 266 522
www.hartlepool.gov.uk

Havering
01708 434 343
www.havering.gov.uk

Herefordshire
01432 260 000
www.herefordshire.gov.uk

Hertfordshire
01923 471 500
www.hertsdirect.org

Hillingdon
01895 250 111
www.hillingdon.gov.uk

Hounslow
020 8583 2000
www.hounslow.gov.uk

Isle of Wight
01983 821 000
www.iwight.com

Isles of Scilly
01720 422 537
www.scilly.gov.uk

Islington
020 7527 2000
www.islington.gov.uk

Kensington & Chelsea
020 7361 3009
www.rbkc.gov.uk

Kent
01622 671 411
www.kent.gov.uk

Kingston upon Thames
020 8547 5757
www.kingston.gov.uk

Kirklees
01484 226 891
www.kirklees.gov.uk

Knowsley
0151 489 6000
www.knowsley.gov.uk

Lambeth
020 7926 1000
www.lambeth.gov.uk

Lancashire
01772 254 868
www.lancashire.gov.uk

Leeds
0113 234 8080
www.leeds.gov.uk

Leicester City
0116 252 7811
www.leicester.gov.uk

Leicestershire
0116 232 3232
www.leics.gov.uk

Lewisham
020 8314 6000
www.lewisham.gov.uk

Lincolnshire
01522 552 222
www.lincolnshire.gov.uk

Liverpool
0151 233 3006
www.liverpool.gov.uk

Luton
01582 546 000
www.luton.gov.uk

Manchester
0161 234 5000
www.manchester.gov.uk

Medway
01634 306 000
www.medway.gov.uk

Merton
020 8274 4901
www.merton.gov.uk

Middlesbrough
01642 245 432
www.middlesbrough.gov.uk

Milton Keynes
01908 691 691
www.miltonkeynes.gov.uk

Newcastle
0191 232 8520
www.newcastle.gov.uk

Newham
020 8430 3165
www.newham.gov.uk

Norfolk
01603 408 426
www.norfolk.gov.uk

North East Lincolnshire
01472 313 131
www.nelincs.gov.uk

North Lincolnshire
01724 296 296
www.northlincs.gov.uk

North Somerset
01934 888 888
www.n-somerset.gov.uk

North Tyneside
0191 200 5006
www.northtyneside.gov.uk

North Yorkshire
0845 872 7374
www.northyorks.gov.uk

Northamptonshire
01604 236 236
www.northamptonshire.gov.uk

Northumberland
01670 533 000
www.northumberland.gov.uk

Nottingham
0115 915 5555
www.nottinghamcity.gov.uk

Oldham
0161 770 3000
www.oldham.gov.uk

Oxfordshire
01865 792 422
www.oxfordshire.gov.uk

Peterborough
01733 747 474
www.peterborough.gov.uk

Plymouth
01752 668 000
www.plymouth.gov.uk

Poole
01202 633 633
www.poole.gov.uk

Portsmouth
023 9283 4092
www.portsmouth.gov.uk

Reading
0118 939 0553
www.reading.gov.uk

Redbridge
020 8554 5000
www.redbridge.gov.uk

Redcar & Cleveland
01642 444 108
www.redcar-cleveland.gov.uk

Richmond upon Thames
020 8891 1411
www.richmond.gov.uk

Rochdale
01706 647 474
www.rochdale.gov.uk

Rotherham
01709 382 121
www.rotherham.gov.uk

Rutland
01572 722 577
www.rutland.gov.uk

Salford
0161 794 4711
www.salford.gov.uk

Sandwell
0845 358 2200
www.sandwell.gov.uk

Sefton
0845 140 0845
www.sefton.gov.uk

Sheffield
0114 273 5028
www.sheffield.gov.uk

Shropshire
0845 678 9000
www.shropshire.gov.uk

Slough
01753 475 111
www.slough.gov.uk

Solihull
0121 704 6000
www.solihull.gov.uk

Somerset
0845 345 9122
www.somerset.gov.uk

South Gloucestershire
01454 868 008
www.southglos.gov.uk

South Tyneside
0191 427 1717
www.southtyneside.gov.uk

Southampton
023 8022 3855
www.southampton.gov.uk

Southend-on-Sea
01702 215 000
www.southend.gov.uk

Southwark
0845 6001 2184
www.southwark.gov.uk

St Helens
01744 456 789
www.sthelens.gov.uk

Staffordshire
01785 223 121
www.staffordshire.gov.uk

Stockport
0161 480 4949
www.stockport.gov.uk

Stockton-on-Tees
01642 393 939
www.stockton.gov.uk

Stoke-on-Trent
01782 234 567
www.stoke.gov.uk

Suffolk
0845 606 6067
www.suffolk.gov.uk

Sunderland
0191 520 5555
www.sunderland.gov.uk

Surrey
08456 009 009
www.surreycc.gov.uk

Sutton
020 8770 5000
www.sutton.gov.uk

Swindon
01793 463 000
www.swindon.gov.uk

Tameside
0161 342 8355
www.tameside.gov.uk

Telford & Wrekin
01952 380 000
www.telford.gov.uk

Thurrock
01375 652 652
www.thurrock.gov.uk

Torbay
01803 201 201
www.torbay.gov.uk

Tower Hamlets
020 7364 5006
www.towerhamlets.gov.uk

Trafford
0161 912 2000
www.trafford.gov.uk

Wakefield
01924 306 090
www.wakefield.gov.uk

Walsall
01922 650 000
www.walsall.gov.uk

Waltham Forest
020 8496 3000
www.lbwf.gov.uk

Wandsworth
020 8871 6394
www.wandsworth.gov.uk

Warrington
01925 443 322
www.warrington.gov.uk

Warwickshire
01926 410 410
www.warwickshire.gov.uk

West Berkshire
01635 519 771
www.westberks.gov.uk

West Sussex
01243 777 100
www.westsussex.gov.uk

Westminster, City of
020 7641 1816/7
www.westminster.gov.uk

Wigan
01942 486 038
www.wigan.gov.uk

Wiltshire
01225 713 000
www.wiltshire.gov.uk

Windsor & Maidenhead
01628 683 870
www.rbwm.gov.uk

Wirral
0151 606 2000
www.wirral.gov.uk

Wokingham
0118 974 6104
www.wokingham.gov.uk

Wolverhampton
01902 551 155
www.wolverhampton.gov.uk

Worcestershire
01905 763 763
www.worcestershire.gov.uk

York
01904 551 550
www.york.gov.uk

Scotland

Aberdeen City Council
01224 522 000
www.aberdeencity.gov.uk

Aberdeenshire Council
01224 664 630
www.aberdeenshire.gov.uk

Buchan Area Office
01779 473 269

Banff Area Office
01261 813 340

Formartine Area Office
01888 562 427

Garioch Area Office
01467 620 981

Marr, Kincardine & Mearns
Area Office
01569 766 960

Angus Council
01307 476 300
www.angus.gov.uk

Argyll & Bute Council
01546 602 127
www.argyll-bute.gov.uk

Clackmannanshire Council
01259 450 000
www.clacksweb.org.uk

Comhairle Nan Eilean Siar
01851 703 773
www.cne-siar.gov.uk

Dumfries & Galloway Council
01387 260 427
www.dumgal.gov.uk

Dundee City Council
01382 433 088
www.dundeecity.gov.uk

East Ayrshire Council
01563 576 121
www.east-ayrshire.gov.uk

East Dunbartonshire Council
0141 578 8000
www.eastdunbarton.gov.uk

East Lothian Council
01620 827 631
www.eastlothian.gov.uk

East Renfrewshire Council
0141 577 3430
www.eastrenfrewshire.gov.uk

Edinburgh Council, City of
0131 469 3032
www.edinburgh.gov.uk

Falkirk Council
01324 506 600
www.falkirk.gov.uk

Fife Council
01592 583 372
www.fife.gov.uk

Glasgow City Council
0141 287 2000
www.glasgow.gov.uk

Highland Council
01463 702 000
www.highland.gov.uk

    Caithness Area Office
    01955 602 362

    Inverness Area Office
    01463 663 800

Lochaber Area Office
01397 702 466

Nairn/Badenoch & Strathspey
Area Office
01540 661 009

Ross & Cromarty Area Office
01349 863 441

Skye & Lochalsh Area Office
01478 613 697

Sutherland Area Office
01408 621 382

Inverclyde Council
01475 717 171
www.inverclyde.gov.uk

Midlothian Council
0131 270 7500
www.midlothian.gov.uk

Moray Council
01343 563 097
www.moray.gov.uk

North Ayrshire Council
0845 603 0590
www.north-ayrshire.gov.uk

North Lanarkshire Council
01236 812 222
www.northlan.gov.uk

Orkney Islands Council
01856 873 535
www.orkney.gov.uk

Perth & Kinross Council
01738 476 200
www.pkc.gov.uk

Renfrewshire Council
0141 840 3477
www.renfrewshire.gov.uk

Scottish Borders Council
01835 824 000
www.scotborders.gov.uk

Shetland Islands Council
01595 744 000
www.shetland.gov.uk

South Ayrshire Council
01292 612 000
www.south-ayrshire.gov.uk

South Lanarkshire Council
0845 740 6080
www.southlanarkshire.gov.uk

Stirling Council
0845 277 7000
www.stirling.gov.uk

West Dunbartonshire Council
01389 737 000
www.wdc.gov.uk

West Lothian Council
01506 776 000
www.westlothian.gov.uk

Wales

Blaenau Gwent
01495 350 555
www.blaenau-gwent.gov.uk

Bridgend
01656 643 643
www.bridgend.gov.uk

Caerphilly
01443 815 588
www.caerphilly.gov.uk

Cardiff
029 2087 2087
www.cardiff.gov.uk

Carmarthenshire
01267 234 567
www.carmarthenshire.gov.uk

Ceredigion
Aberaeron 01545 570 881
Aberystwyth 01970 617 911
www.ceredigion.gov.uk

Conwy
01492 574 000
www.conwy.gov.uk

Denbighshire
01824 706 101
www.denbighshire.gov.uk

Flintshire
01352 752 121
www.flintshire.gov.uk

Gwynedd
01286 672 255
www.gwynedd.gov.uk

Isle of Anglesey
01248 752 900
www.anglesey.gov.uk

Merthyr Tydfil
01685 725 000
www.merthyr.gov.uk

Monmouthshire
01633 644 644
www.monmouthshire.gov.uk

Neath Port Talbot
01639 763 333
www.neath-porttalbot.gov.uk

Newport
01633 656 656
www.newport.gov.uk

Pembrokeshire
01437 764 551
www.pembrokeshire.gov.uk

Powys
01597 826 000
www.powys.gov.uk

Rhondda Cynon Taff
01443 424 000
www.rhondda-cynon-taff.gov.uk

Swansea
01792 636 000
www.swansea.gov.uk

Torfaen
01495 762 200
www.torfaen.gov.uk

Vale of Glamorgan
01446 700 111
www.valeofglamorgan.gov.uk

Wrexham
01978 292 000
www.wrexham.gov.uk

Appendix 9

Useful website addresses

- **Administrative Justice & Tribunals Council**
  Oversees the practice of tribunals, including independent appeal panels
  www.ajtc.gov.uk

- **Advisory Centre for Education (ACE)**
  A charity which provides advice and information on school admissions, and admission and exclusion appeals
  www.ace-ed.org.uk

- **Assessment and Qualifications Alliance (AQA)**
  Promotes education for the public benefit
  www.aqa.org.uk

- **Association of Educational Psychologists (AEP)**
  The voice of the educational psychology profession
  www.aep.org.uk

- **BBC**
  Provides advice and information on education and facilities
  www.bbc.co.uk/education

- **Boarding Schools' Association (BSA)**
  Provides information and advice on over 500 boarding schools
  www.boarding.org.uk

- **British Dyslexia Association (BDA)**

  The voice of dyslexic people

  www.bdadyslexia.org.uk

- **British Psychological Society**

  The representative of psychology and psychologists

  www.bps.org.uk

- **Bullying UK**

  Provides advice and guidance for parents whose children are being bullied

  www.bullying.co.uk

- **Childline**

  Provides a 24-hour service for children in distress or danger

  www.childline.org.uk

- **Children's Legal Centre**

  A national charity concerned with law and policy for children and young people

  www.childrenslegalcentre.com

- **Choir Schools' Association (CSA)**

  Represents 44 schools attached to cathedrals, churches and college chapels

  www.choirschools.org.uk

- **Community Legal Advice**

  Provides independent legal advice for parents whose children are having problems at school

  www.clsdirect.org.uk

- **Contact a Family**

  Provides advice and guidance for parents with disabled children

  www.cafamily.org.uk

- **Department for Children, Education, Lifelong Learning and Skills**

  The Welsh government's department for education

  www.learning.wales.gov.uk

- **Department for Children, Schools and Families**

  The English government department for education

  www.dcsf.gov.uk

- **Edexcel**
  Helps deliver qualifications to two million learners worldwide
  www.edexcel.org.uk

- **Education Otherwise**
  Provides advice for parents whose children are being educated outside
  of school
  www.education-otherwise.org

- **Fatherhood Institute**
  Provides help, support and advice for fathers
  www.fathersdirect.com

- **Girls' Day School Trust**
  Provides broad education in independent schools
  www.gdst.net

- **Girls' Schools Association (GSA)**
  Represents heads of independent girls' schools
  www.gsa.uk.com

- **Good Schools Guide**
  A comprehensive guide on all schools in the UK
  www.goodschoolsguide.co.uk

- **Governornet**
  A website for governors
  www.governornet.gov.uk

- **Guardian newspaper**
  Provides a mix of education news and features
  www.guardian.co.uk

- **Headmasters' & Headmistresses' Conference**
  Represents 250 independent schools
  www.hmc.org.uk

- **Her Majesty's Chief Inspector of Education and Training in Wales (Estyn)**
  Provides inspection reports for Welsh schools
  www.estyn.gov.uk

- **Her Majesty's Inspectorate of Education in Scotland**
  Provides inspection reports for Scottish schools
  www.hmie.gov.uk

- **Home Education Advisory Service (HEAS)**
  Gives advice about home education
  www.heas.org.uk

- **Independent Association of Prep Schools**
  Promotes excellence in education for over 600 independent schools
  www.iaps.org.uk

- **Independent Panel for Special Education Advice**
  Gives advice for children with special educational needs in England and Wales
  www.ipsea.org.uk

- **Independent Schools Association (ISA)**
  Provides support for head teachers of independent schools
  www.isaschools.org.uk

- **Independent Schools Inspectorate (ISI)**
  Provides inspection reports for independent schools
  www.isi.net

- **Kidscape**
  A charity established to keep children safe from abuse
  www.kidscape.org.uk

- **Local Government Ombudsman**
  Provides independent investigations into complaints about school appeals
  www.lgo.org.uk

- **National Curriculum online**
  Provides details online about the National Curriculum
  www.nc.uk.net

- **Netmums**
  Provides help, advice and support for mothers
  www.netmums.com

- **Network 81**

  A network of parents working for inclusive education for children with special educational needs

  www.network81.org

- **Office of the Schools Adjudicator (OSA)**

  Considers objections to school admission arrangements and resolves disagreements on statutory proposals in England

  www.schoolsadjudicator.gov.uk

- **Ofsted**

  The office for standards in education in England

  www.ofsted.gov.uk

- **Oxford Cambridge and RSA Examinations (OCR)**

  Provides qualifications that engage learners of all ages

  www.ocr.org.uk

- **Parentline Plus**

  A charity that provides help for parents

  www.parentlineplus.org.uk

- **Public Services Ombudsman for Wales**

  Provides independent investigations into complaints about school appeals

  www.ombudsman-wales.org.uk

- **Qualifications and Curriculum Authority (QCA)**

  Provides information about the curriculum

  www.qca.org.uk

- **Raising Kids**

  Provides help and guidance for all parents

  www.raisingkids.co.uk

- **Research and Information on State Education (RISE)**

  Promotes and encourages research into state education

  www.risetrust.org.uk

- **School Appeals**

  Provides one-to-one help to assist you in winning school appeals

  www.schoolappeals.org.uk

- **Schoolsnet**

  Provides detailed profiles on 27,000 schools

  www.schoolsnet.com

- **Scottish Council of Independent Schools (SCIS)**

  Provides information and profiles on independent schools in Scotland

  www.scis.org.uk

- **Scottish Executive Education Department**

  The Scottish government's department for education

  www.scotland.gov.uk

- **Scottish Qualifications Authority (SQA)**

  Responsible for the development, accreditation and assessment of qualifications in Scotland

  www.sqa.org.uk

- **Society of Headmasters and Headmistresses of Independent Schools**

  Provides support for heads of about 100 independent schools

  www.shmis.org.uk

- **State Boarding Schools' Association (SBSA)**

  Provides advice about boarding schools

  www.sbsa.org.uk

- **Teachernet**

  Provides advice and guidance on a range of educational issues

  www.teachernet.gov.uk

- **Telegraph newspaper**

  Provides a mix of education news and features

  www.telegraph.co.uk

- **Times newspaper**

  Provides a mix of education news and features

  www.timesonline.co.uk/education

- **Which School Limited**

  The directory of independent schools in the British Isles

  www.isbi.com

- **WJEC**

  Refers to various websites about various educational issues

  www.wjec.org.uk

- **YoungMinds**

  A charity committed to improving the mental health of children and young people

  www.youngminds.org.uk

Glossary

- ### Academies
  Academies are independently managed, all ability schools set up by sponsors from business, faith or voluntary groups in partnership with the DCSF and the local authority. Together they fund the land and buildings, with the government covering the running costs. All new academies are covered by the Codes of Practice and the independent appeals process, but some of the original academies are not.

- ### Admission authority
  This is the authority responsible for setting the admission criteria. For community and voluntary controlled schools, it is the Local Education Authority (LEA), although some LEAs have delegated this decision to the governing body of the schools. For all other schools, the governing body of the school concerned is the admission authority.

- ### Admission criteria
  These are the priorities established by the admission authority to determine which pupils will be offered school places for oversubscribed schools, where there are more applications than places available.

- ### Admission forums
  They have a key role in ensuring a fair admissions system that promotes social equity, does not disadvantage one child compared to another, and which is straightforward and easy to understand for parents. Forums are also responsible for monitoring compliance with the Code. Membership of the forum is restricted to local councillors, head teachers and other persons with an interest in education. Members are either elected or appointed.

- **Admissions booklet**

  This is the annual publication issued by the LEA which sets out the admission arrangements and also details the admission criteria for schools within its administrative boundaries.

- **Admissions round**

  This commences at the start of the academic year before admission and it finishes when the offers are made. For secondary schools, this will be on 1 March and for primary schools, a date determined by the local authority. This does not apply in Scotland, where the timetables are different.

- **Allocated school**

  The school determined by the LEA that the child should attend, if it is not possible for the authority to allocate him to any of the parent's preferred schools.

- **Balancing exercise**

  This is the process where the appeal panel considers whether the issues raised by the parent outweigh the case put forward by the admission authority. This is used for normal prejudice appeals in England and Wales.

- **Banding**

  Banding is an increasingly popular method of achieving an intake that reflects the range of abilities of the children applying to a particular school or group of schools, or of children in the local authority or country. It is not a way to select children by high academic ability or aptitude for a particular subject. Banding is an oversubscription criterion and can only be used when there are more applications than places available; it cannot be used to keep places open if, for example, some bands are oversubscribed and some are not. Admission authorities proposing to use banding to allocate places must set out in their published admission arrangements how this will work and what other oversubscription criteria will be used within each band.

- **Catchment area**

  This is the geographical area defined by the admission authority where children living within it will be given priority for places at the school. The catchment area is defined before applications are sought.

- **Children in public care, looked after children and children in care**

  Children who are in the care of the local authority, as defined by section 22 of the Children Act 1999. A looked after child is only considered as such if the local authority confirms that he will be in public care when he is admitted to the school.

- **Choice advisors**

An independent service commissioned by local authorities to support families who need the most help during the admissions round in order for the parents to make the best and most realistic choice of secondary schools for their children. Choice advisors assist parents through the decision-making process, but they must not take the decision for them. This applies in England only.

- **Choosing a school**

A guidance note issued by the Scottish Assembly for schools in Scotland.

- **City technology colleges**

These are independently managed, non fee-paying schools in urban areas for pupils of all abilities aged 11 to 18. They are geared towards science, technology and the world of work, offering a range of vocational qualifications, as well as GCSEs and A-levels. The Codes may not apply to the colleges, but this matter does need to be checked.

- **Class size appeals**

This appeal is where the admission authority argues that the admission of an additional pupil will require the school to employ another teacher or provide additional accommodation so that the statutory class size of 30 is not exceeded for children aged five, six and seven.

- **Clerk**

The person appointed by the admission authority to advise all parties to the appeal about procedures, the law and any matters arising out of the appeal process. The Clerk is independent and he will write to the parent to advise him of the appeal panel's decision.

- **Code on School Admission Appeals**

Statutory guidance issued by the DCSF for admission authorities to follow when they are arranging admission appeals.

- **Code on School Admissions**

Statutory guidance issued by the DCSF for admission authorities to follow when they are arranging admissions.

- **Common application form**

  The local authority form which parents must complete to express their preferences. The minimum number of schools a parent can choose is three, but some authorities allow a parent to express up to six preferences. The form has to be returned by the closing date nominated by the LEA for it to be treated as an on-time application. These forms can now be completed online. This applies to applications in England and Wales.

- **Community schools**

  These are schools that are run and maintained by the LEA.

- **Composite prospectus**

  This is commonly referred to as the admissions booklet published by the LEA, which provides details about the admission arrangements for each of the schools within their jurisdiction. It will usually be published at the beginning of the academic year before admissions or transfers will take place. It sets out details about the schools, including the closing date for applications.

- **Comprehensive schools**

  This is a general term that refers to schools that do not select by ability.

- **Contextual value added (CVA)**

  CVA has been introduced by the government to illustrate the progress made by pupils at school. This is because it has been argued that performance figures can be misleading because no allowance is made for the ability of the children when they are admitted to the school. You could get a situation where pupils achieve good marks but, in fact, their progress is slower than some other schools that started from a lower level when they were admitted to the school. CVA takes this into account and it has been promoted as a more accurate assessment of pupil's progress.

- **Co-ordinated schemes**

  These are the schemes agreed by LEAs which set out how they will deal with applications. They must be consulted upon across all relevant admission authorities and determined in the year before they apply. All LEAs are required to co-ordinate secondary and primary admissions for all schools in their area. Although individual admission authorities rank all applicants in order of priority for admission, offers are sent out by the LEA on 1 March for secondary schools and on an agreed date for primary schools. This applies to applications in England and Wales only.

- **Dedicated Schools Grant**

  This is the funding provided by the government to assist local authorities in providing education facilities in their area.

- **Department for Children, Schools and Families (DCSF)**

  The government department responsible for setting and implementing government policy in England.

- **Excepted pupils**

  These are pupils that are not counted when deciding if a class size has exceeded 30 or a ratio of 30 to 1 for pupils aged five, six and seven. There are five exceptions referred to in the Code of Practice on School Admissions, published by the DCSF.

- **Faith schools**

  Faith schools are mostly run in the same way as other state schools. However, their faith status may be reflected in their religious education curriculum, admission criteria and staffing policies. Faith schools are usually voluntary aided or controlled schools.

- **Foundation schools**

  Formerly referred to as 'grant-maintained schools'. The governing body is responsible for setting and implementing the published admission criteria.

- **Funding formula**

  This is the method used by local authorities to allocate funds to the schools in their area.

- **Geographical areas**

  This applies to England and Wales. The geographical area is determined after applications have been received from applicants and it is drawn up after higher priority places have been allocated. This is a subjective assessment and it is generally being phased out.

- **Governing body**

  The group of people elected or appointed to oversee the management and budget of the school.

- ### Grammar schools (designated)

  There are 164 schools designated as grammar schools by virtue of section 104(5) of the School Standards and Framework Act 1998. A grammar school is defined in section 104(2) of the Act as a school that selects all (or substantially all) of its pupils on the basis of academic ability.

- ### Home–school agreements

  This is a statement explaining the school's aims and values; the school's responsibilities towards its pupils who are of compulsory school age; the parents' responsibilities; and what the school expects of its pupils.

- ### Independent appeal panel

  The group of people appointed to hear appeals in accordance with the Code of Practice on School Appeals. Panel members are appointed by the admission authority and are independent. Panel members should receive regular training.

- ### Infant class size appeals

  This is where the admission authority refuses a school place because it would result in a class size of more than 30 for children aged five, six and seven, or a ratio of more than 30 children to one teacher.

- ### Key Stage 1

  This is defined by the National Curriculum. Children aged five, six and seven come within this category. This covers academic Years 1 and 2. Reception classes are also referred to as foundation classes.

- ### Key Stage 2

  Children in Years 3 to 6.

- ### Key Stage 3

  Children in Years 7 to 9.

- ### Key Stage 4

  Children in Years 10 and 11.

- ### Local Education Authority (LEA)

  The council/local authority responsible for setting and determining local education policy and management.

- **Local Government Ombudsman (LGO)**

  An independent and impartial body that investigates complaints about maladministration of certain public bodies. This is a free service.

- **Maintained schools**

  This includes all community, voluntary controlled, foundation and voluntary aided schools. Academies are not included, as they have separate funding agreements with the government.

- **Maladministration**

  This is where the approved and published procedures for admission of pupils and the appeal process have not been followed, and have caused injustice as a result. Cases of maladministration are investigated by the LGO in England and Wales and by the Public Service Ombudsman in Scotland.

- **National Assembly for Wales**

  The government responsible for setting and implementing government policy in Wales.

- **National Curriculum**

  This is the education programme that each school is required to follow and it is determined by the government.

- **National offer day**

  This is 1 March and it applies to secondary schools in England.

- **Net capacity**

  The net capacity of a school is the number of places that the governing body of the school has adopted, which it believes the school can accommodate without causing problems for the school. The net capacity is intended to provide a robust and consistent method of assessing the capacity of schools. It does not apply in Scotland.

- **Ofsted report**

  A report produced by a team of school inspectors to assess how a school is performing against a range of predetermined targets in England. It is usually held at least every four years. Reports are now based on self-assessment.

- **Oversubscription/oversubscribed**

  This occurs when the number of applications for school places exceeds the number available.

- **Placing request**

  The method used in Scotland that allows parents to express a preference as to where their child is educated.

- **Plenary session**

  This is the part of the appeal hearing where the admission authority presents its case for prejudice before a group of parents or all parents/guardians who are appealing for a particular school.

- **Points systems**

  Some foundation and voluntary aided schools use points systems as part of their admission criteria to determine places. Such points systems can take many forms, but usually points will be awarded for regular attendance at church and also taking part in church activities. Such pointing systems can be very complicated and difficult to understand. Such systems are discouraged because of their complexity.

- **Preferred school**

  This is the school that a parent would like his child to attend.

- **Prejudice appeals**

  This is where the admission authority refuses a school place because it believes the admission of one more pupil would have an adverse effect on the efficient use of resources and/or the efficient education of the children already at the school.

- **Prospectus**

  The publication issued by the school setting out the policies, principles and ethos of the school.

- **Published admission number/limit**

  The maximum number of pupils per year group to be admitted agreed between the admission authority and the governing body of the school.

- **Qualifying measures**

  These are the measures that the school would have to take if it admitted any more pupils in Key Stage 1, which would result in the class size limit of 30 being breached. Qualifying measures are either the employment of an additional teacher or the provision of additional accommodation.

- **Reception class**

  This is defined in section 142 of the School Standards and Framework Act 1998. It is a class for primary children who will become five years of age during the academic year. It is also referred to as the foundation year.

- **Relevant age group**

  This is the age group to which children will normally be admitted. Children will join the year for their chronological year group. Each relevant year group must have admission arrangements, including a published admission number.

- **Relevant area**

  The area for a school (determined by its local authority and then reviewed every two years) within which the admission authority for that school must consult all other prescribed schools on its admission arrangements.

- **'Rising fives'**

  This is the term that refers to a child who will be four years of age at the beginning of the academic year, but will reach the age of five before the end of that academic year.

- **School days**

  This includes days when the school is open and excludes days when the school is closed. School holidays are excluded.

- **Schools Adjudicator**

  An officer appointed by the Secretary of State for Children, Schools and Families, but who is independent. The Adjudicator decides on objections to published admission arrangements and variations of already determined admission arrangements. The Schools Adjudicator comes under the Administrative Justice & Tribunals Council.

- **Scottish Executive Education Department**

  The government department responsible for setting and implementing government policy on education in Scotland.

- **Special educational needs**

  Children with special educational needs come into three categories. The first is defined as 'School Action'. This means that children have been identified as needing extra support which can be either educational or behavioural. The need is not considered to be substantial and it can be dealt with from within the school's existing resources. The second is 'School Action Plus'. This is where the identified need is more serious than 'School Action' and it requires the intervention of outside agencies. The third is children with a statement of educational needs. These children have severe needs and will be subject to a formal statement process, where a school will be identified for the child. Children on 'School Action' and 'School Action Plus' will not be given priority in the admission arrangements. Children with 'statements' will be offered places, even if this means that the school will exceed its published admission number.

- **Standard number**

  The number arrived at by the DCSF by its applying a formula to determine the maximum number of pupils to be accommodated at a school (note that this term has been replaced by net capacity, but it is still often referred to by admission authorities in statements to appeal panels).

- **Statement**

  This is the written paper issued by the admission authority summarising how the admission arrangements for the school apply to the application, the relevant background information and a summary for the reasons given for the decision. The admission authority should send the parent this statement and other papers for the appeal nine working days before the date of the hearing.

- **Statement of special educational needs**

  A statutory document issued by the LEA specifying the particular needs, resources and provision required to support a child, and it can include a named school that is suitable for providing education for that child.

- **Statutory walking distance**

  This has been determined as two miles for children under the age of eight and three miles for children aged eight and over. If a parent is allocated a school by the LEA, which is not an expressed preference and which is located further than the statutory walking distance, then he will qualify for financial assistance with transport to and from school. This is usually provided in the form of a bus or rail pass. If such services are not available in the more rural parts of the country, then the transport may be in the form of a taxi. Some LEAs may provide assistance, even if the school allocated is an expressed preference, but this is a matter for local discretion.

- **Trust schools**

  These are foundation schools and are popularly known as 'trust schools'.

- **Twice excluded pupil**

  A pupil that has been excluded twice from two or more maintained schools. If this occurs, the parent loses the right to express a preference for a period of two years from the date of the last exclusion.

- **Voluntary aided school**

  A school where the governing body is the admission authority and it sets the admission criteria for the school. It is usually a school with a religious ethos.

- **Voluntary controlled schools**

  These schools are similar to voluntary aided schools, but the LEA is the admission authority for this type of school.

- **Waiting list**

  The list established by the admission authority to determine places at a school if they become available after the main round of admissions. They are normally based on the admission criteria.

- **Working days**

  Includes Mondays to Fridays, but not Saturdays and Sundays. It also excludes public and bank holidays.

Index